THE LIFE AND TRUTH OF
GEORGE R. STEWART

THE LIFE AND TRUTH OF GEORGE R. STEWART

A Literary Biography of the Author of *Earth Abides*

Donald M. Scott

McFarland & Company, Inc., Publishers
Jefferson, North Carolina, and London

All photographs are courtesy the Anna Evenson/Jill Stewart Evenson Collection unless otherwise noted.

LIBRARY OF CONGRESS ONLINE CATALOG DATA

Scott, Donald M.
   The life and truth of George R. Stewart : a literary biography of the author of Earth abides / Donald M. Scott.
     p.   cm.
   Includes bibliographical references and index.

   ISBN 978-0-7864-6799-0
   softcover : acid free paper ∞

   1. Stewart, George R., 1895–1980.   2. Stewart, George R., 1895–1980. Earth abides.   3. Authors. American—20th century—Biography.   I. Title.
   PS3537 .T48545 Z74 2012
   [B]   2012275062

BRITISH LIBRARY CATALOGUING DATA ARE AVAILABLE

On the cover: George and Ted Stewart in 1924 (photograph from the Anna Evenson / Stewart family collection)

Manufactured in the United States of America

McFarland & Company, Inc., Publishers
  Box 611, Jefferson, North Carolina 28640
  www.mcfarlandpub.com

To

LIBRARIANS AND TEACHERS,
Keepers of the Light

BILL AND KEN AND FAMILIES,
Keepers of our Light

and

KEITE DAVIS SCOTT,
For too short a time, bearer of our light

... If there is to be a poet in these modern times, he must go out for himself and must gain much wisdom. He must look deeply into the world, and far into time, even though he sees both the world and time from some little microcosm like Sheep Rock Spring.

— George R. Stewart, *Sheep Rock*

Table of Contents

Acknowledgments

In a way, this book about George R. Stewart is like Stewart's *Sheep Rock*. Many people contributed their knowledge or support. I am simply the weaver of the tale. So my deepest thanks to:

The Nourishers: Many kind people offered nourishment for body and soul — good fellowship, meals, lodging, good spirits and conversations over spirits or beer during the writing of this book. They helped make this book and deserve thanks: the Byrnes, Lopezes, Farmers, Paynes, Baronis, Barneys, Aabergs, Harrisons, Showmans, Actons, DeMartinis, Amunruds, Goldbergs, Rases, Panaros, Valens, Swetts, Lapachets, Stouts, Mosses, Wongs, Donna Nunes, Dennis Allen, and Bert and Diana Solle, Jack and Joyce Stewart, Bill and Laura Scott, Ken and Keite Scott, Ray and Anna, Irene and Paul Sterling, Gary and Aleli Anderson, John and Angela Lucia, Richard and Mila Payne, Larry and Jan Payne, Dee and Barney, Dale and Dixie Myers, Warren and Theresa, Jack and Leslie, Auntie Bennie, Dan Ryan, Phil and Jenny, Marc and Chris, Casey and Josh, John Mattly, John Evans and crew, the Mario's crew, Steve Rudolph of the National Park Service, Jeff Ellison and the Rangers of Yosemite's Mather District, Lori Robertson of the United States Forest Service, Paula Garrett of the Public Lands Institute of the University of Nevada at Las Vegas, and Megan and Kaitlin Scott.

While writing the book I had the privilege of living as Guest Writer in "Stegner House," the Wallace Stegner Boyhood Home, in Eastend, Saskatchewan, Canada, three times. My thanks go to Stegner House manager Ethel Wills, and Ken Wills; and also to the Tokaryks, the Banfords, the Websters and all the good people of Eastend.

Another Canadian, Dr. Allen Tough, convinced me I could undertake a project of this nature as an independent scholar.

The Encouragers: Various colleagues and friends along the way encouraged, discussed, or otherwise intellectually nourished the work: Larry Gilbert, Chris McKay, Penny Boston, Greg Bear, Joel Hagen, Michael Sims, Gus Frederick, Mary Valleau, Sandy McPherson, Dr. Helmut Grimm, Paul Im, Oliver Morton, G. David Nordley, Poul Anderson, Bob Valen, Ted Stout, Kees Veenenbos,

Jim Funaro, Richard Brong, Philip Aaberg, Dee O'Hara, Will Golden, Russ Nelson, Joe Demers, Judy Demers, Bob Norby, and Ron Sopp. Special thanks to Jim Funaro, and the Board and members of CONTACT for sponsoring the first George R. Stewart Symposium. Tom Becker and Karen Schaffer extended an invitation to join the *Earth Abides* panel at Potlatch 20, and shared meals along the way. David Poindexter of MacAdam-Cage found merit in the initial idea and encouraged the writing of the book. Michael Ward did a wonderful job creating the George R. Stewart web pages. And Greg Bear said, "You don't think about writing a book; you either write the book or you don't write the book."

Sadly, some of the greatest friends of the book did not live to see it finished. In part, it is a memorial for them. Bob Broughton, Garth Hull, Ron Kelsey ("Tuffy"), Charlie Goulet, Allen Tough, Russ Nelson, Earnest Callenbach, Noel Perrin, Michael Rossman, Ed De Martini, Ted Everts, and Keite Davis Scott all helped immensely with the book, as they helped many others during (and in Keite's case, thanks to organ donations, after) their lives.

The Librarians: Irene Moran, Walter Brem, Anthony Bliss, Susan Snyder, and Baiba Strads of the Bancroft Library gave invaluable help with the research and writing of this book. Other librarians included Dr. Stanley Olson of the *University of Utah* Marriott Library Special Collections Manuscript Division, Walt Disney archivist David Smith, and the keepers of the websites which have been so important in researching this work. Noah Belikoff and Baiba Strads went above and beyond the call of duty to help with last-minute research.

The Readers: readers of the manuscript included Dr. Joseph Illick of San Francisco State University, Dr. Albert H. Harrison of the University of California, Davis, Dr. Philip Hull of Kansas State University, Ranger Philip Butler, former rangers Nicholas J. Lee, John Lucia, and Angela Lucia, Jack Stewart and Jill Stewart Evenson. Stewart Scholars Steven Williams and Bob Lyon read it with special consideration to details of Stewart's influence on others. I thank them all.

The Sharers of stories: Quoted by their kind permission, and enriching the book, are the following people: Dr. John H. Stewart, Jill Stewart Evenson, Dr. Jeff Gritzner, Kim Stanley Robinson, Page Stegner, James Sallis, Hartmut Bitomsky, Bob Broughton, Philip Aaberg, Bill Cassady, Bob Lyon, Steve Williams, Ken Carpenter, Anthony Bliss, and Baiba Strads. Others, not quoted but nonetheless important contributors, also deserve thanks: Frank Brusca, Tim Gorelangton, Peter Hart and Carol Field, Dr. Noel Perrin, Richard Brenneman, Keith Ferrell, and Lynne Hollander Savio.

The Stewart Family: This book would not have been written without the support of Stewart family members: Jill Stewart Evenson, Anna Evenson, Jack Stewart, and Erik Evenson. Anna Evenson shared and gave permission to use her collection of Stewart photographs.

The Editors and other helpers: Dinah Showman put many hours into the task of editing the early manuscript. Denise Lapachet Barney also edited an early version, lightly, with literary eyes. Nicholas Clifford's fine online guide to indexing helped greatly with that necessary but onerous process.

The Endorsers: Thanks to Page Stegner, James Sallis, Anthony Bliss, Greg Bear, Philip Aaberg, Kim Stanley Robinson, Dr. James D. Burke, Dr. John H. Stewart, Keith Ferrell and Dr. Paul F. Starrs for endorsing the book.

The Mid-wife: Literary agent Sally Van Haitsma gave good and useful advice about the book at all stages, and she encouraged the project when publication seemed unlikely.

Finally, thanks to all the good teachers and librarians, from Stockport, Ohio, to the Bancroft Library in Berkeley. Especially that unknown librarian in the old Sunnyvale County Library who said, as she placed *Earth Abides* in my hands, "Here. I think you'll like this book."

In addition to interviews with those who knew George R. Stewart or were influenced by him, I used the following sources:

Irving Stone's *Let There Be Light*, John Caldwell's *Number 46 of the Western Writer Series* and Wallace Stegner's essay, "George R. Stewart and the American Land," were invaluable. Other essays on Stewart and his work, especially those by James Sallis, Noel Perrin and Larry McMurtry, have been very helpful. I've used them all, gratefully.

Archival material in the *Wallace Earle Stegner Papers* at the University of Utah, the film collection at the Utah State University Library, the *George R. Stewart Collection* at the University of Nevada, Reno, Special Collections Library, and the *George Rippey Stewart Papers* in the Bancroft Library at the University of California, Berkeley, were equally invaluable.

The many books Stewart wrote reveal his intellectual progression and give clues to his life and inner thoughts.

I visited many of the towns where Stewart lived and worked, and traveled the highways he described, in order to get a flesh and blood sense of the places of his life.

Finally, I had the rare honor of knowing George R. Stewart and Theodosia Burton Stewart, and their family and some of their friends. I talked with him about his work and ideas. After he passed away, I learned important details of their lives from Mrs. Stewart.

Now, I pass this book along, for the enlightenment of future readers — a small thanks for the gifts given by teachers, librarians, friends, colleagues, family, and George R. Stewart.

Preface

In *The Shadow of the Wind* Carlos Ruiz Zafon writes about the power of the first book that finds its way into the soul of a reader. Even when he or she thinks it's been forgotten, some unexpected reminder will reawaken its memory. Such a book directs the reader's life.[1]

Thus it was for me, as for so many others, with George R. Stewart's *Earth Abides*. I read and reread the novel. Each reading took me more deeply into Stewart's mind, and I began to understand the system of his ideas—which could integrate art and science, automobiles and ecology, fiction, and the truths of his time. Then I moved beyond his books, to examine Stewart's life, and the historical influences on him. His ancestry was Scots Presbyterian and "deeply American," so I studied the intellectual history of the Scottish Enlightenment and the young United States to find clues to his way of thinking. He was a professor of English at the University of California, Berkeley, so I studied the university's intellectual foundations. Then, by coincidence (or synchronicity?) I met George R. Stewart. I asked him about his work and his ideas, learning much, but not enough. I knew there was, somewhere, a deep truth about Stewart and his work, and I intended to find it.

So while this is a biography of ecological novelist and historian George R. Stewart, a consideration of his rich and influential body of work, and a memoir, it is also the story of a quest to find the deepest truth about Stewart and his work. The book spends many pages on his life, his books, and the historical influences on him, because it is in those places that clues to this truth are found. Then, at the end of the book the object of the quest rises, to surface like a hungry trout. Like a good fisherman, I hook it. It drags me through rushing waters of thought, into the deep, to the ultimate truth about George R. Stewart.

1

Prologue:
Of Librarians and Libraries

Late in the summer of 1956, just before my 13th birthday, Mom fired up the black, wood-trimmed, 1950 Ford station wagon, and nosed it onto Highway 9. She and brother Ray and I drove through Santa Clara Valley (not yet Silicon), its orchards ripening in the hot summer sun. We passed our familiar landmarks: Cali Brothers Feed & Grain, Mariani Orchards, Fremont Union High School, El Camino Real. And then we were there, at the Sunnyvale Library.

I went in and walked over to the desk.

"I'm looking for a book by an author named 'Stuart'—*Forbidden Planet?*"

The librarian smiled. "We don't have that book. But we do have a very good book by another 'Stewart.'"

She took me into the stacks and pulled out one of the books. "Here. I think you'll like this." *Earth Abides*, by George R. Stewart.

It was summer vacation, and that was a good thing, because I did not sleep until I'd read the whole novel. By the time school opened in September I'd read all of Stewart's books to be found in that old Sunnyvale Library. I still remember the force of his ecological novels *Storm* and *Fire*, but *Earth Abides* was the work that found its way into my soul. I did not know the word then, but *Earth Abides* carried the gift of epiphany. Nor did I realize that the epiphany had set me off on a "saunter"—that is, a pilgrimage, *a Sainte-Terre*, "to a Holy Land."

As high school began and friendships developed, I put George R. Stewart's books away. Then, in 1960, visiting my high school friend Tom Vale, I spotted *Earth Abides* in his family library. When I mentioned that I'd read the book Tom said, "So you know about ecology? Conservation? The Sierra Club?" No. I knew nothing of those things. So for the next hour, Tom and his family educated me. Tom handed *Earth Abides* to me and said, "Here—now read this again."

Re-reading it, I began to see beneath the work's surface. To glimpse the structure that gives the book its power. To understand the ideas behind the beauty of Stewart's language. To learn the definitions of words like *ecology*. Thanks to Tom Vale, an epiphany had become an enlightenment.

All else since, including this book, has come from those gifts: from the librarian, the Vales, and the works of George R. Stewart.

I. Wandering Toward Wisdom

1

The first great American appreciation for wilderness came in the mid–19th century. Henry David Thoreau wrote many works about the re-creation he found in nature. By the end of his life, he had developed his feeling into a statement of faith: "In Wildness is the preservation of the world."[1]

Thoreau and his friends matched their love of wildness with an equal love for liberty. When he refused to pay his poll tax as a protest against the illegal invasion of Mexico by the United States, Thoreau was tossed into the town jail for a night. The experience produced his "Essay on Civil Disobedience," which would become a worldwide call to courage in the quest for civil rights and political freedom. It was also a moral and spiritual challenge to like-minded people, like his friend Ralph Waldo Emerson. (Emerson is supposed to have visited Thoreau in jail, asking, "Henry, what are you doing in there?" and Thoreau is supposed to have replied, "Waldo, the question is: What are you doing out there?"[2]) There would be continuous, nationally divisive battles over civil liberties, right down to today's debates over "Patriot Acts" and undeclared wars, and Thoreau's essay is as fresh as ever. But the love of Wildness and the scientific appreciation of the ecosystem would become less and less controversial, and more and more a quality of American national character.

By the early twentieth century, the idea had spread. As John Muir wrote, "Thousands of tired, nerve-shaken, over-civilized people are beginning to find out that going to the mountains is going home; that wilderness is a necessity; and that mountain parks and reservations are useful not only as fountains of timber and irrigating rivers, but as fountains of life."[3] By the time Muir wrote the passage, in 1901, Americans had made an unprecedented choice: to preserve vast areas of their wild lands in vast national parks, for scientific study and personal "re-creation." Horace Albright, second director of the National Park Service, summed up the idea when he directed his rangers to "keep these bits of primitive America for those who seek peace and rest in the silent places; keep them for the hardy climbers of the crags and peaks; keep them for the horseman and the pack train; keep them for the scientist and student of nature; keep them for all who would use their minds and hearts to know what God had created ... so that centuries from now people of our world, or *perhaps of other worlds*, may see and understand what is unique to our earth, never changing, eternal."[4] (Emphasis added.)

By the mid–20th century, the parks, forest wildernesses, and other great public lands, and the ideas on which they were founded, had shaped our national intellectual and personal character. Yet traveling to the isolated parks required time and money, both of which most working people lacked. (As hard as it is to believe in this day and age, one of the biggest concerns of Stephen Mather, the first director of the National Park Service, was getting enough visitors into the parks to justify their cost.) The same was true of the ideas underlying the parks and other protected ecosystems. Most of the writings about ecology were published in magazines read by a few highly literate people — a well-educated elite.

Travel to the parks eventually increased. By the late 1940s people began visiting the parks in huge numbers, thanks to the postwar availability of good jobs, good roads, good cars, and vacations for the then-large middle class. At the same time, in the 1940s and 1950s, these new travelers through the natural world were getting an understanding of ecology by reading a series of novels written by a professor of English at the University of California, Berkeley: George R. Stewart. The first of these — the first *ecological* novel — was *Storm*.

There comes a moment in each human life when the struggles pay off and the dream is realized. For George Stewart, that moment came in 1941, at the edge of the Grand Canyon. Theodosia Burton Stewart ["Ted"] remembered: "In September we took a trip to the Southwest. Along the way, George and I would go into the shops where they sold Hopi, Navajo, and Pueblo art, look at some beautiful piece, and say 'Wouldn't it be nice if we could afford that?' One of our stops was at the El Tovar Hotel, at Grand Canyon. While we were there, a telegram came — *Storm* had been chosen as a Book-of-the-Month Club main selection!" An excited Ted telegraphed her daughter Jill with the news.

"For the rest of that trip," Ted recalled, "we'd look at some beautiful pottery or jewelry, and say, 'Wouldn't it be fine if we could afford that?' Then we'd look at each other, laugh, and say, 'But we CAN afford it!'"[5]

As the novel changed the Stewarts' lives, it also changed the lives of its readers. Stewart's precise description of events, which he based on careful research, introduced the ecological view to readers. His style — sometimes dramatic narrative, sometimes poetic flight of description — gave readers a *feeling* for his ecological vision. It's no exaggeration to say that the novel gave an ecological epiphany to its readers. And through them, *Storm* changed the rest of us. The effect of the book on human society is best shown in one simple, profound change: following Stewart's example, the National Weather Service (and the rest of us) began naming storms.

With the success of *Storm*, Stewart must have realized another truth. The back and forth of his life, which may often have seemed a wander toward an unknown wisdom, was actually a *saunter*. Stewart's life experiences — bad ones, like childhood emotional problems, the death of a brother, his own near-death, the family's uprooting and emigration — and good ones, like his discovery of nature and maps and books, his epic wanders, the joy that came from being appreciated for his writing, his marriage to Ted — all these things led to *Storm* and its success. Later, as an old man writing his unpublished autobiography, he would develop an equation to help make sense of the chaotic mix of experience that shaped his life and created his character: $L = H+E+X$, a life is the sum of the influences of heredity, environment, and the unknown vicissitudes of fate or luck. [6]

Like the equation, this saunter through Stewart's life begins with *Heredity*.

2

Like Stewart, we're pilgrims here, on a saunter: in our case through the life and work of George R. Stewart. Our quest is to understand the sources of Stewart's vision and the deepest truth of his work. Ours won't be a straight line saunter — when a side road promises help with the main quest, we'll explore it. But we'll more or less follow Stewart's *Autobiography*, which begins with his H factor. With heredity, in this case his deep heredity, from old Scotland.

The old Scots said, *Cuimhnich air na daoine o'n d'thàinig thu*: "Remember the men from whom you have come." Stewart spent many pages of his autobiography doing just that. In the early eighteenth century those old Scots — artists, scientists, teachers, thinkers, explorers, poets, lovers of knowledge, and warriors as need be — created an enlightenment which changed the world. George R. Stewart's life and values reflected that enlightenment. To understand him, it's necessary to understand the Scottish Enlightenment and those who created it. So our saunter starts in Edinburgh, defeated capital of an isolated country.

In the early eighteenth century Scottish engineers built good roads. Scottish Presbyterians built a church founded on a belief in universal education, and then created the first national system of public schools. Schools, libraries and universities spread learning throughout the country, along the new roads. Thinkers educated by church and school traveled the roads, to Edinburgh. In Edinburgh, they formed clubs, like the Oyster Club, where men like James Watt, Adam Smith, David Hume, James Hutton, Benjamin Franklin and others shared ideas in free and friendly discussion, and the Scottish Enlightenment was born.[1]

In the space of a few years, Edinburgh's thinkers produced capitalism, a poetry of the common man, horsepower, the science of geology, and the Encyclopedia Britannica. The beginnings of the modern world — based on education, machines, capital, science, and a democracy of the common people — had emerged from the Scottish Enlightenment. "Progress" and "Human History," as we know the terms, are Scottish ideas. So are "capitalism," "popular sovereignty," and free public education. *We* believe education, capitalism, technology, engineering, and science should be the foundations of society's progress because *they* believed it. We use "common sense" because Scotland produced a philosophy called *Common Sense*.

The ideas poured out of Scotland, to sweep the European and American continents. Voltaire summarized the effect of the Scottish thought when he wrote, "It is to Scotland that we look for our idea of civilization."[2] The Scottish Enlightenment may even have inspired the American Revolution, since in the critical decade before the Declaration of Independence Benjamin Franklin received an honorary doctorate from Scotland's St. Andrews University, fellow Philadelphian Benjamin Rush studied medicine at the University of Edinburgh, and Thomas Jefferson's teacher, the Scottish Enlightenment's Dr. William Small, "probably" — as Jefferson put it — "fixed the destinies of my life."[3]

Two men influenced by the Scottish Enlightenment carried its ideas to the New World. Both came to create — or recreate — educational institutions. The first man failed, but another university would be founded using his name and his ideas. The other man was successful. He created a new kind of university in America. Both men would shape the educational system of the United States, and thus the work and ideas of George R. Stewart.

Although Irish Bishop George Berkeley didn't live in Scotland, he was involved in the Scottish Enlightenment. Berkeley was one of the founders of the philosophical movement called "empiricism," the idea that something existed only if an ordinary person could perceive it. *Esse est percepi*, "To be perceived is to be," is his great statement of the idea. When Edinburgh's David Hume added his ideas to Berkeley's, a basic principle of modern science was born: scientists must base knowledge on observation.

Berkeley has been called the first great American philosopher. In the early eighteenth century, he moved to Rhode Island, hoping to use it as a base to raise money to build a college in the Bahamas. The funding didn't come through, so he returned to Ireland. But he left his mark here. He divided his library between Yale and Harvard, and gave his farm to Harvard.

America also left its mark on the bishop. The wilderness of eighteenth century New England exhilarated him. Inspired, Berkeley wrote a poem about a new kind of society, based on nature. Today, one line from that poem is often quoted as an example of the eighteenth century imperialistic mind: "Westward the course of empire takes its way." Yet read more of Berkeley's *Verse on the Prospect of Planting Arts and Learning in America*, and you will see that it is actually an idealistic vision of a better society, based on the natural world. A society where:

> The force of art by nature seems outdone,
> And fancied beauties by the true:...
> Where nature guides, and virtue rules;
> Where men shall not impose for truth and sense
> The pedantry of courts and schools.
> There shall be sung another golden age,
> The rise of empire and arts,
> The good and great inspiring epic rage,
> The wisest heads and noblest hearts.
> Not such as Europe breeds in her decay;
> Such as she bred when fresh and young,
> When heavenly flame did animate her clay,
> By future poets shall be sung.
> Westward the course of empire takes its way:
> The four first acts already past,
> A fifth shall close the drama with the day:
> Time's noblest offspring is the last.[4]

Berkeley's ideas about the value of wilderness and the importance of scientific observation would be fundamental to the work of the great university where George R. Stewart would make his career.

The other transplanted member of the Scottish Enlightenment was Scottish Presbyterian John Witherspoon. After fighting a losing battle against Anglican encroachment in Scotland, he left Edinburgh to seek religious freedom in the American colonies. (Later, he would sign the Declaration of Independence.) With the support of Dr. Benjamin Rush of Philadelphia, Witherspoon became president of the Presbyterian College of New Jersey in 1768. He brought a new way of teaching to the college, one based on the system used in Scottish universities. Professors specialized in a particular discipline; students "majored" in a specialized area, but always worked within a generalist context so they could see the relationship of one discipline to another.[5]

The College of New Jersey, founded on Witherspoon's ideas of interdisciplinary study and academic freedom, was renamed Princeton University in 1896. It was the university George R. Stewart would attend, in the early twentieth century — arriving on a train pulled by a steam engine based on a design by James Watt, another member of the Scottish Enlightenment.

Robert Louis Stevenson once wrote, "The happiest lot on earth is to be born a Scotchman. You must pay for it in many ways, as for all other advantages on earth. You have to learn the Paraphrases and the Shorter Catechism; you generally take to drink; your youth … is a time of louder war against society, of more outcry and tears and turmoil…. But somehow life is warmer and closer; the hearth burns more readily, the lights of home shine softer on the rainy street; the very names, endeared in verse and music, cling nearer round our hearts."[6] George R. Stewart wasn't born in Scotland, but he learned his Presbyterian catechism, drank his share of the "water of life," *Uisgebethea* (whisky), and knew his turmoils. He enjoyed the warmth of the hearth or the campfire, and learned to love the names of places. After Princeton, he would become an educator, interdisciplinary scholar, fighter for freedom, and author. Inheriting the Scottish love of geography, he would write about the land. Like the members of the Oyster Club, Stewart would work with colleagues in many disciplines. In all these ways, George R. Stewart would follow his ancestors, those of the Scottish Enlightenment.

There was a closer ancestry as well, which also helped make George R. Stewart the man he became. His American roots went back to 1616, when a Dutch ancestor settled in what would later become Manhattan. So he called himself "Deeply American." Since his paternal ancestors kept good records,

and his maternal grandfather, Andrew Wilkins Wilson, left his own memoirs, Stewart knew his American ancestry well.[7] Andrew Wilson's book included the stories of those who came before him, beginning with his grandfather — George R. Stewart Jr.'s great-great-grandfather — Joseph Wilson, a tough Irish freedom fighter who came to the United States after his acts against British occupiers in Ireland went awry. Joseph married a woman of similarly strong and independent character, and together they scratched out a bare living on hilly farmland in Pennsylvania. It was a hard life, with little time for such niceties as education. Yet in the best Scots-Irish tradition, Joseph had enough "l'arnin" to read two complex theological works.

The "Mother Spring." Andrew Wilkins Wilson: George R. Stewart's maternal grandfather, writer, educator and businessman, who inspired the young Stewart.

One of his favorite recreations was to discuss those works. His other recreation was the consumption of quantities of whisky so it's safe to assume that discussion was interspersed with drinking.

Whisky or not, hardscrabble life or not, Wilson could be called enlightened. He could think, and ideas were his passions.

Joseph encouraged his son Samuel to become a teacher in the local school. But hardship — he lost his wife and his farm and had to see his children scattered out to various relatives — took him away from the classroom. Still, he encouraged the family love of learning, insisting that his children be educated. So 14-year-old Andrew kept at his studies even after he went to work (earning $5 a month) — often studying, like Lincoln, by candlelight after a hard day. Eventually, Andrew learned his grammar, math, even Latin.

Andrew became a teacher. He soon joined with another teacher to found a school (now the prestigious Kiski Prep School). But he couldn't make enough money to support his family, so he left the profession to take a job at Sutton and Moore's store in nearby Indiana. There, he prospered, eventually becoming co-owner of the store. He never lost his interest in education. Wilson helped found Indiana Normal School, now Indiana University of Pennsylvania, where a campus building carries his name. Appropriately, the Andrew Wilson Building was the original home of the university's Model School, a place for teachers to learn new ways to teach. Like his ancestors, Wilson was an enlightened man who never let money or self-interest get in the way of learning.

Dr. John H. (Jack) Stewart, George R. Stewart Jr.'s son and Andrew Wilson's great-grandson, has given Wilson's autobiography considerable study. He writes, "I had the feeling that [Andrew Wilson] really was an intellectual and scholar, but didn't have the time to pursue it while making a living. I had the feeling that he had the genes that passed down to GRS. I certainly had the impression that I had found the mother spring."[8] Jack Stewart's father agreed. In his own autobiography, George R. Stewart wrote that he believed his talent for writing came from his grandfather.

Although George R. Stewart's father, George R. Stewart, Sr., collected family records that dated back to the 1600s, Stewart's paternal side left no work as polished as the Wilson Autobiography. But if George R. Stewart Jr. had known nothing of his paternal line except the Civil War journal of his uncle, John H. Stewart, it would have been enough. Reading the journal today still brings to life the scent of gunpowder, and the terror and the courage of the Civil War. Here is the journal, published (I believe) for the first time.[9] Spelling and grammar are the Lieutenant's:

(**May 5, 10 AM**) Gen Hancock orders us to attack the enemies left. This was a hard march. I think it could not have been less than 5 m. It rained nearly all the way and mud half way to the knees. when ... within one mile of Fort McGruder

& Williamsburg, we came to a river very much swollen which had to be crossed on a dam. After 2 pieces of artillery ... & 3 regiments—6 Main 5 Wis + 49 Pa had got over the dam gave way leaving 3 pieces of artillery + one regiment— 43[NY?] behind. We were completely cut off from the main body of the army and no chance to help us. The only thing to do was to fight.... After the line was formed we rested in place for about one hour—when Gen Early with 8000 men (?) made his appearance from a woods on our right—+ front—His march was oblique. Gen Hancock who had been looking for someone to appear ... road down the line ordering us to fall in. The bugle also sounded for fall in. After all were in rank and the reg't dressed up we were ordered to fall back which was done in good order about 100 paces when a new line was formed the right resting on a Reble Fort that had been evacuated By falling back it compelled Gen Early to show his whole front. Our line was formed as accurately as if we [were having?] Dress Parade. The Rebles at this time were yelling Run Bull Run or G———D

All this time Gen H was in front of his Com.d giving his orders in person. He seemed to have forgotten that he had ades for that purpose. Lt. Parker, ade rode up and asked the gen if he had not better go to the rear he said the Johnis are fireing directly at you. He turned to him on his horse and said Mr. Parker will you please go to hell go and tell Col Cobb to ... dressup the left of his Regt. The Gen then put spurs to his horse and rode the line and charged the men not to fire until they got orders ... and when they did fire to fire for the knees. He then went to the rear. The artillery was set for an oblique fire. When the rebls got within 100 or 150 feet of our lines Gen H gives the command Ready Aim Fire The Artillery opened an oblique fire with grape and canister. Gaps ... were mowed through the enemy that reminded me of a wheat field that the Cradle had gone through. The fireing was kept up for about one hour. The rebls in the mean time ... close up & advancing until they got their hands on our cannon. The cannoniers had drawn their sabors to protect them when Gen H yells out Now Gentlemen we will charge the enemy. Seeing the Bayonets come down making a solid front of steel and massing to charge was more than they could face They turned and ran a great many throwing away their guns. A great many of the enemy were shot while running. A great many who saw they could not get away dropped down along side of their dead and wounded.... Gen Early + his men that could got under cover into the woods. We closed up our lines and got ready for an other attack Just about this time the brigade was dressed Rebl Cavalry appeared from woods in front and to our left ... once our men took off their caps and beckoned for them to come up but they would not venture. We were well drilled in the Hollow Square Movement—so if they had under taken to charge us they would have stood a poor chance for victory. About 6 [P.M.?] all was quiet except the cries of the wounded for water.[?]—Gen Hancock rode the line slowly and thanked us for the way we had acted and told us that this was what 8 months drill + Curssing had done. As soon as it was dark Pickets were thrown out in [advance?] of the battle field and men detailed to look after the prisoners + wounded. The rations the men had in their Haversacks was generally given up to give to the wounded so we did not get anything to eat until morning. It rained nearly all night. The wounded I think were nearly all put into a large barn on right of the line during the night. We all wondered what morning would bring forth. We knew from the amount of rain that had fallen that the stream in our

rear must be high and could not think that it would be possible to receive any
ade before morning and then it might be too late if the Rebles would attack us
with an overwhelming force.

Morning May 6 A bright morning and surrounded with [friendly] troops
that had slipped in during the night. McGruder at the same time evacuated
at Williamsburg and Marched for Richmond. Received rations about 6 A.M.
While eating our hardtack and washing it down with coffee Gen McClelland
[*sic*] came into our camp He got off his horse thanked us for what we have done
and catching Gen Hancock by both shoulders shaking him and I think calling
him superb —

After a few months in battle, Lieutenant Stewart fell ill. He was put on
light duty; then pensioned off. Never married, he moved in with George R.
Stewart's family when he was elderly. George Stewart, Jr., remembered him as
senile and difficult to live with, and was glad to see him go to a state hospital.
Yet Lieutenant Stewart would have his influence on young Stewart. Reading
his uncle's journal young George Stewart felt the call to adventure — and of
the need, sometimes, to go up against the guns.

George's father seemed less adventurous than his brother John. An engineer who understood machines better than humans, he was silent and dispassionate in his dealings with others. Yet there was a depth to him. He had a passionate side, and courage not unlike that of those facing enemy fire. He would need it all — passion, courage, depth — when, in his forties, he romanced young Ella Wilson. Ella was 19 years younger than Stewart and an accomplished woman in her own right. Andrew Wilson had passed the family passion for education along to his chil-

Ella M. Wilson at Vassar. Wilson's daughter, she became a Greek teacher, married
George R. Stewart Senior, and would be George R. Stewart's mother. She taught her
son several languages, including Greek, during the summer before his senior year of
high school.

dren; four of his sons went to college and three became educators. Remarkable for the time, four of Wilson's daughters, including Ella, also went to college. Ella Wilson graduated from Vassar to become a teacher of Greek in a preparatory school.

Ella was not to be trifled with. Stewart's letters to her, written with a careful, restrained approach, show how much he respected her. But the letters also have a stick-to-it-iveness that shows his courage and determination.

He began his courtship in a letter dated October 31, 1889, that closed with a revealing quote from Robert Burns:

> Miss Ella M. Wilson:
> Dear Friend;
> Without any preliminaries, I will let my subject introduce itself.
> If agreeable to you, it would give me great pleasure to have you correspond with me.
> I have hesitated to ask such a favor, because I am so poor a correspondent and so little gifted in the "art," but in the hope that, in this respect, I do not "see myself as others see me"....
> "Your Friend, Geo. R Stewart"[10]

For a time he continued to salute her as "Miss Wilson: Dear Friend." Then, in a moment of boldness, in one letter Stewart addressed her as "Dear Ella." But in the next, perhaps feeling he had been too forward, he returned to *"Miss Wilson, Dear Friend."*

From a modern perspective, a courtship of such formality and respect seems simple-minded. Yet there is beauty in it, as the hard-shelled engineer was softened by his love for this woman. There is courage in it, as the shy, older man courted a much younger woman. And there is wisdom in it — George R. Stewart, Sr. had progressive ideas about relationships between men and women. He chose a woman with a degree and a career, one not to be taken lightly.

Ella agreed to marry him, perhaps because she saw in him the same strength of character his brother John showed when he marched against enemy guns. George Stewart, Sr. had had his share of reverses, but he'd also had the courage to pick himself up and move forward again. She knew she'd have her work cut out for her, making the old bachelor into a husband and father. Yet since she herself was not traditional, an untraditional husband was what she wanted.

They married. He continued his work, engineering the extensions of the interurban railway systems and gas lines to the new suburbs growing up outside Pittsburgh. He did well enough to afford a fine home in one of those suburbs, Sewickley. There, the couple began to raise a family, the heirs to the near and far ancestry of the Stewarts.

3

Sewickley, Pennsylvania, was a literary town. Willa Cather spent some time there and left an idea of the town when she wrote, in "A Gold Slipper"[1] "to be mounted upon the stage in this fashion, as if he were a 'highbrow' from Sewickley ... was ludicrous." Mystery writer Mary Roberts Rinehart, who inspired the phrase "The butler did it," lived in Sewickley.[1] And Robinson Jeffers, the great twentieth century American environmentalist poet, spent his early childhood there, where his parents were friends and neighbors of the Stewarts.[2] So Sewickley was a writers' town. But the only future writer *born* there — on May 31, 1895 — was George R. Stewart.

Baby Stewart's stay in Sewickley was even briefer than that of young Robinson Jeffers. When George Jr. was about a year old, financial reverses forced the Stewart family to move from Sewickley to Indiana, Pennsylvania. There, his mother's relatives could help them through the hard times. So Indiana, Pennsylvania, would be the first place George R. Stewart knew, the place where he had his first memory: of looking out a window at a panorama of the town.[3] For the next few years of his life, Stewart's boyhood years, that environment of town and family and friends — Stewart's E factor — would shape his character. (But Stewart's X factor would also be in play.)

George R. Stewart's boyhood town was so archetypically American that it could pass for George Bailey's Bedford Falls in Frank Capra's *It's A Wonderful Life*. In fact, the town *was* Bedford Falls — at least for the movie's male star. Indiana, Pennsylvania, was also the boyhood home of James Stewart, who played George Bailey in Capra's 1946 film. Although the movie's Bedford Falls was built on a studio backlot in the San Fernando Valley, Jimmy Stewart said that when he walked onto the set for the first time he almost expected to hear the bells of his home church in Indiana.[4]

Although nothing in the papers or books of George R. Stewart mentions James Stewart, and there is no record of their having met in Indiana — unlikely, since George left the year Jimmy was born (1908) — both Stewarts shared the common heritage of that small American town. As they went out into their separate careers, they reflected the experience and the values of the place in their work. Jimmy Stewart, by portraying the common person reaching uncommon heights — Mr. Smith in Washington, Lindbergh crossing the Atlantic, George Bailey keeping his town decent and kind. George Stewart, by writing about people like the Donner Party's Reed family, fictional graduate student Isherwood Williams, and the "many heroes" of the Westward Movement — common people of uncommon accomplishment. The qualities of good character, self-reliance, optimism, and faith — values like those of the people of Indiana, Pennsylvania — would be as essential to George Stewart's books as they would be to Jimmy Stewart's portrayal of George Bailey.

It is no coincidence that Walt Disney, who would later film two of George R. Stewart's novels, modeled his greatest work of art on a small town like Indiana, Pennsylvania. Disneyland's Main Street, USA is lined with the storefronts of commerce common to Stewart's Indiana or Disney's boyhood town of Marceline, Missouri. At the end of Disney's Main Street is a park with paths leading to adventures like those found in literature and education in the schools and libraries of American small towns: Peter Pan's Never-Never Land, a cruise through the jungles of the world, pirates, trips to the imagined future. In the same way, Indiana's citizens, like Andrew Wilson, used commerce as the engine to drive the life of the town, but never forgot that business had a higher calling. The income from the town's businesses funded the library, the churches, the school, and the college — places of knowledge and enlightenment for the townspeople.

Life in an early twentieth century town like Indiana, Pennsylvania, might seem dull.[5] No malls, no TV, no radio, video games or computers. People couldn't jump into a jet plane or automobile to travel easily to distant places. It was not a perfect era — there was no penicillin to cure the killer diseases, and no psychiatry to cure depression or other mental illnesses — but life was certainly *not* dull. (Think of Garrison Keillor's Lake Wobegon.)

Holidays and festivals, which followed the cycle of the seasons, offered frequent diversions. On Valentine's Day, with its hint of spring and lengthening days, the people of Indiana exchanged cards and wishes. On Decoration Day — today's Memorial Day — veterans of the Civil War marched, accompanied by the local Greeneville Band, and the townspeople knew that summer was nigh. Summer was the beloved season, the time of growing crops and kindly weather. For boys, allowed more freedom to explore dangerous things in those days, Independence Day was the summer's highlight. One could fire off firecrackers. Make loud noises. Get hurt. (George Stewart wrote that he wore his fireworks burns like honorable scars.)

As the year moved back toward school, and the air cooled, the youngsters prepared for another celebration. Riding with their families in buggies over autumn roads, they watched farm folks stir huge vats of apple butter. Back in town, they helped put up their families' canned vegetables and fruit, meats, jams, and jellies. It was a sign that the biggest festival of the year — the County Fair — was close at hand. There, city folks and country folks competed to see who had the best preserves or brandied mincemeat or pies. Fair time was also visiting time, when farm and city friends separated by the miles could meet and catch up on each other's news. After the competitions and the visits, country and townsfolk alike could enjoy the spectacles: displays, sideshows, the merry-go-round, mock military battles and the ascension of hot air balloons. When the fair was over, children and parents had enough good memories to last until the next holiday.

Thanksgiving was quiet, religious. But Christmas, like the fair and the Fourth, was a full pulling-out of all stops at year's end. There were presents and a feast and California grapes on the table. Then, as the days began to lengthen again, and the New Year's Day passed, the people of Indiana began preparing for the festivals of the coming year.

But life was not all fairs and festivals. There was plenty of time for the self-made adventures of the young. The great gift of the pre-media days *was* time. Youngsters could enjoy each day to its fullest, creating their own adventures — some of which could lead to experiences as delicious and deadly as any offered by today's adventure travel agencies. And as those of us lucky enough to have lived when we made our own music know, a boy can get in as much trouble in the few square miles around a small town as an adult can in the entire U.S.A. Every small town has haunted houses and small but nonetheless interesting wildernesses to explore.

Stewart began creating his own adventures as soon as he could walk.[6] In the summer of 1898, his third year, two stand out. First was the Adventure of the Penny. Given a penny and cautioned to keep it out of his mouth, Stewart put it on his tongue. He was warned not to swallow it. Of course, he swallowed it. Afraid of what he'd done, he tried to ask for help, but it was beyond his three-year-old vocabulary. The adults listening understood that he was afraid. Finally, they figured out it had something to do with the now-vanished penny. After searching the room, they realized there was only one place the penny could be. The next day, as they say, everything worked itself out: they put him on the potty and found the penny.

Stewart's Adventure in Red began when he noticed workmen painting a house across the street. The Stewart house was a sedate off-white. The painters' red was a more interesting color. When the child walked over for a closer look, one of the workmen (who probably laughed about this for weeks) gave young Stewart a brush and a little paint. The boy was able to paint about 12 inches of the front of the house before the paint ran out. His parents took it well and left young George's first masterwork on the house.

Stewart learned a never-forgotten lesson from his adventures: consider consequences. Think before you paint. Most important, and essential to the man he would become, *learn to communicate*. From the day of the penny until the end of his life, Stewart worked to master language.

But he was not deterred from adventuring. When he was four, he decided to cross a flooded river on a shaky bridge. His father came to rescue him, but hesitated, afraid the old bridge wouldn't hold his weight. He shouted a warning, but young George, by now in the middle of the bridge, was too frightened to move. Then, for the first time in Stewart's memory, the X Factor came into play. A boy from an "other-side-of-the-tracks" family, known as "Nigger Dan," went out onto the bridge and led Stewart back to the riverbank. Dan walked

Stewart to a safe bridge, put the boy on his back and, like St. Christopher, carried him across the flood to his father. Stewart never forgot the lesson of that day: a "bad" person may do good deeds. Later, "Nigger Dan" would be transformed into one of Stewart's most heroic characters in the novel *Earth Abides.*[7]

The closer environment, of family, would also shape his character. But it would be a difficult shaping. He recalled his childhood as secure and happy. But he had his reservations about it. He was loved, and felt loved, yet he was emotionally undernourished by the dynamics of the Stewart family.[8]

One reason was that Stewart's family was atypical for its time. There were only three children, and the children were born a respectable and manageable three years apart. The family was also one of the first with a wife and mother whose professional life equaled that of her husband's. Today we value such families; but during his childhood, Stewart recalled, he often felt "different" from his friends.

Other problems came from his place in the birth order. His older brother Andrew was the favored heir-apparent, who lorded himself over George. George's status as the baby of the family protected the younger Stewart for a time, but when George was three, John Harris Stewart was born. After John's birth, big brother Andrew had the honored position of first-born and little brother John that of being last-born. Young George moved into that forlorn region reserved for the middle child. His first response was to become a crybaby, using tears to get back attention now lost to his baby brother. When the tactic failed, he withdrew into himself, into a secret world filled by fantasies which often stretched over weeks. He withdrew to such an extent that he later believed he had been nearly schizophrenic.[9]

He was saved by the companionship of books. Before he could read, others read to him, speaking the words so he heard their music. His nurse, Neenie, was a Southerner who read Uncle Remus in dialect, with the languid cadences of Southern speech. His engineer father read George a natural history book filled with technical language, and the child heard a different rhythm of words. His mother probably read to him in Greek; if so, he would have realized that every language has its own music.

As soon as he learned to read for himself, young George began an addictive devouring of books. One of the first was the King James Version of the Bible. (Not wanting to seem unmanly, he hid when he read it.) It was not the easiest of books to read, with its ancient language and complex tales, but he loved the stories, of epic adventures and journeys and battles, and so he mastered it. He read it more for those tales than the religious ideas, but the ideas would stay with him, as would the King James Bible's beautiful use of the English language.

George R. Stewart (front), Andrew Wilson Stewart, and Neenie, circa 1897. Neenie was the boys' nurse, from the South, who read Uncle Remus stories to the boys in dialect.

His favorite books were adventure novels. He read most of the books written by the now-largely forgotten boys' author George Alfred Henty, a kind of a *Master and Commander* author for boys. Henty used his historical novels to teach the values necessary for good character — battle onward, respect your opponent, care for the innocent — and Stewart imbibed those values with the stories. He also read Jack London and Kipling. But it was another author, a Scot, who would have the greatest influence of all.

One day, Stewart was rummaging around in the attic. It was (we can imagine, in this largely post-attic age) a dark unpainted place, with shafts of sunlight streaming in through one or two small windows, its bare wood floor piled around with wooden boxes, barrels, old trunks. The young boy opened each box or trunk with care. He looked through the contents, pulling objects out, examining them, then replacing them as they were: Old letters. Faded

George R. Stewart, 1905. Young Stewart would have been in the full glory of his archetypical American boyhood in Indiana, Pennsylvania.

photographs. Old toys saved for the memory of the pleasures they brought, or for the memory of their owner.

Young George noticed a shelf filled with books. He scanned the titles. One caught his eye. He pulled it out, opened it, looked it over. It was the one thing in the attic that he did not put back. He headed back down stairs with his find, found a comfortable place, and began reading Robert Louis Stevenson's *Treasure Island*.

As his own novel *Earth Abides* would change so many lives, *Treasure Island* changed Stewart's. Stevenson's books carried a more sophisticated understanding of the human heart than Henty's (who once wrote Stevenson suggesting that he write with "less psychology and more claymores"[10]). By reading Stevenson, Stewart was growing beyond Henty's books, to learn the complexity of adult feelings.

He also learned something about the writing of books. Once, Stevenson changed narrators in mid-stream. Young Stewart was perplexed. But then he realized that the shift *worked*. For the first time, he became conscious of the use of literary technique to help tell a story. It was an important lesson for a future writer.

Above all, Stewart learned the value of a good map. *Treasure Island* is a book based on mapping, its story told through a map. The tale begins when young Jim Hawkins finds the treasure map. Throughout the story, the map frequently reappears, a reminder that the land is a character in the book.

Maps were everything to Stevenson. "It is my contention — my superstition, if you like — that he who is faithful to his map, and consults it, and draws from it his inspiration, daily and hourly, gains positive support.... The tale has a root there: it grows in that soil; it has a spine of its own behind the words.... As he studies [the map], relations will appear that he had not thought upon."[11] Stevenson drew the map of Treasure Island before he wrote his book, then let his characters interact through the map to tell the story.

After he read *Treasure Island*, Stewart always thought with this mapmaker's sense of the world. As a child, he drew his school maps with love and precision. As an adult, he based his books on a well-mapped sense of place. Since maps can also put one *idea* in relation to another Stewart also became a mapmaker of the geography of thought. His working maps would become more and more complex visualizations of how the disciplines connected in telling the stories of places. Maps also helped him develop this understanding: There can be no honest consideration of human events without knowledge of the geographies of those events.

Treasure Island had given Stewart an epiphany, fundamental to everything in his work that followed.

Books and maps, family and town, friends and festivals and adventures, the making of music by families: joyful things for children, in those days before television and computers. But there was another influence on those born in the nineteenth or early twentieth century, a much darker influence: the incurable diseases. When the doctor leaned over to the spouse or parent and said, quietly, "Typhoid" or "Scarlet fever" or "Pneumonia," there was nothing to do but pray, and wait. The disease names may mean little to those under 40, but in Stewart's day they were the names of death. Those diseases could not be cured until the invention of sulfa drugs, penicillin, and antibiotics in the 1930s. Rest and liquids, warmth and time were the only medicines available.[12]

Young George thought his little brother John might have become the musician of the family. The boy loved music. A photograph shows him playing a drum almost as large as himself. But in January 1906 typhoid fever struck John Harris Stewart. He survived, weakened. Then pneumonia hit. On January 6, 1906, the little boy died.

It was not ended. Later that year, pneumonia struck George Stewart, Sr. For a time, an almost-endless time, his life hung in the balance. The elder Stewart survived, but he was severely weakened.[13]

Two of five in the tiny family affected and one of those dead — it was the handwriting on the wall. To stay in the damp, cold Eastern winter was to play dice with death. The only long-range cure would be escape to a warmer, drier place. So, at the age of 61, when most men were planning their retirement, George Stewart Senior decided to move his family to Southern California, where he hoped he could become a successful farmer.

Like the period at the end of a paragraph, the move to California would signal a great change in this saunter — the end of young George's childhood. The boy was about to emigrate from place and time, leaving Pennsylvania for California, and boyhood for adolescence.

So this is a good place to pause, and reflect on his boyhood.

Stewart had been shaped by all three factors in his equation of life, E, H,

Johnnie Stewart with drum, circa 1905. This was George R. Stewart's younger brother, who died when he was five.

and X. And he'd been lucky: All three factors had worked to his advantage. He'd had some adventures, which taught him important lessons, but he survived their dangers. He'd discovered books, and the rhythm of language. He'd become a lover of maps, and a maker of maps. When he thought about his childhood decades later, he regretted only one thing about his years in Indiana — perfect scores in school behavior. He feared he'd missed out on the honored "Huck Finn" tradition, and that he might lack the wild and wooly spirit required of an archetypical American boyhood.

He would soon find spirit. He was entering an epic geography, one sure to inspire a young maker of maps. He was moving from the tame innocence of an Eastern boyhood to manhood in the vastnesses and wildernesses of the American West. There, and on the journey into adulthood, he would find dangers and wonders, battles and victories, characters and heroes, worthy of great stories.

4

In the early twentieth century, a transcontinental move to the Western United States was not undertaken lightly. In those days, crossing 2,800 miles of America, even by railroad, was daunting. Emigrants had to leave friends and family behind, and the leave-taking was often final. As *im*migrants to the West, the travelers entered a new world, where strange faces and places replaced those well known, and the locals spoke an English that included Spanish and Indian words. Even the landscape, with its vast deserts and huge mountains, its sere prairies, was alien to a people from the moist Eastern prairies and the low Appalachian Mountains.

Because those who emigrated West were often never seen again, "gone west" became a synonym for death. But death had already touched the Stewart family, and threatened it again. So in the autumn of 1907, George Stewart, Sr. and his oldest son, Andrew, traveled West to reconnoiter. Housing was hard to come by — it was a boom time — but the pioneers found a simple place in Azusa, settled in and started their new business.

While his father and brother were establishing themselves in California, 12-year-old George was traveling on the East Coast with his mother and aunt. The trio traveled to Princeton, New Jersey, to visit George's uncle, Dr. Robert Wilson. Wilson, professor of Semitic languages at Princeton Theological Seminary, was a close friend of poet Robinson Jeffer's father William Hamilton Jeffers. After a pleasant visit and a look at Princeton University, young George and his mother and aunt went on to Philadelphia and New York — the boy's first visit to either city.

Stewart recalled Princeton as pleasant, but New York and Philadelphia impressed the boy. Mother and Aunt took him to see four plays, two of which he never forgot. One starred the great David Warfield, so effective an actor that Stewart could quote lines from the play all his life. The other was a musical, the first American production of *The Merry Widow*. Stewart also had another New York experience, a romantic holdover from the nineteenth century: after one of the plays, the ladies and the lad rode home through the snowy streets of New York in a horse-drawn Hansom cab.

Not long after that New York trip, mother and son heard from father, now well enough established in Southern California to send for the rest of the family. So in February 1908 young George and his mother boarded the train, and followed his brother and father West. The Santa Fe Railroad's *Scout* was not the crack *Super Chief* of later years. It was a slow train which stopped three

George R. Stewart (standing) with (left to right) his father, Mrs. Cain, Ella Wilson Stewart (George's mother), Andrew Wilson Stewart and Paul Cain at Mt. Wilson 1910.

times a day so passengers could rush through Harvey House meals. But crossing the country at a leisurely pace was a great adventure for a boy from a small Eastern town. Seven decades later he still recalled "the endlessly-stretching fields of wintry Kansas ... its poor and half-frontier villages ... in the corner of Colorado, the Rocky Mountains.... At Albuquerque there really were Indians.... [The desert's] thin growth looked strange and inadequate to a boy from the verdant hills of Pennsylvania."[1]

But the West had its own adequacy. The names on the land, for example. Cañon Del Diablo carried the flavor of the Southwest and fascinated Stewart; he made the crossing of the Canyon a highlight of his trip. Decades later he remembered his first view of other places with romantic names, like Flagstaff and the Painted Desert, which flashed by the train's window. He already had a passion for place names. His trip would foster that passion and help shape his life's work.

Stewart was eager to see the lush citrus groves surrounding his new home. But his first view of California, south of Cajon Pass, was that of wild desert and wilder mountains. It was not a disappointment. A stalled train gave him the chance to get out and explore the wonderland. He wandered through the desert near the tracks, its plants more exotic than any flora young George Stewart had known.

What he saw, close and far, is still one of the best American viewscapes. Plants of the California desert frame the view. The tough sandstone layers of the Mormon Rocks, similar to nearby and oft-filmed Vasquez Rocks, thrust their fantastic shapes up near the tracks. To the west the landscape is backed by the San Gabriel Mountains (today's Cucamonga and Sheep Mountain Wildernesses). High peaks like Mount San Antonio, pine-covered, often snowy, rise more than 10,000 feet. It is a setting so archetypically American and Western that it is often used in films. Young Stewart was so entranced by the scene that he wandered away from the train. When its whistle signaled, he had to race back. But those few minutes changed him. At that unplanned stop on the southern side of Cajon Pass, George R. Stewart had discovered the grand geography of his manhood.

George and his mother arrived in Los Angeles, where George's father and brother met them. Their new home, a simple frame house, would be in Azusa, a few miles to the east at the foot of the San Gabriel Mountains. A rural town founded during the California Agricultural Rush of the 1880s, it was less than 30 years old when the Stewarts moved in.

The Stewarts' first California years were not easy. They were still grieving over the death of a child. They missed friends and family in the East. Even with the kinder climate the senior Stewart's health was a worry. And the move west was expensive. So the family knew tight times as George's father tried one and then another agricultural scheme to make money. He heard that sweet potatoes were a good investment and planted acres, but rabbits got them. He sold the potato land and bought an orange grove in nearby Ontario. But the grove was not very productive and his father did not know much about the growing of oranges.

George had his own concerns. He was still lonely, and his family was not much help. His parents, grieving over John's death and struggling to make ends meet, had their energy directed elsewhere. And when George refused to join Andrew in get-rich schemes, his brother bullied or ignored him. Young George also had the experience of all young people who move: his childhood friends were 2,500 miles away. He could not turn to them as sounding boards, confidants, or advisors. So if anything, in these early California years, he was even more withdrawn than he had been in Pennsylvania.

Stewart turned loneliness into an advantage, using his spare time for his school work. Given an assignment to fill in the maps in freshman workbooks, he took extra time to color and label them with an almost adult precision. It was such satisfying work that he kept two of the books all his life. The pleasure it brought him helped take some of the edge off his loneliness. Years later, he remembered how much he had enjoyed coloring the maps.

Then, slowly, shy young George Jr. began to make some friends. One would be a friend for life. "Buddy" lived with his mother, a vaudeville performer and actress, in the town's railroad hotel. A bit of a character, he was always composing slightly bawdy compositions, which he'd sing surreptitiously at school for the amusement of other students. It was just the sort of friendship to bring George out of his doldrums.

George "Buddy" DeSylva went on to become one of the great songwriters of the twentieth century. We still hum his songs today: "April Showers," "Look For the Silver Lining," "You're the Cream in My Coffee," "If You Knew Susie," "Button Up Your Overcoat," "The Birth of the Blues." He also became a producer and was key in introducing Shirley Temple to the world. (In *The Littlest Rebel*, DeSylva's young star closes the films singing one of his songs: "Polly Wolly Doodle.") DeSylva's songs defined his time, that Golden California time of perpetual sun, movies, citrus and dates, and the casual life.[2]

One DeSylva song, "California, Here I Come," could have been written for the Stewarts. But another, "The Best Things in Life Are Free," would have been a better anthem for young George. He was about to receive a gift, won through sweat and courage, from the wild Earth.

Azusa sits at the foot of towering mountains. The town sits at about 600 feet above sea level. The summit of Mount San Antonio, 15 miles northeast, is over 10,000 feet. In those pre-smog days the summits and the forests below them were visible most of the time. With neat orange groves backed by snowy mountains, it was a postcard of a place. But the pretty postcard view was deceptive.

That place had power. When winter storms blew in there was no doubting it. Peaks disappeared behind clouds and the continuous drenching of California storms. When the storms cleared, the rivers were roaring-full and the peaks were covered to a depth of feet with snow.

Wander up the canyons from Azusa today on the right trail, up the East Fork of the San Gabriel River toward the Sheep Mountain Wilderness, and you will find evidence of that mountain-storm power. Drop down to the river, and hike until you turn a corner and run smack-dab into a huge highway bridge. No highway, just a state-of-the-art 1930s highway bridge over the San Gabriel. Powers-that-would-be tried to build a highway up this canyon. But beyond the bridge San Gabriel Canyon becomes the deepest gorge in Southern California — 3,000 feet deep, nearly two-thirds the depth of the Grand Canyon. In a storm it fills with water, roaring its way down to the Pacific. In 1938, one great storm brought four days of heavy rain. *Canyon* became *cannon*, firing water downhill. The flood took out what had been built of the highway, but left the bridge.[3]

Gazing upward at the snowy, forested mountains, young George could sense the power behind their beauty. Yet it did not terrify him. It exhilarated him, and overwhelmed his loneliness. Looking up, filled with the energy of young manhood, would he not be called by those mountains?

5

The Stewart home in Azusa was about a mile from the mouth of San Gabriel Canyon. When the San Gabriel River and its tributary creeks were not filled with great floods — and it was dry most of the year in the semi-desert climate of southern California — the canyon was a pathway into the wild mountains. With his friend and hiking companion Paul Cain, Stewart often headed up the dry creek beds into the Transverse Ranges. Each hike held its lessons. Once, for example, George and Paul found their path blocked by a large rattler. At first they panicked. But they recovered, and found a way around the snake. Once past the danger they stoned the snake and took the rattles. (Stewart never forgot the incident: the rattler would reappear in *Earth Abides*.)

Short hikes whetted Stewart's appetite for wilderness. So, at 16, he joined his cousin Steele and a friend named Fitzpatrick on a long camping trip in the San Bernardino Mountains. The three young men left Redlands, borrowed burro in tow, and headed toward the peaks. The inexperienced young men had to stop frequently to repack the animal, but they managed to reach the base of the mountains that day. There, for the first time, Stewart slept under the open sky in a camp he had helped set up.

After that first shakedown cruise of a day they had a fine trip. We don't know their precise route. (Stewart later wrote that they followed a stage road so hot and dry they found a horse dead from thirst and exhaustion, but in summer that would describe almost any road heading up into the high mountains from Redlands.) However they went, it was strenuous. If they went to Running Springs, the logical destination since the town is directly above Redlands, they gained 4,500 feet in 14 hot miles. But it was well worth the effort. Along the way they learned how to pack, how to tie a diamond hitch to keep the pack on their burro, how to set up camp — which in those days meant cutting poles for the tent and making beds from cushions of boughs or sand. Eventually they found a lake — probably Big Bear Lake. "Wilderness!" the young men thought — until they saw a movie company. But they unpacked the mule, set up camp, and stretched out, surrounded by the high mountain forest.

For days, they wandered through the cool, alpine forests, climbed the mountains, and swam in the lakes. For George R. Stewart, it was another life-changing experience. Decades later he wrote: "For the first time ... to move freely in good mountain-country, to make camp and break it, to see untouched landscape, and to hear running water and the wind moving in pines.... Even a sixteen-year-old can know ... he thus touches something very ancient."[1]

Stewart had felt the first exhilaration (and surely some of the terror) of the Earth's wild places. Like his discovery of maps and the names of places, his meeting with the ancient wilderness brought an epiphany. He had come to understand, in his soul, the power of the Earth.

As if that wilderness epiphany was the only reason for their stay in Azusa, Stewart's family moved as soon as the young hikers returned from the mountains. George's father had sold his first orange grove at a profit and bought a better grove near Anaheim, in Orange County. With more income, they could afford the move to a better town.

On September 26, 1911, the family moved to Pasadena. Pasadena was a civilized town, with Throop University (now Caltech) as its intellectual center and the Mid-Winter Parade (today's Rose Parade) its annual celebration of art and culture. But civilized as Pasadena was, its architecture celebrated the wilderness of the high San Gabriel Mountains which rose behind it. Moving there meant an immersion in nature.

Pasadena's architectural firm, Greene and Greene, a leader in the Arts and Crafts movement, designed homes to look like rustic mountain houses. With stone fireplaces, natural wood tones, and unpainted timbered interiors, the homes seemed to grow out of their natural surroundings. Since Greene and Greene's simple "California bungalow" designs were priced "democratically," most families could afford one, and it was said that every block in Pasadena had at least one of these nature-based houses. The Stewarts lived in one on Jackson Street. Even his home reinforced young George's new passion for nature.[2]

The Stewart family business was also rooted in nature — at least the nearly natural world of an orange grove. One summer Stewart worked in the grove, just west of Anaheim (about 35 miles south of Pasadena). He usually walked the two miles from town to orchard on a pleasant country road (now a main route to Disneyland) without meeting a vehicle. He later remembered "neat and friendly rows of majestic rounded trees, grown so large that they almost touched — glossy green all year; at times, sprinkled thickly with white and fragrant blossoms; again, bountifully hung with orange globes."[3] His wild mountains were never far, and on a clear day, while he worked in the grove, Stewart could gaze north to see the 10,000-foot mountains above Pasadena.

Stewart was a student at Pasadena High School for two years. He had some interesting classmates — Howard Hawks, for example, who would become one of the great American film directors — but, at first, little time to develop strong friendships. Yet these years would define his professional life, thanks to the hard work of good teachers and the inspiration of a few words.

Stewart had a lifelong interest in toponymy and etymology — the history of names and the history of words. Since that would be central to his work, this is a good time for a short side trip in our saunter: to a consideration of the meaning of words.

The word we write as "teach" is one of the oldest in our language.[4] It is part of our "native vocabulary," words used in Proto-Indo-European at least 6,000 years ago and still around in one form or another in all modern Indo-European languages. At least six millennia ago, *deik* (or *deig*) meant what *teach* means today, "To show." In that same ancient time, *Ghedh* meant "to join, or fit together." Thus a "good teacher" shows students skills, knowledge or abilities which fit them well for the needs of their lives.

Deuk, found in e*duc*ate, meant anciently "to lead." The similarity of spellings, *deik* and *deuk*, suggests another idea — a powerful one: the qualities of character called for by two human tasks, teaching and leading, are very similar. Thus, a good teacher will also be a leader. At Pasadena High School, Stewart heard that idea for the first time when a motivational speaker defined *educate* as "to lead out."[5] After the talk, Stewart knew what he wanted to do: to "lead others" out of dark ignorance, into enlightenment. Like his mother, George R. Stewart would become an educator.

But he would not teach just any discipline. Some disciplines encouraged enlightenment, but others did not, and he would avoid those. He learned how he did *not* want to teach from his math classes. Stewart found math classes dull and boring: "Problem-solving, infinitely repetitious … infinitely foolish … taught by conscientious men and women." Schools justified the math curriculum as a way of "training the mind."[6]

Words again: *Train*, often used as a synonym for education, actually means the opposite: "to drag along behind."[7] In a training environment, no child is left behind — or allowed to go ahead. Students are dragged along, learning repetitive skills, allowed little thought and few questions. Training may have its purposes, but George R. Stewart did not want to be trained, or to train, so he avoided disciplines like math which were based on training. He considered only those subjects which he could *teach*.

But *what* to teach? Two good teachers showed him the answer.

Senior Literature Teacher Ida Williams showed Stewart how ideas, art, and events are interconnected. He learned that the various disciplines of knowledge are connected to each other

George R. Stewart, Pasadena High School yearbook photograph. About 1913.

and influence each other. It encouraged him to start exploring different disciplines. He became especially interested in his science classes. He might even have become a scientist, he thought, but no science teacher took a personal interest in him. The good teacher, or in this case the lack of one, made the difference.

Another English teacher taught Stewart the most important lesson of all: that he had a way with words. The teacher asked the students to write a poem. George took the task lightly, knocking out a poem about the school's star receiver with the refrain "And Gibbs got a forward pass."[8] Impressed by the poem, the teacher asked George to read it to the class. The class loved it. So the teacher took the poem to the principal, who thought enough of the work to ask George to read it at the weekly football rally. When George read the poem to the gathering, the students of Pasadena High School brought down the roof with cheers of praise.

It was a turning point in his life.

As a lonely child, Stewart read and created fantasy tales. He developed his own world. There, in his world, he began to live the life of a scholar and a weaver of words. But on that transcendental day at Pasadena High School, which he later described as the most important day of his life, he discovered that he had a great gift. He could *write*.

Success led to success. Stewart became a star on the tennis team (where, in keeping with his new status, he played against another future author, Thornton Wilder.) He acted in the school play. He was elected to student body office and presided over student body meetings. Once, he was even carried on the shoulders of cheering admirers, in adulation, from a debating victory. He became social, even developing a strong friendship with his fellow student Gladys Knowlton. And — most important — he saw his first story published, in the Pasadena High School student magazine.

All through these years, his interest in language and his skills in writing grew. George's mother began to teach him the ancient and modern Western languages, and he was soon fluent in Latin, Greek, and German. Learning the rhythms of these (and later other) languages helped him understand the music of English. He also learned how English words had evolved from words in earlier languages. He read Isaac Taylor's *Words and Places*, which helped focus his interest in the history of words.

When all was said and done, he had a good idea of what he would teach. His mother had shown him the beauty of other languages. Taylor's book encouraged and focused his interest in the names of places. English teachers taught him that he could write, about any discipline, and that his words could sway an audience. Now, he decided, he would carry the light of these good

Opposite: **Unknown person (left), Gladys Knowlton, George R. Stewart, Mt Baldy. Stewart had become quite a mountaineer after moving to California, circa 1913–1915.**

teachers onward, teaching others about words and language. George R. Stewart would teach English. But his English courses and his English scholarship would always reflect his interest in science and love of wilderness.

6

After graduation from Pasadena High, Stewart took another transcontinental train ride, to Princeton University where he would do his undergraduate studies. Princeton was not his first choice. Stewart wanted to attend the University of California, Berkeley. But his Vassar-educated mother viewed the place as a rustic frontier school. Besides, the Stewarts were good Presbyterians, and in those days Princeton University had close ties to Presbyterianism. His brother, Andrew, had preceded him at the university, and done well there. So there was no question about it, and George R. Stewart went to Princeton. But if the family stories are to be believed, he went in his own adventurous way — "by the rods," or hoboing his way east.

He had some remarkable classmates in the class of 1917. Stewart ran a relay race with one of them — F. Scott Fitzgerald. But in Princeton's stratified society, running the same race did not mean being on equal footing. Fitzgerald — Francis Scott Key Fitzgerald, named for a famous ancestor who composed "The Star-Spangled Banner"—had, like most other students, attended prep school before Princeton. Stewart, raised in the more egalitarian society of the West, was a graduate of the democracy of a public high school. So he would always be an outsider. Or, as he put it, one of the "wanderers around the edge."[1]

Yet the edge was not necessarily a bad place to be. In fact, there were advantages to being on the edge, if you knew how to work it to your benefit. Fitzgerald later wrote that the few students who came to Princeton from public high schools were hard workers, and eventually became the student leaders.[2] Stewart, with his experience in turning solitude into scholarship, used his Princeton time well: working hard, he graduated third in the Class of 1917.

Stewart did have some social success. He was invited to join one of the Princeton dining clubs. He learned to mix with the high and mighty, or those who would become high and mighty, like Fitzgerald. He even made a few life-long friends. Classmate Harold Osmer eventually became Stewart's neighbor in Berkeley, thus gaining a kind of immortality as a character in *Earth Abides*. Another classmate, Chauncey Leake, moved to the San Francisco area long after the Princeton years and became a clubmate of Stewart.

So Stewart was not lonely at Princeton. But he found the place lacked a serious intellectual climate or any sense of political or social duty. The limited curriculum wasn't of university quality. (Geography, which would become a foundation of the books he later wrote, wasn't even offered at Princeton.) Most classes bored him. As in high school, he found the math professor to be the worst teacher of his college career "grinding us through innumerable problems that we solved essentially by learning, like clever monkeys, to push the proper buttons."[3]

All this, even though the university was going through a small flowering. Sophomores were questioning the elitist nature of Princeton dining clubs, and Fitzgerald was writing stories, which he later worked into one of his novels, for the Nassau Literary magazine. Stewart felt the energy in the air. It encouraged him to get involved in university activities. He joined the Orphic Order,

Princeton's Arch club; George R. Stewart lower left. Although not very social by nature, Stewart was invited to join a dining club at Princeton. (Others not identified.)

Princeton's version of a University Orchestra, where he played the flute. He also became a member of the oldest political, literary, and debating society on any college campus in the world.[4]

The American Whig-Cliosophic Society grew from the merger of two other societies founded just before the Revolutionary War. The name "Whig" is rooted in the Scottish Enlightenment: the Covenanters, battling for religious freedom, yelled "Whiggam!" to urge their horses forward. The Whigs, a liberal British political party that supported American independence, believed history was progressing toward a system of parliamentary democracy which guaranteed individual freedom. ("Liberal" and "liberty," first cousins to each other, both descend from the Latin word for *freedom*.) It's safe to say that Stewart found that the liberal views of Whig-Clio fit well with his Scottish-American love of freedom. The interdisciplinary interests of the club, in literature as well as politics, would also have appealed to his way of thinking. And the Whig way of telling history, as an epic with many heroes, would shape his ideas about human progress.

All in all, Stewart prospered at Princeton. Believing that education should open new fields to the mind, he took many electives. With few social demands on his schedule, he had plenty of time to study, so he received high grades in most classes. He earned High Honors in English, and won the prize for philology (the study of historical linguistics). He was elected to Phi Beta Kappa, an American philosophical society founded at William and Mary — by Princeton's John Witherspoon among others — the same year the Declaration of Independence was signed. (The name of the society comes from the Greek: Φιλοσοφία Βιοῦ Κυβερνήτης, or "philosophia biou kybernetes." Which means, more or less, "Love of wisdom steers life." That was certainly true for Stewart.)

Stewart felt he'd received a good education at the school, and left, ready for life.

As he entered adulthood, Stewart could again consider his equation about life, $H+E+X=L$. Of the three factors, luck would prove the most important in the years to come. Sabers were rattling in Europe. America would get involved. He might well become a casualty on the battlefield. Luck would determine that.

7

On February 7, 1917, George Stewart's mother wrote to her son:

My Dear George:
Your letter certainly was a shock and yet from some remarks made last summer it should perhaps have been not entirely unexpected.
I hardly know what to say.... Yet if it seems the right thing for you to go and you feel that you can be of service and are willing to run the risk, you must go....

... I am a good deal of a Presbyterian. When one is in the path of duty or doing what seems right, one is about as safe in one place as another....
With much love, Mama[1]

George R. Stewart, Jr., had joined the Army.

When the United States entered World War I in April 1917, a patriotic fever swept through the United States. Promised immediate assignment to France, Stewart and several Princeton friends enlisted in the Army before they graduated. His father supported the decision, encouraging his son to get to France as soon as possible so he would have a sense of the War before bad weather hit. He volunteered money to help his son with his expenses.

After basic training, Private First Class Stewart was assigned to Section 565 of the U.S. Army Ambulance Corps. It was quite a change from Princeton. In a letter to his friend Gladys Knowlton he wrote of working alongside his friends Bill Nye and Sumner Reynolds at that oldest of Army occupations, ditch digging: "Sumner supplies the muscle and Bill the entertainment; I enjoy the results of both."[2]

As things turned out, there would be plenty of time to dig ditches. Overseas orders never came. The generals sent the infantry over in large numbers but held the ambulance drivers back.

The Ambulance Corps' staging center for Europe at Allentown, Pennsylvania, was soon overcrowded. Base commanders decided one way to reduce camp boredom would be to send the Ambulance Corps out on local training missions. Stewart saw much of eastern Pennsylvania in 1917. As always, Stewart worked the experience to his benefit. On a three-day campout to Gettysburg, where the soldiers bivouacked in pup tents near the ground of Pickett's Charge, the soldier-scholar spent as much time as he could wandering around the battlefield, history book in his hand.[3] (The experience would inspire his book about Pickett's Charge.) He used his spare time to prepare for his post–Army graduate work, spending much of his time at the base library. He taught himself Anglo-Saxon so he could read *Beowulf* in the original tongue.[4]

The X Factor, chance or providence or luck, seemed to be working to his advantage, giving him time to study and keeping him from the guns. But then another kind of luck almost took him. The great Spanish Influenza Epidemic of 1918 swept the Earth without respect for geographic or cultural boundaries. Called the worst epidemic in history, it killed more than 20 million people worldwide. At least 600,000 of those deaths were in the United States. For some reason, young, healthy adults were more susceptible than older people. Army camps were hit hard.

Stewart contracted pneumonia, probably as a result of the flu. Once again the X Factor worked in his favor, and Stewart survived. He never completely recovered, and one lung would bother him for decades. (Eventually he would

"Myself with ambulances." George R. Stewart poses by the unit's ambulance fleet, circa 1917–18.

have it removed.) So Stewart's military career ended like that of his ancestor Lieutenant John H. Stewart — discharged, with a pension for disability.

But the disease didn't keep him from adventure. In a letter written years later to author George R. Stewart, Justin A. Wood asked if he might be the same George Stewart with whom Wood roomed in army quarters at Yale University.[5] The Stewart whom Wood knew had planned to hitchhike home to California after his discharge. A dangerous plan, thought Wood, since his roommate had a tuberculosis-like cough and he did not expect him to live very long.

Of course, it was the same George R. Stewart, coughing from lingering effects of his pneumonia. Never one to let adversity or ill health hold him down, Stewart headed out, hitchhiking west, as soon as the spring of 1919 opened Miss Gentry's new transcontinental road.

8

Before the Interstate highways there were the U. S. highways: even numbered east-to-west — U.S. 80, Route 66, U.S. 40; odd-numbered north-to-south, from U.S. 1 to U.S. 99. But before the numbered U.S. highways, there were more than 200 privately funded, *named* highways. The Lincoln Highway was, and is, the best known. Others included the Yellowstone Trail, the Theodore Roosevelt International Highway, and the Dixie-Overland Highway.

But none of these roads, not even the famous Lincoln, was the first transcontinental highway. Miss Gentry's was the first.

Chairwoman of the Jackson County, Missouri, Good Roads Committee and a member of the Daughters of the American Revolution, Elizabeth Butler Gentry — always addressed as "Miss Gentry" — proposed a coast-to-coast highway that would follow historic trails through the middle of the country. Her suggested route followed the National Road from Baltimore to Vandalia, Illinois, Boone's Lick Road from Saint Louis to Kansas City, the Santa Fe Trail to Santa Fe, New Mexico, and what she called the "Kearney Route" from Santa Fe to Los Angeles — a road which would provide for the convenience of travelers and memorialize American history. She proposed that the highway be named "The National Old Trails Road."

In 1911, Miss Gentry published a pamphlet, booming for the new road: "The fascination of the road is known to all travelers, whether it be by camel, stage coach or motor car, and the call of the road to its lovers is as insistent a note as the call of the sea to the sailor."[1] Inspired by her words and leadership, men and women met in 1912 to found the National Old Trails Road Association. Six months before the first meeting of the Lincoln Highway Association, Miss Gentry's proposal was well down the road, so to speak, toward realization. By 1914, the National Old Trails Road even had its first signs, placed by an expedition from the Automobile Club of Southern California.

The story of that expedition gives an idea of how tough it was to travel on those early highways. In the West, the truck carrying the signs and equipment followed a "road" that existed mainly in the mind: sandy desert trails better suited to mules in some places; narrow and dangerous roads over the southern Rocky Mountains in others. Whenever they crossed a river or a stream, expedition members had to find a ford — the primitive bridges couldn't hold the truck's weight. Slowed by the obstacles, the crew was on the road to Kansas City long enough to feel winter's approach. They reported weather so cold that "each night all water is drawn from the radiator and the hose line between the radiator and the pump is disconnected and drained. The pump is then drained also and the motor run dry for a minute or two. In the morning it is necessary to pour hot water over the pump to free the shaft enough to crank the motor, then each cylinder is primed and, after replacing the hose connection on the radiator, the carburetor is flooded and the motor is started without water in the radiator. The next step is to pour warm water into the radiator, followed by hot water until it is filled."[2]

It should be no surprise that the pioneering sign crew didn't reach Kansas City that first year. Still, they managed to sign hundreds of miles of the new route, and eventually finished the job: five years later George R. Stewart took a photograph of an Auto Club of Southern California's National Old Trails sign near Indianapolis. The new road signs encouraged motorists. In all of

1914, before the signs had been placed, Holbrook, Arizona, counted less than 200 transcontinental drivers passing through. In May of 1915 alone, after the signage, 216 cars went through Holbrook on the new road.

Signed or not, the National Old Trails Road was a long way from the modern idea of a highway. Most improved stretches were in or near major cities. Rural sections, in those days used by horse and wagon for local transportation, were graded dirt — which meant dust or mud most of the time. Property lines took precedence over road routing. (Even today, travelers on some secondary or rural routes still come across sections where a road makes a 90-degree turn left, then a 90-degree turn right, another 90-degree turn right, and another 90-degree turn left, to go around someone's farm. In 1919, such zigs and zags were the rule.) And engineers didn't know much about designing roads for automobiles. The engineering philosophy of the day was that the needs of the road had priority over the needs of the automobile. So,

for example, roads were designed with high-crowned centers to let rainwater drain. But if a tall Model T went a little too fast around a sharp corner on a crowned road, say, maybe 20 miles an hour, a rollover could result. Stewart described one in his hitchhiking journal: "4/16.... Came to Ford ... overturned rolled clear 180° but no one hurt. Loaded too heavily and running too fast on crested road. We tipped it up straight and she ran like a clock. Man foolishly went on for K.C."[3] (Stewart saw several rollovers during his days on the road.)

George R. Stewart hitchhiking, April 1919. After surviving pneumonia associated with the 1918 flu, George R. Stewart decided to hitchhike home to Pasadena. He made it as far as Garden City, Kansas, and then took a train the rest of the way.

Yet, primitive and dangerous or not, in 1919 Miss Gentry's road was the most established transcontinental highway, and an almost direct route from New York City to the Stewart home in Pasadena. It was the logical route for George R. Stewart to use on his hitchhiking trip. So in the month of pilgrimages, Chaucer's Aprille, he put on his army uniform, gathered up his kit, and stuck out his thumb.[4]

Stewart photographed the adventure. The pictures show the young man in Army uniform at various places along the way. He was creative, too. One photo shows his distinctive silhouette shadowed across the road.

He also kept a journal of the trip.[5] It gives a realistic idea of highway travel in times often sentimentalized as the "good old days":

4/11/1919 Marshall to Effingham (Illinois)
Worst day of all. Hit road @ 7.30 hoping to make 100 mi or at least 80.... Rode few miles with ... Co. School Supt. To Martinsville where he gave exam ... picked Ford with old lady and young fellow. Old lady friendly, lost boy last fall ... of flu.... Stopped at X-roads and sit in shelter of road machine; put on overcoat.... Walked on, cannot recall how I got to Casey ... cold and wind. Walked a good deal with maybe short ride....

Got lift of about ½ mile in lousy F ... at various stages, read a little Plato ... decided to walk to Greenville although it was after 5. Walked 4 mi in 50 min 10 min rest walked on rather tired.... Apparently good fellow ... carried me to Teutopolis ... started walking to Effingham to test the country; the country almost called my bluff ... almost dark. Picked [up] ... on bridge by oil truck and to Effingham....

4/17/19 Edgerton to Burrton followed old trail first & waited. [The National Old Trails route split west of Kansas City.] Came back & debated. Finally took new trail in time to be picked by a dealer in a Liberty car. [Then] ... picked by old settler ... Drove very slowly and very dangerously (I am getting nervous about Fords). Told about the old days — ... buffalo by Wichita, prairie chickens everywhere. Great hunter; has last desire to shoot a mountain lion before he dies. Going ... to California. Anxious to have me keep on with him but I was not anxious. At Waverly ... steak etc, huckleberry pie. Out and waited by culvert, passed several times, picked by man ... thought he was going further than to Burrton.... Roads fair. He took me to a little hotel he called landlady by first name. Oil lamp in room.

Years later, when his friend Charles Camp asked him if it had been hard to get a ride, he answered that it wasn't hard to get a lift, but "in those days there weren't very many cars. If you made a hundred miles in one car that was a Big Ride. You rarely did that."[6]

He didn't make it all the way home to Pasadena. The after-effects of the pneumonia finally caught up with him in Kansas and he abandoned his hitchhiking at Garden City. He took the train the rest of the way, a prudent choice. The hardest part of the road lay ahead and the "Great American Desert" was no place to be sick or exhausted.

Even though the trip was cut short, it had been a fine adventure. Stewart hitchhiked more than halfway across the United States, through towns with names like Old Peculiar, Greenup, and Kingdom City, and across the Hundredth Meridian, gateway to the West. He enjoyed the company of fellow wanderers, people brought together by the democracy of the American highway: "Jewish" travelers, "crude" farmers, drummers (salesmen), a beautiful woman in a Cadillac. He traveled the old trails, the National Road and the Santa Fe Trail, and the new automobile road that followed them. It was good preparation for books he would later write about place names, trails, and highways.

After resting in Pasadena, he stuck his thumb out again. This time, he followed the "Pacific High-

George R. Stewart — hitchhiking to UCB, 1919. After a short rest, Stewart hitchhiked from Pasadena to Berkeley to begin his graduate study in English.

way" along the route of another historic trail, El Camino Real. Again he photographed his trip: A stretch of wild coast, an old oak near San Miguel where he camped. A photo of himself on a small dirt road — probably one of the better stretches of the Pacific Highway of 1919 — with his "kit" on his back.[7] It took Stewart a few days to get to Berkeley by thumb. Once there, he checked into a hotel, cleaned up, and headed over to the University of California campus.

At Berkeley, Stewart would continue his study of English. He would also

Opposite: Soldiers in Albuquerque, circa 1919; George R. Stewart is on the right.

open new regions of thought by combining bookish work on literature and history with field research. In doing this, he would be working in the best tradition of the University of California. For in its formative years, the University of California had given birth to a new way of thinking, a *California* enlightenment, which combined "the land" with the book. Since that is critical to Stewart's story, it's time for another detour on this saunter.

9 *Fiat Lux*

The United States of America was the first nation founded on the ideas of the Enlightenment, especially the eighteenth century Scottish Enlightenment. The founders of the United States built many of the ideas of the Scottish Enlightenment into the government, the financial system, and the schools of the United States. They did so because they believed, as Jefferson wrote, "Enlighten the people generally, and tyranny and oppression of body and mind will vanish like evil spirits at the dawn of day."[1]

Almost as soon as the nation was founded, Jefferson sent the Corps of Discovery west. Lewis, Clark, and party carried with them a set of instructions from Jefferson which directed them to learn all they could about the natural history and human culture in the Louisiana Territory — a mission of enlightenment. It would also operate along relatively democratic lines: the captains, Lewis and Clark, held votes when critical decisions needed to be made. At least once, the voters included Sacagawea — the first time a woman or a Native American voted in an American election — reflecting the marriage between liberal democracy and science that was the hallmark of the Enlightenment.

Shortly after the Corps of Discovery set out on their journey, Jefferson received a letter from one of the great scientists of the day:

> Mr. President,
> For moral reasons I could not resist seeing the United States and enjoying the consoling aspects of a people who understand the precious gift of Liberty. I hope to be able to present my personal respects and admiration to one who contemplates philosophically the troubles of two continents.... I am quite unaware whether you know of me already through my work on galvanism and my publications in the memoirs of the Institut National in Paris. As a friend of science, you will excuse the indulgence of my admiration. I would love to talk to you about a subject that you have treated so ingeniously in your work on Virginia, the teeth of mammoth which we too discovered in the Andes.[2]

Alexander von Humboldt had just returned from his own scientific expedition, a five-year exploration of Mexico, Cuba, and South America, the first to explore much of the region. It was also the first expedition which examined a place from a *holistic* scientific perspective. Von Humboldt did not study life-forms and landforms of an area in isolation from another. Instead, he studied a place; then observed how all its elements — of land, air, water, and life — interconnect with and influence each other. His work is considered one of the foundations of the modern science known as biogeography.

Scientist-President Jefferson, who knew of von Humboldt's work, sent the German scientist an invitation to the White House. Their audience became a lengthy visit at the White House, and later, Monticello. The two men spent days discussing science and liberty. Although Von Humboldt disagreed with Jefferson on the issue of slavery, he generally agreed with him politically. The two men agreed enthusiastically on matters of science and exploration. They even discussed the Lewis and Clark Expedition, which excited von Humboldt as much as it excited Jefferson. When von Humboldt left the United States, American author Margaret Bayard Smith gave him the highest of praise: "An enlightened mind has already made him an American."[3]

Widely read in the United States, Von Humboldt's books soon had Americans discussing one of his main ideas: κόσμος. "Cosmos." He wrote, "I have the crazy notion to depict the entire material universe, all that we know of the phenomena of universe and earth, from spiral nebulae to the geography of mosses and granite rocks, in one work — and in a vivid language that will stimulate and elicit feeling.... But it is not to be taken as a physical description of earth; it comprises heaven and earth, the whole of creation." Von Humboldt was writing a work encouraging humans to see the universal — the cosmos — which underlies all knowledge, a work which would reveal how "everything is interrelated."[4]

He published the first volume of *Cosmos* in 1845. An international best-seller, it brought von Humboldt's ideas about the unity of nature and the importance of holistic field science to its many readers. But it also had a deeper message. As one of its reviewers wrote, "If the world is ever to be harmonized it must be through a community of knowledge, for there is no other universal ... principle in the nature of man.... [The first chapters of *Cosmos* reveal] the very spirit of liberal culture."[5]

Von Humboldt's ideas were very much at home in the United States. So as the emigrants headed west, traveling for a time along the river named for the scientist, his ideas traveled with them. The idea of cosmos, of nature studied on site and in an interdisciplinary way, had become a part of American enlightened thought.

In 1868, nine years after the *New York Times* devoted its front page to American celebrations of von Humboldt's centennial, a group of men who had emigrated from the old states founded the college that would become the University of California. As they stood on what is now known as Founder's Rock and gazed west out the Golden Gate, one of them quoted Bishop Berkeley's poem: "Westward the course of empire makes its way." That inspired another founder, Frederick Billings: "Eureka! Berkeley said that! And that saying fits this location.... Berkeley would be a good name."[6] So the new town, which would soon house the university, was named for a philosopher—one who helped develop empirical science, judged that any new civilization would succeed only in a place where "nature guides and virtue rules," and believed America was that place. And it was named in a time when the ideas of Jefferson and von Humboldt, the ideas of enlightenment, liberal thought, and cosmic understanding, were driving the search for knowledge.

Without realizing it, the founders had struck their own intellectual mother lode—because in founding the college that would become the University of California at Berkeley along the lines envisioned by Bishop Berkeley, and in the time of *Cosmos*, they would also found a new enlightenment. It would carry forward the work of the older Enlightenments, of Europe and Scotland, but it would add a new idea: since it is in untamed wildernesses that scientists like von Humboldt or explorers like Lewis and Clark can best seek *cosmos*, huge wildernesses should be preserved. This idea, of the necessity of wilderness, gave the new enlightenment its own Californian character. So call this the *California* Enlightenment, if you will.

The motto chosen for the university which would give birth to the California Enlightenment was, fittingly, *Fiat Lux*: "Let There Be Light."

Almost as soon as the university opened its doors, hands-on study of wild nature became part of its program. Its first professor, physics Professor John LeConte (who would later become university president), built his curricula around Bishop Berkeley's idea of empirical observation of nature. LeConte's brother, geology professor Joseph LeConte, deeply religious and a passionate scientist, believed humans must study two books of God: scripture and nature. Joseph LeConte would work to preserve God's book of nature for science—especially after John Muir inspired him.

Scottish-born John Muir arrived in San Francisco, on March 28, 1868—five days after the University of California was founded.[7] Four days later, he walked from San Francisco to Yosemite. The great, ancient valley, with its half-mile-high waterfalls, its verdant swales and meadows, and its interplay of light and life and rock, staggered him. "The Range of Light," he called it. He found work, settled in, and became an apostle for wilderness, ready to preach to any visitor to Yosemite who came his way.

One of the great geological controversies of the time was boiling around four Sierra valleys. Josiah Whitney, considered the greatest geologist of the age and leader of the first survey of California geology, held to the "catastrophic theory"—the idea that giant cataclysms caused the formation of Hetch Hetchy, Yosemite, Tehipite Valley, and Kings Canyon. But field research in Yosemite convinced Muir that glaciers did the work. Muir believed he had discovered remnant glaciers in the highest peaks of the Yosemite.

Word of the debate between the eminent geologist and the untrained "self-styled poetico-tramp-geologist-bot. and ornith-natural, etc.!!!," as Muir once described himself, reached Joseph LeConte's ears.[8] Who was right? LeConte wanted to go and see for himself.

He soon had the opportunity. In 1870, when the university was two years old, several of its students decided to spend part of their summer mountaineering in the Yosemite. The "University Excursion Party" invited geology Professor Joseph LeConte to join them. In Yosemite Valley LeConte and the students were buttonholed by the rough, intense young Muir. He told the party he could show them glaciers. "Why not join us?" the students suggested. So Muir went along, all the way across the Sierra, to the high desert beyond Mono Pass. On the way he used that great natural laboratory to make his case, showing the students and their professor clear evidence of glaciation.

Muir also argued for the value of wild places. One night, he took Professor LeConte to Tenaya Lake. LeConte remembered:

> I went with Mr. Muir and sat on a rock jutting into the lake. It was full moon. I never saw a more delightful scene. The deep stillness of the night; the silvery light and deep shadows of the mountains; the reflection on the water, broken into thousands of glittering points by the ruffled surface; the gentle lapping of the wavelets upon the rocky shore — all these seemed exquisitely harmonized with one another and the grand harmony made answering music in our hearts. Gradually the lake surface became quiet and mirror-like, and the exquisite surrounding scenery was seen double. For an hour we remained sitting in silent enjoyment of this delicious scene, which we reluctantly left to go to bed.[9]

LeConte's field work convinced him that Muir was right. He returned to the university and published in favor of Muir's ideas. LeConte was also convinced of the value of field studies in wilderness areas, and thus of the need to preserve wild places. LeConte later joined with Muir and others to found the Sierra Club to preserve wildernesses for research and recreation.

The ideas of Muir and LeConte, about the value of wilderness, would be a foundation of the California Enlightenment. Institutions born from Muir and LeConte's ideas — like the Sierra Club, and the National Park Service — would be the offspring of the California Enlightenment.

Another foundation of the California Enlightenment was a collection of books, maps, drawings, and oral histories amassed by Hubert Howe Bancroft.[10] Ohioan Bancroft came to San Francisco as West Coast representative for New York bookseller George H. Derby. He was so successful that he soon opened his own bookstore and publishing house.

After work, relaxing in the restaurants and bars of the city, Bancroft often heard 49ers talk about overlanding to California and their days in the mining camps. Bancroft realized he could use the stories to write a history of California, and began organizing the recording of hundreds of oral histories from the Gold Rush and Overland Movement. He also began to collect the pioneers' journals and letters. In time, he had 60,000 items, most of them primary sources. It was the first great record of thousands of people entering a new land where the main character they'd interact with would be the land itself. It was also a detailed record of how those people were changed by the interactions. After he published his history, Bancroft gave the collection to the University of California, Berkeley. The journals, letters, oral histories, maps, and sketches became the foundation for one of the great research libraries of the world, the Bancroft — first library to preserve such a vast literature of wild places.

By the time George R. Stewart arrived at Berkeley, in the academic year 1919-20, to earn his Master's Degree in English at the University of California, the California Enlightenment was well established. The Bancroft Library was there, with its wonderful collections of wilderness literature. Professors, like Herbert Bolton, were teaching history as a function of landscape. Even the look of the campus, founded in the work and ideas of Frederick Law Olmsted, reflected the importance of the natural world. And there was still nearby wild land to explore.

Stewart would fit well with the principles of the university's Enlightenment. He would mine the resources of the library; but his greatest scholarly discovery would be found in the field. That is, George R. Stewart's work would join literature and land.

10

The morning after he arrived in Berkeley, George R. Stewart walked from his hotel to the University of California campus, Princeton Bachelor of Arts degree in hand, and registered at a table near the Northeast Corner of the Life Sciences Building. The young women who examined Stewart's Princeton diploma commented on the beauty of its orange-and-black lettering, then checked him in. Stewart had joined the intellectual community of the University of California.

Stewart was entering one of the best English departments in the United States. Under Charles Mills Gayley, the Department of English at the University of California, Berkeley, had become a national leader in the teaching of English. Although the department began to decline in the early twentieth century — University President Wheeler, insisting that English departments should stick to teaching English composition, cut the staff— the department was still better than before Gayley took over, and still a national leader in the discipline.

Gayley is mythologized at Berkeley, where he's remembered as someone who wrote college songs to boost the spirit of the Golden Bear, offered classes popular enough to require use of the Greek Theatre, and generally boomed his way through 34 years in the department. Gayley Drive, which leads to California Memorial Stadium, is named for his ability to work Cal students up before a game. (Gayley was a great fan of Cal football.) He encouraged a well-rounded life for his students and professors, teaching the idea by example: Gayley championed the cause of black Americans, defended Irish Home Rule, and in his spare time organized a volunteer ambulance company. But Gayley was always The English Professor. When a teacher from the Anna Head School, a girls' school, presented an assigned paper about an Elizabethan comedy, *The Honest Whore,* she mispronounced "whore." Gayley corrected her: "Whore — *whore*—WHORE! It is pronounced *WHORE!* ... Even your little girls down at the school know how to pronounce that word!"[1]

George R. Stewart remembered Gayley with great affection. One of Gayley's favorite lines, which the professor frequently quoted, stayed with Stewart until the end of his days. The line was from Kipling: "After me cometh a builder — tell him, I too have known." Decades later Gayley's quotation would wander into Stewart's novel, *Sheep Rock.* And Stewart would end his history of the Department of English with a reference to Galey and the quote.

Wheeler's "English-as-composition" philosophy was not necessarily bad for Stewart. With less staff to supervise students doing creative work in English literature, students were able to work independently. Stewart had almost complete freedom to do his work the way he wanted to do it. Such benign neglect is a great gift, for the gifted.

He also had good teachers. Professor Chauncey Wells did not publish, and had no degree beyond Bachelor's. But he could teach. By the time Stewart left Wells' American Literature essay-writing class, he had the elements of his style down.

Stewart discovered *what* he would write in Herbert Bolton's class. Bolton was one of those people who define an area of study — in this case, California history. Students were mesmerized by his lectures. Bolton insisted that field research be part of their work. And Bolton had a forceful message for students: California history needed bards and scholars — or scholarly bards — to preserve and teach it. To dig into that history would be to pioneer a rush for *literary* gold. And the pioneers were still alive! To go out into that still-wild landscape, to *feel* the land while the pioneers told you about their adventures in that land! Why, it would be a great work, to preserve their stories — and a fine career for those who undertook the quest!

Inspired, Stewart decided to do a thesis that combined California history with literature. There was one hurdle: in those days, serious students of literature were supposed to study European authors — not raw American frontier writers. Stewart figured out how to get around the obstacle. He chose "Robert Louis Stevenson in California" as his topic. Stevenson was a European writer of acceptable reputation who had visited frontier California. Writing about him, Stewart would please the department, and satisfy his own interest in California history.

In 1879, Stevenson headed to California in pursuit of a woman. Fanny Osbourne was married, but not very well married, and she and Robert Louis Stevenson had come to love each other in France. Against his wealthy family's wishes, he chased her west to the Central Coast of California, to Monterey. One day, reading a news story while watching the Pacific waves roll upon the wild coast, Stevenson learned that a coin from a buried treasure had been dug up. It gave him the idea for a tale, and he made some notes.

Then he returned to his primary business: Fanny. After a lonely Christmas in San Francisco, Stevenson finally persuaded Fanny to marry him. His parents disapproved, and cut off his remittance. But Robert and Fanny were happy. They honeymooned at the abandoned "Juan Silverado Mine" high on flat-topped Mount St. Helena above the "long green strath" of Napa Valley. It was a long, leisurely, working honeymoon, as Stevenson wrote to make up for his lost income.

In 1880, Stevenson and Fanny returned to Scotland. Fanny captivated the Stevenson family, who welcomed her, forgave him, and restored Stevenson's inheritance. Fanny and Robert had 14 happy years together after their California interlude, years in which Stevenson wrote some of the best-loved books of his time. One of those was the tale that had come to mind in Monterey as he read of the treasure coin: *Treasure Island*, which Stevenson wrote in 1883.

The hero of the novel, young Jim Hawkins, travels with pirate Long John Silver and others to an island of sandy beaches and oak trees and a flat-topped mountain. He and his companions find (and get to keep) a pirates' treasure. Stewart believed there was something of the place called California, disguised, in *Treasure Island*. Stevenson himself had written, "The scenery is Californian in part,"[2] and it was clear that *Treasure Island*'s landscapes were not those of Scotland. There were other clues, too: *Treasure Island*'s most memorable character, for example, was Long John Silver. But where in California might the landscapes be found? The key certainly lies in the tale.

Treasure Island:
> The hills ran up clear above the vegetation in spires of naked rock. All were strangely shaped, and the Spy-glass, which was by three or four hundred feet the tallest on the island, was likewise the strangest in configuration, running up sheer

from almost every side then suddenly cut off at the top like a pedestal to put a statue on....

... I had now come out upon the skirts of an open piece of undulating, sandy country ... dotted with a few pines, and a great number of contorted trees not unlike the oak in growth."

... I turned hither and thither among the trees. Here and there were flowering plants, unknown to me; here and there I saw snakes, and one raised his head from a ledge of rock and hissed at me with a noise not unlike the spinning of a top. Little did I suppose that he was a deadly enemy, and that the noise was the famous rattle.

Then I came to a long thicket of these oak-like trees — live, or evergreen, oaks, I heard afterwards they should be called — which grew low along the sand like brambles, the boughs curiously twisted, the foliage compact, like thatch. The thicket stretched down from the top of one of the sandy knolls, spreading and growing taller as it went, until it reached the margin of the broad, reedy fen, through which the nearest of the little rivers soaked its way into the anchorage. The marsh was steaming in the strong sun, and the outline of the Spy-glass trembled through the haze....

... great rollers would be running along all the external coast, thundering and thundering by day and night.[3]

Rattlesnakes, live oaks, undulating sandy country, coastal marshes, a distinctive flat-topped mountain, great rolling waves along the coast: all clues, like a pirates' map, that Stewart figured pointed to real places. To find out *which* places, Stewart compared *The Silverado Squatters*, Stevenson's non-fiction story of his time in California, with *Treasure Island*. Then, in the best manner of the California Enlightenment, Stewart went into the field to look at places Stevenson had described in *The Silverado Squatters*.

When he put the literary clues and the field research together, Stewart knew he'd discovered Treasure Island. The Island's sandy beach, oaks, winding rivers, and marshes were the landscapes near Monterey. Spyglass Hill was Mt. St. Helena, the mountain where Fanny and Robert Louis Stevenson honeymooned. And Long John Silver sprang from the couple's honeymoon lodgings, the abandoned Juan Silverado Mine.

Stewart's thesis, "Stevenson in California," was original work of the first order. It easily earned him his Master of Arts degree in English. It also brought him to the attention of other writers and historians. The thesis is still considered a landmark of research and writing. James D. Hart, for example, cites Stewart's work in his Introduction to a 1966 edition of *The Silverado Squatters*.

But it was not his only achievement, in Stewart's first University of California year.

While working on *Treasure Island*, Stewart discovered that Stevenson was the author of an article printed in the Monterey newspaper of his day. "The San Carlos Day Essay," by Stevenson, was republished with an introduction by Stewart in the prestigious *Scribner's Magazine* — George R. Stewart's first

George R. Stewart in Yosemite, June, 1919. This is probably taken at Glacier Point, and probably by the mysterious Rose.

publication in a national magazine. To top things off, Stewart's poem, "A Ballade of Railroad Folders," was published in the old *Life Magazine.*

Stewart later considered the academic year of 1919-20 to be the most important in his professional life. In one year, he had done groundbreaking research on Stevenson, written it up in his master's thesis, been published in two national magazines, and become familiar with the campus that would become his scholarly home. Yet as important as the accomplishments were, an idea that came out of the year was much more important. The research on Stevenson had convinced Stewart that place must be primary in his own work.

On May 12, 1920, the University of California, Berkeley, awarded Stewart his M.A. in English. He went to Columbia to earn his Ph.D. But it was a poor first year. The professor directing his dissertation, Carl Van Doren, wanted him to study how the English view American writers. Stewart felt Van Doren had given him too large a topic with no guidance as to how to cut it down. He had little luck with his research.

Romance may have been working against him as well. His friendship with Gladys Knowlton had lasted long enough — more than four years — to make it a prelude to marriage. They had become very close — there are photos of the couple hiking Mt. Baldy and boating on the Potomac, and the letter from Stewart to Gladys Knowlton which he wrote during his time in the army. But the couple did not marry, and Gladys returned his letter to him. So there may have been a breakup at the same time he was going through his first year at

Columbia. There's also evidence, scant but interesting, of another love: The Anna Evenson Photo Collection holds a few faded photographs of George Stewart in Yosemite with a young woman named Rose. There's nothing else about Rose in any of the papers or the oral history. But it seems that she and he cared enough for each other, for a time at least, to travel to Yosemite and hike together through its mountains. That, too, may have been troubling George Stewart during his first year at Columbia.

Whether caused by a broken heart, or two broken hearts, or simply his year of fits-and-starts at Columbia, Stewart decided that he needed a time of recreation. So he planned an exploration of a new and challenging landscape, and, as usual, planned to do it his own way.

11

The tradition of the "Grand Tour" began in the 17th century when rich young men traveled to the capitals of the western world so they could experience places they'd studied. By the nineteenth and early twentieth century, middle-class tourists — especially teachers — joined the rich, journeying to as many of the great sites of western civilization as they could afford. But, by the early twentieth century, the tour had become routine. It lacked the adventure of the early days, when, for example, those on the tour needed to disassemble their carriages in order to cross the Alps. To recapture the sense of adventure Stewart decided to do his Grand Tour by bicycle.

Bicycling through Europe would be a challenge today. In 1921, it was a brave venture. No freeze-dried food, no backpacker's stoves, no lightweight tents. No Gore-Tex for riding through the frequent rains and mists. No Lycra, no cycling shoes, no helmets. Campgrounds did not exist. There were no fast-food restaurants. No credit cards. Cycling technology was primitive. And roads were bad: many of Europe's roads were merely improved wagon tracks, and some still carried damage from World War I.

Keeping healthy would be a challenge. In a Europe recovering from war, sanitary conditions were questionable. The danger of bad food or drink was high. In fact, Stewart would suffer "road gut" three times in attacks severe enough to lay him low. Stewart also risked a flare-up of his lung disease when he rode, exposed, through wind and rain or over icy mountain passes.

Stewart did have his resources. His treks in the San Bernardino Mountains and hitchhikes across the United States had toughened him and taught him self-reliance. He carried the invaluable Baedeker Guides, with information about roads, sites to see, and places to stay. Most of all, he had the will to do it. After the frustrating year at Columbia, he was up for the trip.

He left a good record of the adventure. Most days, Stewart sent a postcard

Milestone: A rest stop for Stewart on his 1921 European bike trip. He rode his bike more than 3800 miles in about five months.

to his parents. On rest days he wrote longer letters. He kept a diary, detailed in Britain. On the Continent, he recorded only his daily mileages and overnight stops. Stewart sometimes added embellishments to the diary: his hand-drawn maps of proposed routes, and diagrams of interesting places he'd visited.

He set out from New York on the S.S. *Adriatic* in May of 1921. His friend Gladys Knowlton came to see him off, fortifying him with a fruit basket; if it was the end of a romantic relationship between George and Gladys, it was certainly a gentle and friendly closure. It was a good sendoff, but the ocean voyage left some things to be desired. The sameness of the horizon did not appeal to the young lover of mountains. The berth was too short for his tall frame. He was seasick. To prepare for England he read *Hard Times*, but found it the poorest of Dickens's books. And his fellow second-class passengers were not the type of people with whom a young scholar could share ideas. He arrived at Southampton anxious for the landing.

The next day Stewart wrote in his diary, "Adventures begin."[1] He started with a shakedown ride on a rented bike, through picture-book England — from Southampton, west to the Bristol Channel country, and through the Salisbury Plain. Stewart expected a gentle ride, but before the first day was over he began to encounter the demands of the road. Hills. Headwinds. Heavy traffic. And he caught a cold. He also learned his first road lessons. To avoid some hills, he tried a route through Cheddar. The detour proved much longer than his planned route; and he still wound up on top of a hill. But not all road lessons are bad — once on the summit, he enjoyed the view of a lovely English landscape. (The road taketh away; but the road also giveth.)

Some 123 miles later, with the shakedown under his belt, Stewart put together a permanent kit. He decided on a three-speed bike — probably a Raleigh, known for its Sturmey-Archer 3-speed gear hub — since it would give him some advantage on hills. He equipped the bike with a rack and a headlight, and made sure his personal gear included a rain cape and a vest. Then, kit complete, George R. Stewart pedaled out of Southampton, headed for Edinburgh. It was 3 P.M. on the 20th of May, 1921. The real adventure was beginning.

His route took him on a winding literary exploration around England: London, Canterbury, Oxford, Stratford-on-Avon. Always the scholar, he stopped at museums along the way so he could research Chaucerian and Anglo-Saxon manuscripts and an original copy of Dr. Samuel Johnson's dictionary. Then he headed to Colwich at a leisurely pace, to keep an appointment with the nobility.

Lord Graham Balfour, a relative of Robert Louis Stevenson who had known the man, wrote the first biography of Stevenson. (One of Stevenson's most memorable characters, David Balfour of *Kidnapped*, was modeled on a distant relative of Lord Balfour.) Learning of the original work that young Stewart had done on *Treasure Island*, Lord and Lady Balfour invited Stewart to visit them. Stewart accepted with excitement, knowing he'd get a sense of the flesh-and-blood Stevenson from Balfour. The Balfours and Stewart spent an enjoyable evening together, discussing the life and work of Stevenson. Education probably entered the conversation since Lord Balfour was the Director of Education for Staffordshire. Drifting off to sleep in the Balfour's house, Stewart surely reflected on how far his encounter with *Treasure Island* had brought him: to his epiphany of the maps, the discovery of the real Treasure Island in California, and now this cordial evening with members of the British nobility, discussing Robert Louis Stevenson.

The next day, after Lady Rhoda Balfour showed Stewart around the local cathedral, Stewart hit his roads at a hard pedal. The geography was more challenging, as the land began to rise when he neared the Lake District and the Scottish Border. He'd had good luck with the weather so far, but now he began riding through "Scotch mists." Yet he found a pleasing wildness along the way. Riding from Shrewsbury to Chester, he came to the River Dee and wrote, "I was glad again to be near a river which made a noise; I want mountain streams such as I am used to; I get tired of sluggish valley streams all full of weed."[2] After touring Liverpool (where he failed in his attempt to buy some BVD underwear), he had a record 62 mile-day. At end of that day, climbing to Kendal in the Lake District, mountain streams again re-vitalized him. And he had another epiphany. "Got in Hills of Westmoreland & had change to rough rocky country with talking streams. From my experience in England with rivers I have decided that I am inherently a Hillman."[3] Stewart was finding himself, along the Way of the Bicycle.

There was "a rather poor day of wandering around ... without getting anywhere or seeing much of anything I set out to see,"[4] yet nine days after he left Lichfield, Stewart arrived in Glasgow. He enjoyed the town and area for a day; then headed up Loch Lomond, over the Grampian Mountains, through Pitlochery, and down to Edinburgh for another encounter with the world of Robert Louis Stevenson.

In Edinburgh, Stewart visited four elderly cousins of Stevenson's, Balfours again, at Pilrig House. As a child, Stevenson had played in the Pilrig House garden. He wrote the house and the family into at least two novels. "I give you here a letter to a namesake of your own, the learned Mr. Balfour of Pilrig, a man whom I esteem. The laird of Pilrig is much looked up to in the Faculty" he wrote in *Kidnapped*.[5] Stewart had tea with Stevenson's cousins, listening closely as they shared their memories of Robert Louis Stevenson.

From Edinburgh, he headed south, over good Scottish roads. Confidence growing, he began to leave his mapped route, writing, "I have not yet decided what road I shall follow. I shall let the future develop itself— which is the best way to travel."[6] He visited Cambridge, but there was a drought in England and the weather was miserably hot. No mechanic himself, he waited four hours in the heat in Ipswich while a man raised his handlebars. Then he headed for Harwich, to catch the boat to Holland.

On July 11, the now-seasoned traveler began his trip around the Continent. He was in good shape, and comfortable with his equipment. But Stewart had a much greater distance to cover on the Continent, massive mountains to cross, and few weeks in which to do it. He stopped keeping a detailed journal, prob-ably so he could use writing time as road time. Mileages began to build up: an average day went from about 34 miles to 47.

He did not stay in Holland for long. The roads were bad and Stewart found the food wanting. (He thought the Dutch ate too much bread.) The country was flat and uninteresting to a Hillman. But he liked the friendly Dutch people, many of whom spoke English. Several of them rode with him for short distances.

Belgium's rough roads slowed him down, but Stewart enjoyed Belgian cities. He took a break in Antwerp (which he found a very pleasant city), staying for a weekend. The highlight was a visit to the museum-house of a turn-of-the-16th century Flemish publisher. Stewart bought a sheet with old typefaces printed on it.

Next was Paris, the midway point of his tour. Stewart spent six days in Paris, sweating through an unusually hot summer as he wandered about the city. He prepared for the rest of his trip, booking passage home, renewing supplies, and figuring up accounts. His daily expenses had been less than $6 a day, so he had enough to finish the trip, but to be on the safe side he asked his father to send additional funds. He was happy to find that meals were reasonable, and he enjoyed the good French food. But there was a down side to cheap meals — they were a result of war's effects on the French economy.

On July 31, Stewart pedaled out of Paris. There had been little effort to clean up the debris of war on the Champaign Plateau and he found the landscape dismal. The sight of the lush Argonne Forest lifted his heart; but on the other side of the forest he entered a plain where the guns had destroyed every village. The heat and the scenes of destruction took their toll on the young traveler, and Stewart rested for a day at Metz.

He rode through constant rain in Germany and Alsace. In spite of the weather, he enjoyed the beauty of the time: "I had a good ride to-day — the Gap of Belfort on my right, the … valley of Alsace behind, the Black Forest rising away on the left beyond the Rhine & in front the Jura beginning to rise up."[7] In top condition, he made a one-day run of 69 miles down the broad valley of the Rhine.

The easy land would soon fall behind him, but the weeks of work, sweat, and dust had prepared him for what lay ahead: crossing the Alps. He was positive about the challenge, writing, "I hope for some good weather and full moon in the Alps."[8] (He would get neither.) He took a rest day in Lucerne, then began his pedal up the long grades toward the Bruning and Gothard Passes.

"Pedal" was optimistic — he walked his bike as much as he rode it. But the road was good, and the views beautiful. The country reminded him of California; it was "like the Merced Canyon below Yosemite but the [river] is a sort of milky white instead of blue like the Merced."[9] Milky water meant he was nearing glacier country. The next night, he stayed in a hotel by the side of the glacier after biking and walking over 7,000-foot Grimsel Pass. It was a milestone. For the first time Stewart was in the Mediterranean drainage.

By the end of the next day, August 20, George R. Stewart had crossed two more passes, the Furka and the San Gottardo, each more than 8,000 feet high, making the crossing in a driving, bitterly cold rain. His pack and his clean laundry were so wet he believed his equipment would never recover. Yet cold, wet, and exhausted as he was, he was exhilarated. He had met the challenge of the Alps.

That night, drying out and warming up in a hotel in Airolo, Stewart knew the high spiritual state of those who win through storm-lashed mountains. He wrote his mother: "I have had a great day all in a hard rain. It was desperately cold at the high altitude. [Although] I have pretty good nerve for mountain roads…. The San Gottardo was about all I could stand on a bicycle. But I have crossed the Alps."[10]

He still had miles to go. Down, into the Plain of Turin, Stewart rode; then through northwestern Italy, along the Riviera, and northwest across France. By the time he reached Le Havre he had pedaled another 1,100 miles, swum in the Mediterranean, visited Chartres and other historic sites, encountered interesting place names like Aignes-mortes, got sick one last time with "road-gut," and generally had quite a satisfying time.

On September 21, George R. Stewart wrote, "Dear Papa: I ended my cycling … 55 miles [pedaled today] from Rouen getting here about 3 P.M. My bicycle is on the boat & I cross to Southampton to-night,"[11] and it was over. When Stewart sold his bike back to the dealer in Southampton (for about half what he paid) he had ridden 3,836 miles.

Stewart's trip proved to be more than exercise, more than therapy, more than Grand Tour. It was a journey of discovery for the young man. Stewart learned again he was a Hillman; that mountains, with their singing streams and great challenges, moved him deeply. He learned he was not afraid to meet challenges. In the struggle over the great Swiss mountain passes he had pushed himself to his psychological and physical limits, and beyond, and he had won through. He would return to his scholarly studies, but he would never again doubt his need for mountains and wilderness: the places where rivers make music.

12

Renewed by the bicycle trip, Stewart finished his formal education. He left American Literature to study the rhythms of poetic verse under Professor Ashley Horace Thorndyke. Like other professors of his time, Thorndyke didn't offer much guidance, but Stewart did a good job on the difficult task. Researching "Modern Metrical Technique," he analyzed the use of meter in all the English poetry published from 1700 to 1900.

Again, his Army pneumonia proved fortunate. Following the lead of German universities, Columbia required publication of all dissertations, but Stewart didn't have the money to publish. Since the Army was helping pay tuition as part of his disability pension, Stewart argued that the army should publish his dissertation. Eventually, the Army agreed, but they printed it in-house without showing him a proof. The result was riddled with typographical errors. "An awful job," Stewart called it, but at least the dissertation was published.[1]

Ph.D. in hand, Stewart applied for positions at the University of Michigan and the University of California. Michigan answered first, with an offer. Stewart accepted, and in September of 1922 began teaching at Ann Arbor. It was a good choice for his entrance into the university community. Michigan was in the process of being revitalized by its new leader, President Marion LeRoy Burton.

Burton was a remarkable man. Redheaded and charismatic, he overcame childhood poverty to become president of three universities: Smith College, the University of Minnesota, and the University of Michigan. At Michigan he updated the curriculum and raised money to modernize campus buildings. He was a leader off campus as well — Burton gave the nomination speech for Calvin Coolidge's presidential bid at the 1924 Republican National Convention.

Burton saw Stewart's potential, and encouraged him in his work. But Stewart received more than professional support from Burton. Stewart told Bancroft Oral History Interviewer Suzanne Riess, "The president's wife gave a tea, and — I think it was pretty good that I went to it."[2] Dr. and Mrs. Burton's daughter Theodosia was helping with the tea.

Theodosia — Teddie or Ted — had inherited her father's bold, outgoing, charismatic personality. And, like her father, she was a born manager — so much so that she even tried (humorously) to manage the nation's Secretary of State. Hughes wrote to her mother:

> My Dear Mrs. Burton,
>   You may tell your daughter that there were many "strange men" on the train — and that they all talked to me — I thought of her injunction many times — wishing that I could observe it.
>   Charles Evans Hughes,
>   Secretary of State[3]

Teddie was used to mixing with the famous and the creative people of the time. American poet Robert Frost and British Poet Laureate Robert Bridges were family friends. So were Henry and Clara Ford.

Theodosia — Ted — circa 1921. This portrait was taken shortly before she met George R. Stewart.

Ted and Dad, Smith College circa 1915. The young girl is Ted (Theodosia), with her father, Marion LeRoy Burton, president of Smith College. Ted would marry George R. Stewart in 1924.

And, like George, Teddie loved nature. Other family photos show her hiking, paddling a canoe, or meditating, at the family's cabin at Minnesota's Cass Lake. Since the Burtons had maids and cooks to keep up their cabin, Ted's "wilderness" was not as primitive as George's. Still, she had learned to appreciate the rigors and the beauty of the natural world.

And, like George, Teddie was a wanderer. She attended college all over the East and Midwest. There was a year at Minnesota. Another at Michigan. A third at Vassar. At Vassar, she got sick. So she took the following year off, staying home to help her mother. So she was serving at the president's tea when she met young George.

Stewart thought Ted's first impression of him had been less than favorable—that she found him awkward and stiff. But she remembered being impressed by the quiet, lanky Westerner. He had earned the respect of her father and could hold a conversation with the best of university scholars. He could also hitchhike across the United States, and pedal 3,800-miles on bicycle through Europe—both while fighting the lingering effects of pneumonia. If he was a scholar, he was a warrior-scholar.

George and Teddie became good friends. They could talk about the things they loved, like the university and the joys of the rustic life. But they also had

Theodosia, George R. Stewart, his first car. The car is an Overland.

that opposition which attracts. She was hearty, outgoing, cheerful, full of passion for life. He was quiet, scholarly, inner-directed. She was raised in Eastern society, and comfortable in the university setting. He was raised in the "Wild West," where he had become a "Hillman."

The two young people grew closer. One of the family photographs shows them in a prophetic pose — seated on the running board of his Overland Touring Car. The caption reads, "T.B. and G.R.S. 1923. His first car."[4] (In years to come, Ted would know much of riding in cars with George.) Ted is smiling; George grinning, ear to ear. It is a happy couple.

Yet Stewart missed California. So when an offer to teach English came from the University of California at Berkeley, he accepted. He would start teaching at Berkeley in the fall of 1923. In taking the job, he would be separated from the person who had become his best friend, so George took action to head off the loneliness. On the steps of the President's House — Ted's home — he knelt before her. He asked the question. And she said, "Yes!"

George R. Stewart had a dramatic introduction to Berkeley. No sooner had he begun to settle in at his new job at the University of California than a huge fire rushed down from the Berkeley Hills and through the city. The Great Berkeley Fire of September 1923 destroyed more than 600 homes and businesses. Fortunately, the campus was spared.

In a strange way, the fire helped Stewart. Volunteering to help with some of the clean-up took his mind off his separation from Ted until the challenge of being a new instructor at Berkeley could keep his loneliness at bay. And the fire inspired his writing, so deeply impressing him that fire would later be central in his books. Stewart's *Fire* is the first novel about fire ecology, and three of his other novels climax with the cleansing effect of fire. In the final scenes of *Earth Abides*, for example, Stewart moves the Berkeley Fire a few decades forward, where it roars through a post-apocalyptical ghost town and ghost university, sweeping its human characters into an unknown future.

Of course Ted was lonely too, but planning the wedding kept her so busy that she had little time to mope. And soon enough winter passed, days lengthened, and George R. Stewart returned to Ann Arbor. The wedding, held in June at the University of Michigan's new Clements Library, was quite an event. One of Stewart's relatives, Allen Wilson, sent another relative, Eleanor Clark, a tongue-in-cheek description of the scene the day before the ceremony. He listed the gifts piled up in the President's House: "pie-knives, small vases for what-in-the-devil, cheese plates ... flat silver in fourteen different styles and a variety of initials, and two waffle irons.... Several ... rugs, a desk, a bookcase, five barrels of glassware ... and two hundred and thirty donations from friends and others." Wilson reported that the Fords gave the bride and groom a "hand-tooled, leather lined, gilded and perfumed" autographed first edition of *Heart of Darkness* by Joseph Conrad. He thought a better gift would have been a Ford truck, to haul all those gifts back to Berkeley.[5]

It was quite a to-do, that wedding, and it attracted a stellar crowd. The Henry Fords were guests; so were English Poet Laureate Robert Bridges and his wife, and architect Albert Kahn (who designed Ford's Rouge River glass plant and the Clements Library) and his wife. Robert Frost, a good friend of the bride's parents and the first Poet Laureate of the University of Michigan, was probably there. The wedding itself, held in the Main Hall of the newly built Clements Library of American History, was elegant without being overdone. The reception was held at the President's House, next to the library. (Always more realistic than romantic, George R. Stewart later recollected that the hundreds of chicken salads served the wedding guests could have fed the newlyweds for a year.)

After the wedding, and a night in a grand hotel, Ted and George Stewart left Michigan by automobile. George described the honeymoon succinctly as "a wild trip in an old Studebaker car.... Terrible roads ... had to camp out three nights by a primitive roadside garage while they sent in ... for a new part."[6]

Ted's version was richer. She'd gone along with his plan for a honeymoon — driving to Berkeley on what passed for highways in 1924 — but she wasn't prepared for her new husband's idea of lodging.[7]

Crowsnest Mountain, 1924. George and Ted Stewart honeymooned by motoring to Berkeley on what passed for highways at that time. They followed a northern route (more or less today's U.S. 2) detouring north through southern Alberta's Crowsnest Pass along the way.

George drove to a general store. He came out with a tarp, blankets, hatchet, cast-iron fry pan, ropes, matches, and some steaks.

"What are you doing, dear?" I asked.

"Why, dear, we're going to camp our way back to California," he answered.

[She told the story with an amazed look on her face.] You must understand that I was the daughter of the President of the University of Michigan! I did NOT camp!

But camp they did. The first night, in a lonely forest on Michigan's Upper Peninsula, George demonstrated his skill in woodcraft. He set up a tent, made a fire, and cooked the steaks. Afterwards, they lay in the tent, Hillman George R. Stewart as happy as he could be.

But Ted couldn't sleep.

There were strange sounds. Scratchings. Snufflings. Moving things in the night. It was awfully scary!

"What's *that*?!" I asked George.

"Nothing, Dear. Raccoons. Go to sleep."

The next morning the Forest Warden came to the camp for a chat. After a few minutes, he asked, "Did you see the wolf pack last night?"

And that is how my life with George began.

Ted remembered nights in small town campgrounds.[8] "And the things you would hear from the other tents — men ranting around.... I remember one man kept saying, '[The campsite] cost me a dollar! [she laughed] ... it was worth it, but it just cost me a dollar!' He said, 'At home I could have got it for a quarter!' [She laughed again].

She remembered one "awful" night — camping in a huge granary. "You could hear the little mice running all over ... squeak, squeak, squeak, all night long!"

She also remembered the kindness of strangers.

> And of course there were no paved roads. It was a horrendous trip! We got stuck in a kind of a mud they call gumbo, in Montana. The tires, the wheels, all had big chains on them.... We got stuck and the tires would go around inside of the chains.... A cowboy type with a fur cap carrying a rifle came down over the hill and saw what was going on and he took the fence, the wire fence, and he wired the chains to the wheels. He tore up the fence and wired our chains to the wheels. [Ted laughed.] When he came I said, "Oh, George, look — there's a man with a gun coming after us!" [She laughed again.] And he fixed it up and we just walked out of the gumbo. It was wonderful."

The couple drove west on roads of Lincoln Highway vintage, in a day when motor travel was "something of a sporting proposition." The Lincoln Highway Association estimated a month or so for a transcontinental auto journey — if you could average the great speed of 18 miles per hour! The Association advised the cross-country automobilist to:

> *Buy gasoline at every opportunity.*
> *Wade through water before fording it.*
> *Carry chains, shovel, axe, jacks, tires and inner tubes, mechanic's tools.*
> *Don't wear new shoes.*[9]

Even though Ted and George didn't follow the Lincoln Highway, it was good advice for any auto traveler in 1924.

George wanted to see the high Northern Rockies at Glacier National Park in Montana. Since the Lincoln crossed the Rockies far south of Glacier, the young couple took a more northerly route. A map of the route sent to Ted's parents has been lost, so we don't know their exact route. But we can make a good guess from clues they left.

• Ted Stewart's memory of the Upper Peninsula and the Montana gumbo road point to a route west from Michigan on the "Theodore Roosevelt International Highway." That's today's U.S. 2 — known as the Hi-Line in Montana because the east-west highway hugs the Canadian border.

• George R. Stewart told interviewer Suzanne Riess that the young couple went north into Canada to cross the Rockies.

• One photograph in Anna Evenson's Stewart Family Collection shows two

Ted, Oregon state line, 1924. The adventurous newlyweds had made it to California! Ted is standing next to the Studebaker at the California/Oregon line.

Ted on ostrich, 1924. A copy of this photograph hangs on the walls of most of George and Ted's descendants' homes. A posed photograph taken at Cawston's Ostrich Farm in South Pasadena.

gravel tracks across a meadow leading toward Crowsnest Mountain, which is near southern Alberta's Crowsnest Pass.

- The Columbia River Highway, more or less on their route, was one of the best and most beautiful roads of the United States in 1924; George R. Stewart, road-lover, would certainly have made it a point to travel that highway.
- A photograph in the Anna Evenson collection shows Ted standing next to road signs announcing the California-Oregon Border and the Del Norte County Line.
- In his oral history, Stewart mentions a mechanical breakdown in Northern California on the Redwood Highway.

They probably drove the well-established Dixie Highway north to Michigan's Upper Peninsula. Then headed west on the Theodore Roosevelt International Highway to Glacier National Park, north, into southern Alberta, west across Crowsnest Pass, south to hit the Roosevelt again. At Spokane, where the Roosevelt and the Park-to-Park Highways divided, they headed southwest on the Roosevelt to drive the well-engineered Columbia River Highway. From Portland, they went south on the Pacific Highway (first transcontinental highway to be paved from end-to-end) to the Redwood Highway. The Redwood Highway took them to the Bay Area.

It was a successful adventure, and they made it to Berkeley in good time. They stopped briefly; then headed south to Stewart's family home in Pasadena. George showed Ted the tourist highlights — like Cawston's Ostrich Farm and Tropical Gardens, where ostriches were raised for their feathers. It was the only ostrich farm in the United States in those days, and quite an attraction. At Cawston's, the young couple was photographed with an ostrich. Slender, bespectacled, sporting a summer suit and Panama hat, the beginning of a mustache on his lip, George is quite a dashing fellow. Teddie wears a loose skirt, a large straw sunhat, white stockings, and comfortable sandal-shoes. They are both smiling, although a bit stiffly. George is the more relaxed of the two. Ted has good reason to be less relaxed — she is sitting on the ostrich. She holds onto the wings of a bird about two feet taller than her, a bird with large feet capable of doing serious damage.

Bancroft Library University Archivist Anthony Bliss, who found a copy of the Cawston brochure in the archives, described how the photographs were made. A bird wrangler would cover the bird's eyes. Blindfolded, the giant bird would allow a person to climb aboard. Then the wrangler would remove the blindfold. The ostrich would turn into a bucking bronco of a bird, squawking, kicking, and otherwise making life interesting for rider and companion. The trick was to get everything set, cock the shutter on the camera, whip the blindfold off, and snap the photo.

So it came to pass that Theodosia Burton Stewart, daughter of the man who nominated Calvin Coolidge for the presidency, a brilliant and accomplished university graduate, was immortalized sitting on a large, reluctant bird, her new husband standing by her side.

The picture says a lot about Ted and George as they were, starting their life together, in that honeymoon summer of 1924. They loved each other, they loved life, and they were not afraid to take a risk, whether on road or on ostrich. It is the way their descendants like to remember them, and the photograph has become a Stewart family keepsake.

Summer ended. The Stewarts said farewell to the family and again pointed the old Studebaker north. In Berkeley, they settled into their first small place, a cottage above California Memorial Stadium in Strawberry Canyon. For the next few years their days would revolve around George's work, the birth of their children, and the search for a house of their own. Hope-filled as the young couple was, the years ahead would not be easy. Events in the world, at the university and in their own lives meant that George and Ted Stewart would know their share of ordeals. But as they would learn, an ordeal is not always a bad thing. An ordeal can test a person's strength, build a person's confidence, lead to new ways of understanding, even encourage the right person — someone like George Stewart — to try a new pathway in life, or to create new kinds of works.

That is to say, ordeals can be gifts.

II. A Gift of Ordeals

13 *The California Enlightenment*

By 1924, when Ted and George returned to Berkeley to stay, the California Enlightenment had begun shaping American society and the University campus. In its first half-century it helped create an architecture which built the value of nature into structures of wood, glass and stone, and it gave birth to an organization — called "the best idea America ever had" — that would change how humans interacted with nature.

Berkeley's Bernard Maybeck, teacher of architectural engineering at the university in 1904, helped create California Arts and Crafts architecture. Maybeck was inspired by his neighbor, Swedenborgian[1] Minister Joseph Worcester, who had, in turn, been inspired by John Muir's cottage in Yosemite. Like Muir, Worcester believed the natural world reflected God, so human works should reflect nature. He built his own cottage, as Muir had built his "Hangnest," so that it appeared to emerge from the Earth. Maybeck and Worcester became good friends. Maybeck borrowed Worcester's ideas, using natural materials in his own work. Later, when Worcester supervised the building of the Church of the New Jerusalem in San Francisco, Maybeck would have a hand in the design. Usually called The Swedenborgian Church, the national historic landmark is considered one of the great works of the Arts and Crafts Movement. The first "Mission-Style" chairs were created for the church.

Maybeck described his architectural principles in a pamphlet about building on hillsides: "A house of natural material repeats the colors of the rocks; made of plaster or concrete, stone, brick, terra-cotta, rough wood, shingles or shakes, stained or natural, it absorbs the light, and, with the help of trellises and vines, hides among the browns and greens of the hill and is finished for all time. We have 'taken nothing away from the hill,' — have grouped with what is there what we add to it."[2] It was a philosophy which reflected the nature-centered California Enlightenment.

Maybeck designed, or helped design, some campus buildings. His best known is probably the 1902 Faculty Club. The shingle and tile-roofed building fits neatly into the small valley known as Faculty Glade, almost hidden behind an ancient oak tree. Nearby Strawberry Creek flows through groves of old trees. Inside the building, the club's Great Hall, its roof timbers exposed and unpainted, is anchored by a grand fireplace at one end. It feels like it belongs in a national park.

That's as it should be, because another child of the California Enlightenment was the National Park Service; and the early Park Service adopted the California Arts and Crafts style for many of its buildings. (Lake District Ranger Station and Norris Museum in Yellowstone and the Rangers' Club in Yosemite are good examples.) The Service itself grew from the wilderness epiphanies of Joseph LeConte and John Muir and the other members of the 1870 Yosemite University Excursion Party.

And an angry letter. Berkeley Alumnus Stephen Mather, appalled by conditions he found on a vacation through several national parks, sent a 26-page letter of complaint to his old Berkeley classmate Franklin Lane.[3] Secretary of the Interior Lane sent a one-sentence reply: "Dear Steve, If you don't like the way the national parks are run, come on down to Washington and run them yourself."[4] Mather was reluctant — he despised government bureaucracy — but he went. Lane introduced him to young Horace Albright, who agreed to take care of the political and bureaucratic details of establishing the Service. Seeing that Mather was still hesitant, Lane added, "He's another University of California man, by the way."[5] Reassured, Mather agreed to work on the project, if Albright would "consider staying and keeping me out of jail."[6]

Mather believed that academia — specifically, the University of California, with its emphasis on the importance of wild places — should be one of the foundations of the Service. So he built his staff in large part from UC professors, students and graduates — like Ansel Hall, George Melendez Wright, and Horace Albright. He convinced the University of California to cosponsor the first park naturalist lectures, at LeConte Memorial Lodge in Yosemite Valley. By the time George R. Stewart returned to the campus to teach, the Service had even established its first national office for education on the Berkeley campus, in Room 333 of Hilgard Hall.

With its emphasis on the land — whether it was the Bancroft's record of the Emigrants' crossing the wilderness, or buildings that seemed to grow out of the wild Earth, or the new National Park Service set up to protect the wilderness — the University of California was the perfect place for Stewart, the Hillman-scholar. Stewart would fit in very well, and in the years to come he would add considerably to the California Enlightenment.

14

Stewart joined the English department faculty at a difficult time.[1] Gayley had retired. Walter Morris Hart, the new Department Head, wanted to upgrade the department, so from 1921 to 1923 he cleaned house, eliminating instructors and professors without Ph.D.s and replacing them with scholars like George R. Stewart. Hart could not change things overnight, so the Department of English was no hotbed of intellectual activity. It still had some of the frontier intellectual insularity Stewart's mother feared when she argued he should attend Princeton.

For his first few years, young Dr. Stewart was too busy learning the job to worry about departmental politics and policies. He had much to learn, especially about the classroom. The quiet and introverted Stewart was, by nature, more scholar than teacher, but as an instructor his job was to teach students. He often wondered if he could measure up to the job.[2]

Fortunately, the record left by students says he met the measure.

Columnist Frances Trimble, his student in the 1930s, remembered him as a brilliant, innovative teacher. The textbook Stewart chose for his Freshman English Composition class showed his originality — he used *Webster's Collegiate Dictionary*. The first assignment was to write an essay about the words on page one of the Dictionary. Next, Stewart assigned each student a different word; the student had to look it up, analyze it, and use it as the theme of a composition. In another activity Stewart asked each student to write a single sentence of 125 words, then made them edit the sentence to 25 words or fewer, keeping the same meaning.

Trimble was impressed with the fact that Stewart treated students as adults, responsible for their own successes or failures: "Our first 'A' in college was given on a paper in that class, and our first 'F' in college was received in that class. We deserved both.... Right was right, and the teacher was a just man and well aware that he was teaching more than English composition. He was preparing us to live and earn in a very tough world" And she honored Stewart as "a thinker, a seeker of truth, and a researcher [who] taught us that, in a world of grays, there is great beauty in black and white."[3]

Writer Robert Galen Fogerty took a class from Stewart in the 1930s thinking it would be an easy grade. "A 'tea-drinker,' I thought," he wrote, remembering how he'd misjudged the professor. But Fogerty soon discovered Stewart was "a wide receiver, agile, intelligent, dynamic." He was so impressed that he went on to take every one of Stewart's classes. Fogerty believed Stewart had a great influence on his life and character — and on the music of the 1960s group Creedence Clearwater Revival, since Creedence founders Tom and John Fogerty were Robert Fogerty's sons.[4]

In the 1950s, tired of other electives, naturalist Joel Hedgpeth took Stewart's course on biography writing. Although Hedgpeth's grades were low, Stewart's use of words — "He never said too much and what he said was significant" — taught Hedgpeth how to write. He considered Stewart's course the most valuable he took at Berkeley. Following the tradition of the California Enlightenment, Hedgpeth eventually became a writer and editor of works that combined science and literature. Best known is his revision of Edward "Doc" Ricketts's classic work on marine biology, *Between Pacific Tides*. Hedgpeth was saddened that Stewart's fame as an author overshadowed his teaching ability. In a letter to Pulitzer Prize-winning author Wallace Stegner, Hedgpeth lamented the fact that, at Stewart's Memorial Service, "There was no one to speak for [Stewart] as a teacher."[5]

While George was developing his ability to teach, Ted was becoming a leader in the university community. Inspired by her mother's example — Nina Burton had founded "section clubs" at Michigan — Ted helped organize the University of California Section Club. The club was actually a group of sections, each appealing to a different interest, for spouses of university faculty members. (The faculty members usually participated as well.) Since she and George enjoyed drama, Ted founded the Drama Section.

The Section Club did some philanthropic work — providing milk for poor children, for example. But its best work was fellowship — the chance it gave young cash-strapped faculty members to socialize with each other. The meetings inevitably led to get-togethers — dinners, picnics, shared trips — and the foundation for years of collegiality.

Ted didn't forget students. She invited her husband's students to evening teas at the Stewart house. On cool winter evenings, a fire roaring in the fireplace, they would share tea, dessert, and ideas about class work with the professor, his wife, and each other. It was an enjoyable touch of home for lonely students.

Ted knew how to manage the affairs. Jill Stewart Evenson, the Stewarts' oldest child, recalls: "The problem was that students wouldn't always leave — they were in awe of the situation and they didn't know *how* to get up and leave." Ted solved the problem. "They hung a little picture by the front door … they'd get the conversation onto this picture and say, 'Oh, you come up and look at this picture' and get them over to the front door," and then they'd usher the students out the door.[6]

It's no wonder students were reluctant to go. Sitting around the Stewart fire, they felt, for a time, the warmth of home. In a time before email, when travel was expensive and slow and long-distance phone calls were rare, that sense of home away from home meant a lot to students. This letter from Marion L. (Tuttle) Lehnert, written 17 years after one such tea, shares student feelings about the get-togethers. "I was a member of your very first course in poetry writing, U. of Cal. 1925…. I remember one evening when I was so homesick for New Hampshire and the fiancée who was waiting for me…. We met that evening at your little home on the hill, there was a fire in the fireplace, and your charming wife served tea. I wish you would please tell her that she will never know what that cup of tea did for me."[7]

Letters like Marion Tuttle Lehnert's put flesh and blood into the brittle pages of archives, and humanity into scholarship. Sometimes, a page dissolves into the writer's soul and there comes an understanding beyond simple words on paper. Here is one such page, a letter from the Stewart Papers in the Bancroft Library. It is the best description of George R. Stewart as the good teacher, so it deserves the last word here.

> Dear Dr. Stewart,
>
> During the long years … I made a promise to myself, that I would … thank you for your interest and your kindness, if I graduated. I did graduate this June and I do want to thank you for your encouragement…. Sometimes things became so very difficult and the remembrance of your kindness helped me through dark times. I really am proud and happy to have finished school….
>
> Now I am learning how to teach remedial reading to young children…. Thank you, Dr. Stewart. You will never really know how much effect and influence your interest and kindness had, and how many many times I was grateful for it.
>
> Yours sincerely,
> Mary Maxwell Hidalgo[8]

15

In September of 1924, as his daughter Teddie and his new son-in-law George are settling into Berkeley, Marion Leroy Burton sits at the cabin by the lake and writes a letter. There is a September feeling in the letter — mellow and warm, carrying the color of autumn leaves. It is a happy letter: During the summer of 1924, he's gained a son-in-law, an adventurer-scholar Burton admires, a perfect husband for Burton's beloved daughter Teddie. The young couple has established their first home, a small house up Berkeley's Strawberry Canyon, above Memorial Stadium and below the Botanical Garden. Burton's son-in-law, George, is beginning his second year as "Instructor, English Department, University of California, Berkeley," with good prospects. He is earning the sum of $2,400.00—in 1925, about three times the cost of a new car, or half the cost of a modest house.

Dr. Burton addresses the first part of his letter to George, colleague to colleague. Stewart has planned to do some comparative research on American and European universities. Burton is enthusiastic about the project. He discusses Stewart's proposal section by section, expressing great interest in the academic issues involved.

After he's written four pages on scholarly matters, Burton's wife steps in. "Mother says that is enough for now on that *subject*" and his pen glissades into family matters.[1] The loving father writes, "Teddie dear your birthday letter warmed my heart." He thanks them for the gift of a "fish" (a small brass sculpture of a fish, which the newlyweds bought in San Francisco's Chinatown, which is still in the family, in Jill Stewart's care), for their letters describing Glacier National Park, and for George's map of their North American honeymoon drive. He comments on his age: "It's great to be 50. Now I have a right to get gray, bold and cranky." He closes with bold plans. "Next year," writes Burton, "we can all spend [my birthday] together 'somewhere in France.'"

But: "If you want to make God laugh, tell him your plans." There would be no birthday trip to France. Burton, the booming optimist, was ignoring reality. He had a severe infection, an inflammation of small structures in the kidneys called Bright's Disease not easily treated, even today. And, as usual, Burton was pushing, pushing, pushing himself to remake the University of Michigan.

He ignored the warning signs. Concerned, family friend Robert Frost wrote to Mrs. Burton. "Tell Mr. Burton when you can how anxious we have been for him. He must get well and then take care of himself."[2] But Frost was too late. The disease flared, the damp, cold Michigan winter settled in, and pneumonia followed. Marion Leroy Burton died — four days after Valentine's Day, on February 18, 1925.

Theodosia Burton Stewart never spoke with me about this time. I find little about it in the Stewart Papers at the Bancroft. Yet it is not hard to imagine its effect. Ted and her father knew the great closeness of hearts that exists between daughters and fathers. One photograph in Anna Evenson's collection captures it: no one looking at the snapshot of Dr. Burton and his young daughter Teddie coming out of a building at Smith College will doubt their love for each other. With the deep love of two men, Dad and George, Ted expected a lifetime of nourishment for the heart. But four days after the day that celebrates love one of the men left her life. Without George to encourage her — to "strengthen her heart" — life would have been dark indeed.

But it is the human condition that when one life goes, another comes. Ted was pregnant, and the small human growing inside her would not let her mourn too much. The child, a girl named Jane (but usually called Jill), was born on September 27, 1925. Now the young couple could move from mourning the loss of father and father-in-law to the building of a family.

Of course, parenthood brought its own problems. The young couple, one a bookish scholar, the other raised in a household where hired help did most of the work, was not fully prepared for the demands of parenthood. The baby, soon to be babies, demanded attention around the clock. And there were other stresses on the young family: They moved frequently, and Stewart's instructor's position was demanding. It was, George R. Stewart later wrote, confusing.

Good news helped. George was promoted to Assistant Professor, which meant his salary increased to $2,700. He would still teach; but he was now considered by the university to be a "teacher of the highest rank." The promotion also moved him into the realm of the professional scholar, with more time for research and publication. It was an important step in his career, and a great psychological boost for both of them.

In the same year family friend Robinson Jeffers, now an accomplished poet, published *The Roan Stallion*. With its powerful imagery of a storm on the California coast, and its emphasis on the role of nature in human events, the poem influenced Stewart's thought and work. He began to see nature as a character in human drama. That idea would eventually lead to a new literature — *ecological* literature.

So 1925, a year that began with heartbreak, ended with hope. If the year, like the years in Stewart's novel *Earth Abides*, had been named, it might have been named The Year of the Death and the Birth. It had been the first year of the ordeals, and the Stewarts had weathered it well.

Now, I want to give you a sense of Stewart's close geography.

Drive over the Bay Bridge from San Francisco, turn north on I-80, and you're soon in Berkeley. The signs say "I-80 East" but I-80, like U.S. 40 before it, runs pretty much north-south along the tidal flats at the edge of San Francisco Bay. The geography of Berkeley's western edge is flat. Take the University Avenue exit, head east, and the road soon begins rising.

The university, like the Parthenon, once sat high and isolated on its hills. Development has crowded in, but the campus and its campanile — especially the campanile, Sather Memorial Tower — still command the view. From any place on the San Francisco or Marin shore with a clear line of sight across the Bay, the campanile stands high and white in the center of the campus, against the green of the hills behind it. Its bells ring out the hours; and, once a day, its carillon plays songs connected with "Cal." (Except during finals. On the Friday before final exams, the campanile plays "They're Hanging Danny Deever in the Morning;" then stands silent during Finals Week.)

Continue east until you reach Oxford Street. Turn left on Oxford, right on Hearst, right on Gayley (named for Gayley of the English Department), left on Stadium Rim Way, and left again on Centennial Drive.

Now the land rises steeply, toward the summit of the Berkeley Hills. Centennial winds up Strawberry Canyon, near the Stewarts' first small rented home. Beyond Memorial Stadium the landscape is undeveloped, except for two fine retreats. The UC Botanical Garden has an arboretum that displays California native plants in their niches — a good place to wander through the Stephen Mather Memorial Grove of Redwoods. In the Memorial Grove, read the plaque honoring Stephen T. Mather: "There will never come an end to the good he has done." It's one of only two "Mather Plaques" placed outside the National Parks.

A little farther uphill is the Lawrence Hall of Science. There's a fine view of the Bay Area, a museum with the first cyclotron (small, built by E.O. Lawrence of UC Berkeley), some interactive science exhibits, and a restaurant. This is a good lunch or coffee stop. While eating, look out over the university and the city of San Francisco, past Mount Tamalpais, and through the Golden Gate. (Reflect, if you will, on Bishop Berkeley's poem, and Billings's enthusiasm for it.)

Beyond Lawrence Hall turn left on Grizzly Peak Boulevard, a winding mountain road with changing views of the Golden Gate and San Francisco Bay on the west and Tilden Regional Park on the east. Turn left again on Marin Street — a roller coaster of a ride downhill. Marin drops along a topographically ignorant straight line, levels out at each intersection, drops again, levels again, drops again. But don't go too far down. Turn right on Santa Barbara, then left on Indian Rock, to San Luis Road.

For those who know and love Stewart's work, this is hallowed ground. Many of his greatest books were written here. His most enduring novel was set here. When I visit, I park, walk San Luis Road past the Stewart house, then head over to nearby Indian Rock Park. The Stewart home is Ish's home in *Earth Abides*, and the neighborhood is the locale of the novel. The Tribe in Stewart's *Earth Abides* carved the years in the rocks in the park. Once in the park, I'll admire the view, have a post-lunch swig of water; and, if it's late afternoon, I might have a wee — but only a wee — dram. And I'll pour most of that on the ground to honor George R. Stewart and the spirits of place.

Back to the car. Head south now, back to Marin Street, over to Oxford, across Virginia, to the University. You have just circumnavigated the geography of home of the Stewarts of Berkeley.

The Stewarts wandered their close geography for nearly a decade, moving about once a year. They would not settle until 1934, after George R. Stewart's success as a writer provided enough extra money to buy the house on San Luis Road. During that decade of wandering, Stewart worked hard to develop his writing skills and his reputation as a writer. He published his first book, and an article still groundbreaking in its ideas, halfway through the decade, in 1930.

In the 15th century, Leonardo DaVinci listed *Arte Y Scientia*—"art and science must work together"— as one his basic principles. Along the same lines, Jeffersonian-agrarian poet Wendell Berry said, in a 1993 interview in *Orion Magazine*, "The separation of art and science is impossible.... It's organized on the superstition that these two things are separate. Another superstition is that they are separable. Science means "knowledge" and art means "doing" or "making." Obviously you can't know without doing or do without knowing."[3]

George R. Stewart agreed. In a 1930 article, long overlooked but still on the leading edge of thought, Stewart wrote about the interdependence of humanities and science. "Color in Science and Poetry" was published in *The Scientific Monthly* in January 1930—an article by an English professor in a magazine devoted to science.

Stewart wrote that until scientists began to introduce new color words in the 17th century, poets composed their poems with almost no sense of color. Their languages were very sophisticated when it came to discussing fine points of law or logic; but they apparently didn't understand the difference between colors like blue and violet.[4] Stewart wondered if ancient people might even have had a form of colorblindness — that they were only able to see those colors for which they had names. Even Chaucer, the poet we identify with April's flowers, mentioned fewer than a dozen colors in all his works. So perhaps poor Chaucer never enjoyed an apricot-colored sunset over an aquamarine sea but only saw red sunsets over a blue ocean.

Yet in the 1920s a group of Stewart's college students could list 35 shades of the color red alone. What happened? The Enlightenment.

People didn't need to distinguish between blue and violet until scientists, more carefully observing the natural world, needed precise descriptions of what they observed. The new color names were so important that they sometimes took precedence over the discoveries of a science. In the article, Stewart considered Newton's work on the spectrum. Newton originally listed only red, yellow, green, and blue. Then he named the new colors he had observed, coining "violet-purple" for one and borrowing the names for a fruit and a dye for the other two. With all colors named, he described his first complete spectrum as RYGBOIV-P — not today's ROY G. BIV. According to Stewart, Sir Isaac Newton had listed the colors of the spectrum in the order he found names for them, not in their place in the spectrum!

In the eighteenth and nineteenth centuries, the scientists called naturalists explored entire continents, cataloguing and describing almost everything. Thomas Jefferson's instructions to Meriwether Lewis detail how much description Lewis and Clark would be expected to do. Jefferson's list gives a good idea of how many descriptive words the explorers might be expected to coin:[5]

> *The soil & face of the country, it's [sic] growth & vegetable*
> *productions, especially those not of the U.S.*
> *the animals of the country generally, & especially those*
> *not known in the U.S. the remains & accounts of any which*
> *may be deemed rare or extinct;*
> *the mineral productions of every kind; but more particularly*
> *metals, limestone, pit coal & saltpetre;*
> *salines & mineral waters, noting the temperature of the last*

& such circumstances as may indicate their character;
volcanic appearances;
climate as characterized by the thermometer, by the
proportion of rainy, cloudy & clear days, by lightening, hail,
snow, ice, by the access & recess of frost, by the winds,
prevailing at different seasons, the dates at which particular
plants put forth or lose their flowers, or leaf, times of
appearance of particular birds, reptiles or insects.

It was a list any of the great explorers of the era would have understood. Following such a list, they would discover many new plant and animal species. Then, to describe what they discovered the scientist-explorers made up dozens of color names. Stewart singled out Dr. John Latham, who invented so many words that he could list 20 colors for one species alone. By 1800 or so, Latham and other naturalists had given the English language its first developed system of colors and color-words.

The chemists followed. W. H. Perkin, trying to synthesize Quinine, accidentally discovered the first chemical dye, "Mauve," named for the similarly colored mallow plant's blossoms. Soon, other chemists were inventing artificial dyes, and naming them. Sometimes the new dyes were named for natural objects. Sometimes descriptively—"Smoke ice" for example. Sometimes for places where great events had taken place: Magenta was a battlefield where the French defeated the Austrians. Hundreds more color words came from the dye chemists' work and science's color vocabulary again increased.

By the nineteenth century, thanks to the naturalists and chemists, the Romantic poets were able to pour color words into their work. Those scientific words had begun to color poetry.

Stewart concluded that W. H. Perkin's discovery in 1856 of phenyl-phenosafranine, $C_{27}H_{25}N_4C$ — the color Mauve — would be considered one of the great events in the history of poetry. Stewart's acknowledgment of his debt to scientists, and his idea that poets learn from scientists and scientists from poets (and thus art and science depend on each other), would be a foundation of his future work.

In the best tradition of the old interdisciplinary Scottish Enlightenment, Stewart's books would follow Leonardo's principle—*Arte y Scientia.*

George R. Stewart's first major book, about the rhythms of the English language, was also published in 1930. *The Technique of English Verse*, published by Henry Holt and Company, is a fine guide to composing English verse, written with a sense of vernacular patterns of speech. The book also holds a deeper meaning for Stewart scholars, because Stewart drops a few clues about the directions his future writing will take. He describes poetry as more restrictive than prose since the poet must follow the outlines of the type of poem being written. Which leads, Stewart writes, to one danger of the form — poetry can be admired for craftsmanship even if it has little value as art. Prose, on the other hand, must be grounded in solid content.

Those comments suggest that, by 1930, Stewart had made an important choice — he would write prose. He wanted the freedom to shape words without prefabricated patterns, and he wanted his books to be solid. But *English Verse* also shows that he understood the importance of poetry to the sweet rendering of the English tongue. So his prose works would carry a master poet's sense of the rhythm and music of language behind each sentence.

By 1930, after six years of marriage, it was time for George and Ted Stewart to take stock of their intertwined lives. All in all, things looked good. George was a successful teacher and writer whose ideas about the integration of art and science were making people think. Published by the trade press, he reached

Passport Photo. 1930. George, Jack, Jill, Ted.

out to an audience that included both scholars and general readers. He and Ted had weathered the first great ordeal of their lives well, the loss of Marion Leroy Burton. They were working together to raise their family, which expanded when son Jack was born, on August 7, 1928.

In 1930, Stewart took his young family along on his first sabbatical. Although finances were tight, Army disability payments for pneumonia made it possible for them to travel; so the family spent the year in England and France. George worked during his sabbatical, researching his next book on the way to Europe and writing the manuscript in Europe. The family enjoyed the vacation.

But the sabbatical would be the period at the end of a sentence. When he returned to Berkeley, Stewart would find that his expected life of regular promotions, increasing work in department and university affairs, and a comfortable academic life was not to be. The next ordeal had begun.

As they say, life is a journey. But remember Steinbeck's wisdom: we don't take the journey of life, the journey takes us. George R. Stewart's journey was about to take him down unexpected roads. In retrospect, thank God for that.

16

The Stewarts returned from their European sabbatical year, to wander again from house to house. Almost as soon as they unpacked from a move, the Stewarts packed again. By the early 1930s George and Ted had lived in six houses in Berkeley and two in Europe. Daughter Jill had lived in five of those houses; son Jack in three. It was unsettling.

Jill Stewart was old enough to remember life in "the house at the top of Virginia Street" as particularly unsettling. One day she heard "a terrifying noise" from the flats of Berkeley — a house leaking natural gas had blown up.[1] Not long after, she heard a crash near the Stewart home and ran out to see a car teetering over the drop-off at the edge of the street. The passengers were sitting in the car, afraid to move. The car was eventually righted without injury to its passengers, but for a long time Jill was afraid to travel in cars. Jill's third memory of the house was the most traumatic: she fell through a glass door. She still carries a small facial scar from the fall. And the terrifying memory of glass breaking sharply around her has never left Jill.

The Department of English was also shattering.

During the late 1920s the department prospered under the leadership of Walter Hart. Hiring the best people he could and helping them develop themselves, Hart laid the foundation for the department of the next four decades. But then Hart went into university administration. At first that was good for the department, since he used his connections with the president to get more resources for his professors. But Hart could not let go of the department's day-to-day management. There was no chance for another leader to arise who could develop a cohesive department with strong *esprit de corps*.

And the English Department professors would soon need all the spirit they could get. Appointed Chair in 1931, Guy Montgomery kept the position for more than a decade — a time George R. Stewart called the "eleven bad years."[2] Montgomery was not a good administrator. Like many who are not good leaders, he became authoritarian. "We might even put it, 'a tyrant,'" Stewart wrote later, in the official history of the department. Montgomery, siding with administration against the professors, became the enemy of his own staff. (Although this was Stewart's view, the fact that it was included in the history of the department indicates that it was a view shared by many department faculty.)

The Depression was the ally of such academic tyrants. There were no jobs elsewhere. People were stuck. The tyrants knew that, and used it against the professors. But the greatest weakness came from within: the professors' desire for the good life in Berkeley, a paycheck, and friends. "We were sometimes in danger of selling our intellectual heritage for a mess of good friends," wrote Stewart.[3] (And is not this desire to be liked deadly, when tyrants are about?) Even death was a foe. One of

George R. Stewart (left) and Jim Caldwell at Sather Gate, 1930s. Caldwell was a colleague in the Department of English at the University of California, Berkeley.

the best people in the department, Robert Utter, walked out of the Faculty Club after dinner one night to be killed by a falling tree. Stewart walked out the other door at the same time and lived. The X factor was still working in Stewart's favor, but Utter's death was a great loss to Berkeley.

From 1931 until 1942, life in the English department was grim. What little *esprit de corps* had been developed under Walter Hart was crushed. The department declined. In spite of the publication of two major books, Stewart was stuck in his assistant professorship, without tenure, for a decade. Colleagues of Stewart's later told him they wondered how he survived.

After five years of the ordeal of the Montgomery Department, with no apparent hope for promotion, Stewart made a decision. If he couldn't expect a decent income from his professorship, he would make money from writing. He would write books that would interest the general public, books that would *sell*. As he told his oral history interviewer, Suzanne Riess, "I got away, strictly speaking, from the departmental field, and got confidence to go ahead along that line.... But I wouldn't ever have done that if things had been going along well for me, probably, in other ways."[4]

Discouraged by his chances of making a professional life in the department, Stewart had begun a lifelong intellectual and creative walkabout. He had been forced into freedom. It was the gift of the ordeal.

17

On December 3, 1931, Henry Holt published Stewart's second book, *Bret Harte: Argonaut and Exile*. Stewart had aimed the work at both scholarly and general audiences, and *Bret Harte* sold well enough to both groups to convince him that he could write beyond the University of California's scholarly community. Good reviews of the book also encouraged him.

Since *Bret Harte* was as much about California history as English literature, Stewart knew that he could write successfully outside of his scholarly discipline. Freed of the need to follow the scholar's calm path of university writing within the confinement of a discipline, he decided to take a bold step. As he told Bancroft Oral History Interviewer Suzanne Reiss, years later, "I pretty consciously said, 'What have I got to lose? I might as well risk something and do this.'"[1]

It was "this," his next book, which would establish Stewart as a great writer. Risky, it was apparently more suited to the university's Department of History than of English. The only authors considered at length in the book were frontier keepers of diaries and writers of letters. But Stewart wrote the history using all the techniques of the poet and the writer. He also worked in the way of the California Enlightenment — using field research to study the places of the tale and taking colleagues from other disciplines along to help.

The result was an extraordinary book which would begin to change how humans think about the place we call home.

His interest in the Westward Movement made that Stewart's logical "broad canvas." Thinking it over one day, he remembered the Donner Party. The Donner Party story is the great tragic tale of the Westward Movement. In all the centuries since the first landings on the coasts, there had been much death in the settling of America — from conflict, disease, starvation, weather, and from just having had it. But this was different. The heart of the tale was in the winter camps near Donner Lake and on the desperate trails between the lake and the Sacramento Valley where, in order to survive, people had to eat the flesh of others who had died. It was the stuff of nightmares.

In 1920, Stewart read the only work about the Donner Party ordeal, a small book by C. F. McGlashan. Stewart found the story to be a good one, but McGlashan's telling of it poor. A new book about the Donner Party might find a readership. He decided he could tell the story better than McGlashan, and in a way that wouldn't cause nightmares. He would write his book about the Donners as the story of a microcosm of human society under duress, a tale of endurance and survival in desperate conditions. He would tell the story objectively, thoroughly, and without terror. He would avoid judging those who suffered it.

Stewart thought he could consult one or two sources, then do the writing in time left over from family and professorial demands. But he soon learned Huck Finn's lesson: "If I'd a knowed what a trouble it was to make a book I wouldn't a tackled it." Like any good creative project, this one would lead Stewart down trails he never imagined. He would follow those trails, and write about what he found there. In the process Stewart would lead his readers to a new understanding which far transcended the story of the Donners.

George R. Stewart had helpers along the way, like his friend Charlie. University paleontology professor Dr. Charles Camp was not bound by disciplines; he began his career as a herpetologist, went into paleontology, then became a distinguished California historian. Camp and Stewart met in 1934 at one of their clubs. Knowing about Camp's expertise in California history, Stewart introduced himself; then asked, "Why didn't they [the Donner Party] have better men?"[2] Camp answered that there were some very good men — C. T. Stanton, for example, who escaped the death camp but returned to bring food to the women and children, sacrificing his own life in the process. Camp's description of such heroism encouraged Stewart to write the book.

There would be other helpers. Artist Ray Boynton, for example, who painted some of the WPA murals in San Francisco's Coit Tower, and others in City Lights Bookstore, sketched the scenes of the tragedy for the book. (He also sketched young Jill Stewart, George and Theodosia Stewart's daughter.[3])

As George began working on the book, in the early 1930s, he and Ted bought a cabin in Dutch Flat, California, as a vacation retreat for the Stewart family. About 50 miles up-Sierra from Sacramento, and near the Donner Party's route from the death camps to the Sacramento Valley, it would also make a fine base camp for field research. While Ted relaxed and the children swam, Stewart could explore the Donners' geography.

To find places and artifacts important to the story, Stewart and his colleagues walked almost every step of the trail. It paid off—Jill Stewart Evenson recalls, "I remember when he came home and said they'd found the Murphy fire. He figured out where it should have been and they dug down and found all these embers. He felt that he'd pin-pointed where it was."[4] Stewart himself mentioned another find, of logs cut off about ten feet above the ground, at the Donner Party camp on Prosser Creek. (He convinced the California Park Service to take them for safekeeping.)[5]

Research done, he sat down to write. But Stewart soon realized the writing would be more difficult than he had thought. The story was complicated in location. There were the two main camps near Donner Lake, separated by a few miles. There were the camps of those attempting to flee to the Sacramento Valley. There were the camps of the rescuers coming to their aid (and then fleeing back to safety). Each camp had its terrors, its dangers, its deaths and its heroism. Sometimes Stewart was juggling five or six strands of the story at once: different human stories in different locations, and individuals' interactions with different settings.

The story was just as complicated in its human drama. There were characters from all over the map of human emotions. Some were remarkable for their courage, integrity, and compassion. Others were remembered for their venality, selfishness, or nastiness. And human characters changed. For example, one man, banished because of a killing, later became one of the great heroes of the epic.

Stewart's challenge was to figure out how to put it all together in a way that would keep the reader's interest. He decided to use some of the techniques of fiction. For example, he would tell the story of one strand in such a way that it would lead a reader into thinking about another strand just before he moved the reader to it. (Stewart used the techniques so effectively that some readers think the history is a novel.) Then Stewart who as a child gloried in the drawing of maps, put his map skill to work. He mapped the Donner story out. He drew lines on paper to show the various strands, figured out where the reader needed to swing from one strand to another, and designed his literary bridges to get the reader across.

As he mapped the story, Stewart had a grand revelation. Thinking about the landscapes, walking the trail himself, he realized it was the Donner Party's ignorance of the land — of the *ecosystem* — that brought the wagon train and the party to the starvation camps. Stewart suddenly understood that the major protagonist in the tale of the Donners was the "land" itself. He wrote, "I have in the telling often stressed the scene until the reader has, I hope, come to feel the land itself as one of the chief characters of the tale."[6]

It was a sea change in thinking. George R. Stewart had realized that the world is not, as Shakespeare wrote, the stage on which humans interact. The world is actually the major *player* in all human drama. The character of human players is revealed by how they relate to the ecosystem and its events. The Donner Party did not understand that, and it nearly destroyed them.

Stewart's epiphany about "the land" is a profound change in understanding, a new paradigm. It is one of his great achievements, and a cornerstone of all his later work. In fact, it is not too far a reach to say that this new understanding, written into a popular book and read by millions, is one of the foundations of the 1960s Environmental Movement.

The book would not be born easily. A letter from his literary agency, Brandt and Brandt, handed the manuscript back to Stewart after listing six publishers who rejected the work. Stewart then sent it directly to publishers with more success. *Ordeal by Hunger* (a title Stewart never liked) was published by Henry Holt in 1936.

Some 25 years later Stewart noted that "the book is still going along, very nicely."[7] Today, more than three quarters of a century after publication, it is still in print. The book is one of three of Stewart's works which still have wide distribution. (The other two are *Pickett's Charge* and *Earth Abides.*) But it is much more than a popular book. It is a book which helped shape our time.

Ordeal by Hunger is the first Whole Earth work, one in which the author tells his story from both within, and outside, of the Earth system. For much of the book, Stewart writes from what might be called a "Ranger's Perspective," from inside the ecosystem, describing, from ground level, the landscapes, the life, and the weather the immigrants encountered. He details how each ecological factor affected the journey, the character of the human players, and their ultimate fate.

This ecological perspective had been used before. But Stewart added a new dimension in his book. In 1936, 25 years before any human would see it, he opened *Ordeal by Hunger* with the "Astronaut's" or "Cosmonaut's Perspective"— the view of Earth from space. The passage describes the view from orbit as precisely as if Stewart had actually seen it.[8]

Thus, *Ordeal by Hunger* is the first detailed literary look at the Earth System from within and without, Earth as microcosm and macrocosm — what we today call the "Whole Earth" vision. Readers of the book learned to understand the relationships between humans and the Earth in a new way. They visualized Earth from space and realized that it was small and precious. They learned the importance of the "land" in human affairs. Since the book is so popular, this new understanding — Stewart's Whole Earth vision — has come to the millions of humans who've read it. In these ways, in *Ordeal by Hunger*, Stewart was preparing his readers for what was to come — our current ecological, Whole Earth understanding.

He would continue to do so in a series of ecological novels written in the 1940s and 1950s. *Storm*, *Fire*, *Earth Abides*, and *Sheep Rock* were bestsellers that changed their readers' ideas about the relationships between humans and the Earth. *Earth Abides*, the story of a young ecologist who survives a massive die-off of humans to observe the resulting changes in the ecosystem, has had a particularly deep and lasting influence on thought. Never out of print, now in 20 languages — a book honored by Stephen King, Carl Sandburg, James Sallis, Keith Ferrell, and Wallace Stegner — *Earth Abides* was listed in July of 2010 by

The "*GeoS*" Image — taken from the International Space Station by Dr. Ed Lu, it shows the area described in the introduction to 1936's *Ordeal by Hunger*: "To observe the scene of this story, the reader must for a moment imagine himself ... raised in space some hundreds of miles above a spot near the center of the state of Nevada.... Far to his left, westward, the onlooker from the sky just catches the glint of the Pacific Ocean; far to his right, on the eastern horizon, high peaks of the Rockies forming the Continental Divide cut off his view. Between horizons lie thirteen degrees of longitude, a thousand miles from east to west." Lake Tahoe is at lower left, Pyramid Lake at upper left; the country described by George R. Stewart tracks east from a point slightly to the north of Lake Tahoe to the cloud-covered Wasatch Range at the right side of the image.

Amazon as number eight on their sales list for twentieth century United States fiction literature. But the ecological, Whole Earth vision which would reach its fulfillment in *Earth Abides* had its beginning in *Ordeal by Hunger*, Stewart's history of the Donner Party.

During Expedition 7 in 2003, astronaut Dr. Ed Lu photographed the Great Basin, the Sierra Nevada, and the Wasatch Range from the International Space Station — from 200 miles above. These photos could be named the *GeoS* images, because they show the scene exactly as George R. Stewart imagined and described the landscape in *Ordeal by Hunger*. Some 70 years after the idea first came to his mind, 67 years after he wrote the view of Earth from space into his book, the rest of us finally caught up with him.[9]

18

Ordeal by Hunger earned Stewart the Silver Medal of the Commonwealth Club of California, given to an author who has written the year's best non-fiction book about California. It was not the only reward. Stewart finally received his promotion to Associate Professor. After 14 years at the university, Professor Stewart was tenured.

Stewart often wondered why Montgomery allowed the promotion. Decades later he discovered that Montgomery had nothing to do with it. A committee of English faculty members, working behind Montgomery's back, had recommended Stewart's promotion to the university president. They wrote, "[George R. Stewart] is esteemed and liked by those who know him best."[1] Stewart, who always considered himself a loner and a bit of a curmudgeon, had more friends than he knew — something to be valued more highly than any medal.

With the extra income from the sales of his books, George and Ted could finally afford a home of their own. They found a fixer-upper, repossessed after months of neglect. Jack Stewart remembers "this sort of derelict house on San Luis Road — I think they'd foreclosed on it.... I remember going and looking at the house ... there were weeds everywhere."[2] The two-story house sat against the bay-facing side of one of the Berkeley hills. Small outside, it was cramped and uncomfortable inside, as Jack recalls, because "the downstairs area had been divided into several tiny rooms." The sloping backyard had only one spot flat enough to hold a picnic. But rundown or not, cramped or not, the place had one advantage — by borrowing to the limit, the Stewarts could afford it.

The house did have its assets. It was high in the Berkeley Hills, on one of those narrow streets that follow the ideas of Bernard Maybeck by paralleling natural contour lines. It had a wonderful view out the Golden Gate, and Ted

Stewart loved views. The backyard's level spot would be fine for picnics. Ted also loved picnics. And it had a tiny basement which could be turned into a writer's lair. Over the next few years, the Stewarts upgraded the house, adding a library and redoing the dining room and kitchen (which became Ted's pride and joy). When the icebox was replaced with that technological marvel called a refrigerator, the family knew they'd passed a milestone.

George designed a small study in the basement. He added a window so he could glance out at the world as he wrote, but it was otherwise as separate from the world as a mediaeval monk's cell. It was like a monk's cell in another way — the closest bathroom was two stories up, so the scholar/author's bathroom was a large mason jar.

The house on San Luis Road would become the Stewarts' first real family home, a pleasant home. Jill and Jack Stewart, now eight and five, would grow up there. The basement room became the workshop for George Stewart's ideas. And in one of the sweet ironies of history, this awkward, once-neglected little ugly duckling of a house would enter literature and legend as the scene of Stewart's most enduring work — a book Pulitzer Prize winner Carl Sandburg called one of the great novels of its time and author James Sallis called one of the greatest American novels of all time. The house on San Luis Road would become Ish's home in *Earth Abides*.

As Stewart told interviewer Suzanne Riess, "That was really a very lucky house."[3]

A successful family moved into the house on San Luis Road, but it was not an untroubled family. In a letter written during the Stewarts' 1937 sabbatical in Mexico, Ted used a good amount of paper and ink describing her concerns about the children.

> The children have been in the American school 2 months now — Jill seems to be getting along well but Jackie has been very miserable. He is not going back after the September vacation. He has been invited to join a small tutoring group run for the two sons of the British Charge D'Affaires in their own house. We are thrilled for him — it is a lovely place, & the teachers have such grand English accents I like to hang around just to hear them. I think Jack will be about the only American there — I hope so! The hours are 9–12 instead of the heathenish 8–1 at the American school which has just been too much for him — they have one short recess — at 10.30 — in that 5 hour stretch! Jill is bearing up — but looks strained & white too.[4]

The Stewart children had problems.

Jill inherited the Stewart tendency to weak lungs. Tests indicated she was "pre-tubercular," which in those days before penicillin was a possible death sentence. So Ted kept Jill in bed for years. It was a well-intentioned treatment in keeping with the pre–sulfa drug medicine of the time. Yet when other children were out and about, playing and building the necessary social networks of childhood, Jill was in bed, and lonely.

Jack was lonely, too. The son of an author, he could not read very well. In fact, his reading was so poor that he was held back two grades. (He still remembers the shame of it.) Like Jill, Jack was studied, examined, and diagnosed. But the science of intelligence was rudimentary in those days and it would be years before he heard any good news about his condition.

The parents' personalities added to the problem. Ted and George, as opposites, were a good match for each other; Ted once said, "If George couldn't handle someone, I could!"[5] But it made life more difficult for the Stewart children. One parent, outspoken, wanted things done *right*, and *right now!* The other, a quiet scholar withdrawn into his work, was hard to talk with.

Jill remembered one episode in the house on San Luis Drive. "I was probably about 10 years old ... he and I were sitting there alone eating lunch in the dining room.... I decided I was going to wait for him to say something.... I waited and I waited and I waited and I waited.... Finally he did say something and I said 'Oh! I decided I wasn't going to say anything until you said something.' And his response was 'You might have had to wait for the whole meal.'"[6]

Theodosia Stewart was the opposite, as verbal and emphatic as George was quiet and withdrawn. She was not someone who would hesitate to give an opinion about politics, a child's life, or anything else. She wanted decisions made, action taken, and things done —*now*. Jill Stewart Evenson said, "And my mother — you knew her, you met her — was very managerial. She just took over my life and the family and I cannot say it was very happy."[7]

Jack Stewart recalled an incident from his childhood that showed Ted's style. Because he was doing poorly in school, his parents suggested he might want to go to private school some distance away from Berkeley. He didn't want to go, so he waffled about the matter. "Finally [my mother] came to me and said, 'Well, we have to make a decision about it today. Why don't you think about it today and I'll come up tonight when you're going to bed and we'll make the final decision.' And then she came up and she was pretty — demanding almost, you know —'Well, what do you think?' I didn't really want to say, because if you say 'yes' then you're going against what you really want to do and if you say 'no' then you're contradicting your parents. I finally said 'No.' And then she said, 'Well, we'll never talk about it again!' ... and stormed out of the room."[8]

Neither George Stewart's withdrawal nor Ted's strong management were done selfishly. George Stewart worked quietly in his author's cell to bring some extra money in for the family during hard economic times. Ted was managerial because she often had to play the role of two parents. Neither parent was abusive. Neither wanted their children to suffer.

In fact, the parents worked hard to solve the children's problems. With deep faith in the healing power of nature, they tried "natural" methods for healing body and mind. Jill recalled, "She had us both in health school in Berkeley. Me first and then (laughs) she decided Jack ought to be there too. It was called a Sunshine School." (Classes were held outdoors in the sun and students given naps in the afternoon.)[9] The parents also tried other nature movements and techniques to help their children grow healthier. For example, the family camped. Since George and Ted had had some of their happiest times in the wilderness of the mountains or the rustic life by the lake, it seemed a good idea to take their children camping. But Jack and Jill remembered the family camping trips as strained by their childhood problems.

Ted and George Stewart never understood that the root of the problem was the neglect often faced by children of the famous, since they are secondary to the careers and friendships of the parents. Meals, activities, all the "stuff" of family, were designed by Ted and George for the Stewarts' adult friends, sophisticated and successful academics, not for the Stewart children. And the parents were not warm and affectionate with their children.[10] Ted and George, well-intentioned as they were, overlooked one important truth about families: with kids, there's no substitute for a little time, or a hug.

Of course, the family had good times as well — especially the summers at Dutch Flat. Neighbor Dan Rogers — an interesting character with a constant thirst but the honesty of a saint — left a clue to the Stewarts' Dutch Flat days when he wrote that he was looking after their place, but "I sure do miss my noisy neighbors."[11] During the day, George often retired to write in his "scholar's tent." But as the sun set, he joined the family and livened up the evenings with song. Ted did the cooking, the housework, and other "typical motherly" things, and joined in the songfests with gusto.

It was the best of times and the best of places for the children. Although she got in trouble once, for going into the water without an adult nearby, Jill loved Dutch Flat's old gravel pit-swimming hole. And she loved the drives through the Sierra foothills with their beautiful views of snow-capped higher peaks. She remembers her father stopping along the way to talk with locals, and his "surprising" way of talking with ordinary people. (His respect for "ordinary" men and women would become a characteristic of his books.) After the drives, in the soft Sierra summer evenings, with fragrant citronella candles perfuming away mosquitoes, family and guests gathered on the cabin deck to sing. George would bring out his accordion and play the old campfire songs of the emigrants. It was as if a wagon train had again camped in Dutch Flat, its pioneers singing their songs of the great overland migration — "Sweet Betsy From Pike," "Oh! Susannah," and the others. The sweet sound would float out over the Dutch Flat air, until the constellations told the singers it was time for sleep.

Those pleasant Dutch Flat days were harbingers of change for Jack and

Jill. Jack remembered that after one such vacation, "They sent me to a summer school. I didn't know at the time, but it was obviously a place to evaluate children. And they had a lot of things you could play with — like covered wagons — and you played with other kids; and they'd try and evaluate you that way. At the end of the session they gave me an IQ test. I guess that startled everybody."[12] What surprised everyone were the results. Jack was not "slow." He had a high IQ. He just couldn't read. In today's terms, he was dyslexic. And he was by nature quiet, shy and introverted. Shyness and dyslexia, not retardation, were the cause of his problems in school.

Jill's tuberculosis scare went away. Her health improved. Jill would carry some of the emotional pain of childhood throughout life, but she picked herself up, moved forward, and prospered. The "eleven bad years" were coming to an end, for the children as well as George R. Stewart and his Department of English colleagues.

As the years of ordeal began to draw to a close, the Stewart family passed another milestone. George R. Stewart, Sr. and Ella Wilson Stewart, Stewart's parents, died within a few months of each other. A generation had ended.

Born before the Civil War, George R. Stewart, Sr. built businesses that helped the nineteenth century's industrial expansion. Then, starting all over again in his sixties, he moved to Southern California to become a citrus rancher. Like his son, George Jr., he was a quiet and restrained man; but he showed his love for his grandchildren. Jill remembers, "He was the only one who ever called me by my given name, Jane. He used to call me 'My little Jane.'"[13] He passed away on February 18, 1937. Ella Wilson Stewart died in late autumn of that same year. A woman of great courage, who helped end the subservience of her gender, she said goodbye to the places of her youth, and her friends and family moved west into a raw and unknown land with her husband and her sons.

The passing of the generation encouraged another change. In 1938, George R. Stewart, Jr. began signing his letters without attaching "Jr." to his name. George R. Stewart had become his own man.

19

In 1936, on his way to give a talk in Santa Rosa, George R. Stewart made a decision. He would write a novel. Writer Stewart was about to become author Stewart.

It's time to consider the meaning of words again. "Writer" originally meant *scratcher* — a perfectly good term, perhaps, for those of us who scratch down histories of others' lives. Stewart, however, now intended to become an "author" — a *creator of works*.[1] He could build on the techniques, like mapping, that he'd begun to develop in *Ordeal by Hunger*. But freed from a foundation in hard facts, his books could become more creative. Besides, in George R. Stewart's time the authoring of a good novel was every writer's goal.

With tenure, and a reputation as a promising new writer worth watching, Stewart could put more time into his research and writing. He used some of that time to figure out how to write good fiction. Jack Stewart remembered his father at home in the evening, reading novels and making notes about their techniques. Then Stewart began writing furiously — for practice, not publication. Writing *A Detective Story* long before he wrote his first published novel, Stewart was developing his craft. (There are four unpublished novels or partial novels in the Stewart Papers at the Bancroft.[2])

George Stewart also moved into an alcove bedroom, separate from Ted, in the late 1930s. It was not a sign of marital problems. George Stewart often woke in the night with ideas or fully worked passages and put them down on paper. Sleeping alone, he could turn on the light and write without disturbing his wife.

He didn't neglect his non-fiction writing. While he was working up his novelist's skills, Stewart wrote another literary biography. *John Phoenix, Esq.*, a biography of George Derby, the first truly American humorist, was published in 1937. Derby is not well known today, but he inspired young Sam Clemens, who adapted one of Derby's stories for his own writing. And Derby's use of a pseudonym, "John Phoenix," may have encouraged Clemens to develop his own pen name. (Stewart even speculated in the book that Derby, who often traveled the Mississippi by steamboat, might have encountered Clemens during his river-piloting days.) *John Phoenix* is largely forgotten, except by scholars. But Stewart had no time to worry about the success of the Derby book. He was well into his next project.

East of the Giants would be Stewart's first published novel. As with *Ordeal by Hunger*, Stewart broke new ground in the book: he told his story from the viewpoint of a woman. Raised in an upper-middle class Eastern family, Judith Hingham Godoy sails west around the horn with her sea-captain father and her mother to visit Monterey in Mexican California. Intoxicated with the wild freedom and the beauty of the California land and its Mexican culture, strong-willed Judith elopes with a ranchero.

The novel follows her through several decades of California history. She faces racism, violence, the loss of people she loves. As the culture of California changes, from Mexican to Yankee to settled modernity, Judith's character also changes. She becomes a Californian.

Judith Godoy is a Stewart archetype, the strong, life-loving female protagonist who appears in most of Stewart's novels. Stewart developed the idea of the strength of frontier women from his research for *Ordeal by Hunger*. Consider the "Snowshoe Party." Ten men and five women left Donner Lake on

December 16, 1846, to struggle to Sutter's Fort to seek help. A full 33 days later, two men and five women arrived at the first settlement in the Sacramento Valley. Eight of the men had died, but none of the women. In the whole Donner story and for much of the Westward Movement this pattern held true — women endured it better than men.

Judith Hingham Godoy's frontier life forces her to take initiative. After she marries the young Mexican Juan Godoy, she moves to his ranch. Suffering from the crude wretchedness of the place, she takes sick. Finally, when she realizes that it'll be up to her to improve the place, Judith gets out of bed and goes to work. Beauty will come in its time. But first, inspired by the casual pooping of a child in the courtyard, Judith becomes a builder of latrines. She has learned a lesson unavoidable on the frontier — you must surmount your own circumstance. You couldn't call a plumber to the Godoy Rancho in 1838.

Books also help Judith. Reading novels about other times and places, Judith can measure her life against the larger human experience. She understands that her life is a microcosm of all human life. Reading *The Lady of the Lake*, she can see the parallels between the life of ancient Scotland and her wild Californian life, and the similarities between the poem's rebel chief, Roderick Dhu, and her husband, Juan Godoy.

But her salvation comes when she embraces the California land. She has endured her husband's casual infidelities, the crude life on the rancho, and the rough and tumultuous times of the early nineteenth century in California. As she wanders the hills and fields of the rancho she finds solace and encouragement in its wild loveliness. Stewart describes the place in human terms — using words like "voluptuous," and writing of "its moods."[3] It is another step on his saunter toward the ecological novel.

Released in a period when historical fiction with strong female characters was very popular — *Gone with the Wind* days — Stewart's novel was a best seller. *East of the Giants* also earned George R. Stewart another honor: the Gold Medal from the Commonwealth Club of California, awarded for the best work of California fiction published in a year. The book was to be made into a movie, starring Irene Dunne.[4] But Pearl Harbor intervened and the project was abandoned.

The loss of the film was of little consequence to Stewart. He had successfully published his novel. Now he could call himself an "author." He noted his new literary status with a slight name change. George R. Stewart had already dropped "Jr." from his signature on letters. Now he dropped it from his published work.

Stewart finished *East of the Giants* on sabbatical in Mexico with three months left before he had to return to the university. So he wrote another novel.

Doctor's Oral is about one of those important tests of life we each must take — the kind of ordeal most readers have a better chance of experiencing than the one faced by the Donner Party. Anyone who has taken a test that will determine the rest of his or her life — driving, apprenticeship, college boards, the Bar exam — knows what the novel's protagonist, Joe Grantland, is going through. But Joe has more than the doctor's oral exam to face, of course. Stewart is wise enough to know that our lives always have complicating factors. A parent is sick, or we're fighting with a lover or spouse, or we can't figure out how to pay the rent, or … (read the book to find out what Joe must deal with.)

In this novel, Stewart focused on a new type of human hero — the supposedly common person who rises to glory when he or she faces the guns of life. He would no longer write of the owners of ranchos, or others of the elite. In the future, his books would celebrate the heroism of the Common Man and Common Woman.

But he would always return to the theme of the land. There is a preview in this novel when Joe Grantland goes to a place where campus buildings give way to the natural world. He almost heads into the wilderness, away from his problems, toward "real things," but he resists temptation and returns to face his ordeals.

Stewart gave into the temptation. He went into the wilderness, intellectually at least, and stayed there for more than decade. Now he would write about real things, about "the land."

Sabbatical finished, Stewart and his family returned to Berkeley. That fall, he taught three courses. In December, he took a trip to Death Valley. In the spring semester, he again taught three courses. He wrote another book, *Take Your Bible in One Hand,* a limited-edition collector's item about the life of William Thomes, beautifully printed by Jane Grabhorn of The Grabhorn Press. That summer, Stewart taught at Duke University and spent some time at Puget Sound.

Clearly, there wasn't much time to go to Dutch Flat. Besides, with his research on the Donner Party done, the cabin seemed superfluous. When student Ed Cassady received his Ph.D., Stewart called him in and said, "Ed, you've earned a rest. We have a cabin up at Dutch Flat that we don't use much anymore. I'll sell it to you for fifty dollars." (Ed's son Bill, who shared this story, still lives in the "Stewart-Cassady" Cabin.)[5]

The decade's ordeals had been a great gift. Forced to turn to writing when his career slowed, Stewart had improved his family's financial situation, and its social standing. He had also begun to develop some remarkable new ideas about the relationships of humans and the ecosystem — the concept of "the land" and the Whole Earth vision. Now those ideas would be the foundation for a groundbreaking book. A hurricane of a book, his third novel would be the working-out of one of the biggest of his ideas. Eventually, Stewart's new novel would become part of humanity's collective wisdom, and thus change the world. And it would do so just in time.

III. The Man Who Named The Storms

20

Stewart remembered Monroe Deutsch, vice-president of the University of California, saying, "Well, you can consider it just as if you were a scientist at work on something, and if you have to take some time off to go to see something, why, that's all right."[1] Deutsch was giving Stewart permission to use half his time for research and writing. The timing was perfect. On Stewart's second Mexican sabbatical, during the winter of 1937-38, he noticed that major storms striking California were front-page news in Mexico. If the storms of California created such widespread interest there could be a book in it. Stewart accepted Deutsch's offer and went to work.

His original idea was to write something like *The Petrified Forest* or *Grand Hotel*, a novel in which a storm forces a diverse group of people into a situation where the stress of the situation reveals character. But thinking over what he had learned while writing *Ordeal by Hunger*, that "the land is a character in the work," he decided to write his novel so that its drama and revelation of character come, not from the interaction of humans with each other, but from their interaction with the storm itself.

Stewart did not write the book from his study — that would not be in the tradition of the University or the California Enlightenment. Instead, he did his research in the wilds of the Sierra Nevada, immersed in the ecosystem's huge storms. "When a big storm came up," recalled Stewart, "Ted and I would cut off and go someplace, most often up to Donner Pass to see what was happening there."[2] Stewart felt the cold, brushed the snowflakes out of his eyes, talked with the people who worked during the storms. At Donner Pass, in the floods of the great Central Valley, and in the storm-lashed cities, he rode with and talked to those who bore the brunt of the storm.[3] He accompanied railroad crews through the snowsheds above Donner Lake, joined the Division of Highways' snowplows at Donner Pass, saw storm damage at the electric

94

company's foothill facilities, and rode with the Highway Patrol on dangerous roads.

Years later, Ted remembered how much she worried over the chances George took to do his research. To get the feeling of a Sierra storm, for example, he rode a locomotive cowcatcher through a snow flurry to the top of Donner Pass. Ted, who had driven to the Pass to meet him, found him almost frozen. But it paid off. By the time the research was done, he could feel the storm in his soul.[4]

He'd learned a great deal. Storms have lives; they are born, grow and prosper, weaken, and die. Storms interact with animals, people, plants, and landforms, the other inhabitants of an ecosystem. The interactions change the storms, and the other life forms and landforms. It is a story of encounter and character as interesting and important as any in novel or drama. So, thought Stewart, why not make the drama of his story the way the storm and the rest of the ecosystem interact?[5]

Why not make the *storm* the protagonist of the drama?

But how can we have an epic tale if the protagonist is described in the precise but inelegant terms used by most meteorologists? To solve the problem, Stewart has his "young meteorologist" name the storm: *Maria*—pronounced in the old way, with a long "i." Now the storm is a character, representing the ecosystem, and *Storm* becomes Maria's biography.[6]

Stewart opens his novel with the first best-selling literary description of Earth's biosphere as seen from space. Then he moves readers into that biosphere — into the ecosystem, and into this storm — to show how Maria interacts with lifeforms or landforms. The book begins with Maria's birth, then tracks the storm's growth. Lifeforms, including human lifeforms, reveal character by their responses to Maria. Wisdom, courage, or foolishness is revealed by how those lifeforms react to the events of the storm.

By the 12th day the storm has died. Stewart closes his story as he opened it, by moving his readers into deep space for another view of the Whole Earth — this time, from a much more distant perspective. Someone on Venus looking at the Earth, Stewart writes, would see no sign that storms (or anything else) ever disturbed the pale blue dot hanging in the night sky.

Stewart's ecological vision and the vast space of the novel's action made the book difficult to write. As with *Ordeal by Hunger*, Stewart had to juggle many characters in many locations. Each individual story, each event, had to be woven together within the tapestry of Maria. Again he turned to mapping. "I'm a very visual person. I like to see things where you can look at them."[7] He drew maps. Then, after his research, he drew more maps. He did this over and over, often scrapping his work, until he had time, event, and place into a proper weave.

As he worked, he realized that maps were more than research tools; they had a place *in* the book as well. So in early editions of *Storm* the endpapers are maps: Maria's "First Day" on the front endpaper; Maria's full "Seventh-Day glory," on the back endpapers. Stewart also wrote maps into the book, describing how the young meteorologist takes great professional pleasure in updating his storm map by hand in those years before the computer.[8]

Storm was the first ecological novel; the first to define its human characters by how they interact with the land, air, water, and other life that are part of the Earth system. For the first time readers had the biosphere visualized for them and they were shown how they function as part of that biosphere. For many of them, perhaps most of them, it was a great and sudden change in understanding — an epiphany as powerful as the one Stewart had known as a teenager, in the mountains of Southern California, when he first felt nature's "something ancient." The book was published and widely read in the 1940s and 1950s, and its epiphany is probably one of the foundations of the rapid explosion of environmental consciousness in the 1960s.

The novel also popularized the practice of naming storms. Readers liked Stewart's idea of naming storms. Meteorologists adopted it. Thus, in naming his storm, Stewart encouraged the naming of all storms. He had become the man who named the storms.[9]

The novel was important in another way, certainly far beyond Stewart's intentions. As Stewart was writing the book, Ernest O. Lawrence and Glenn T. Seaborg were also at work on the university campus. Their interest was not in the land, but in the ultimate building blocks of the land. They, too, wandered through the field, but in their case, the field was infinitesimally small. And their wandering would be done, not in the great wildernesses a hundred miles to the east of Berkeley, but through ultimate machines set in the natural beauty of the Berkeley campus.[10]

Lawrence had begun studying radiation in the late 1920s with the idea of building machines to save lives by burning cancers away. Convinced that outside funding would be necessary to the research, he approached several corporate giants. His appeals seemed to pay off at a meeting held at the privately run Bohemian Club's Redwood Grove when businessmen agreed to help fund his research. Lawrence used the funds to develop larger and larger "cyclotrons" to split the atom. But splitting atoms had the potential to do much more than burn cancers. Since it released tremendous energies, atom-smashing could also be used to build huge bombs.[11]

Lawrence's colleague Glenn T. Seaborg came to Berkeley in the 1930s to work in the new field of nuclear physics, which merged chemistry and physics. Seaborg believed nuclear physicists could use Lawrence's cyclotron to create new elements of matter. Those new elements could fill out or even expand the

Periodic Table of the Elements. In 1940, Seaborg's idea paid off when the Berkeley team used the cyclotron to create the first element beyond those of nature.

The next year, in Room 307 of Gilman Hall, Seaborg and co-workers Arthur Wahl and Joseph Kennedy created and identified Element 94. That element, for better or worse, was plutonium — the stuff of the Bomb. The deadly element was discovered on February 23, 1941, in the midst of a great California winter storm. Think of the scene at the moment of the creation of Frankenstein's monster and you will have the right image in your mind: in the laboratory, the scientists are discovering a thing that may become the destroyer of worlds, while outside the greater power of a storm, not made by men, rages against the laboratory's windows.

But something else, infinitely hopeful, was happening in that storm. As plutonium was discovered, in storm-smashed Gilman Hall's Room 307, George R. Stewart was in the depths of the same storm doing research, or writing the results of his research into his new book. He and Ted were driving through the storm — near the sentinels of the coast, or the summits of the Coast Ranges that rise from the ocean to meet the storm, or the cities of the plain, or Donner Pass in the long Sierra, where the storm was at its most violent. Or he was in his Monk's cell as the storm lashed the windows, sharp-penciling the power of the ecosystem into a novel — one whose ideas would reach around the world, and, like the discovery of plutonium, change human society forever.

The book's belief in the endurance of the ecosystem would counterbalance the potential of nuclear weapons to destroy all life on Earth. In a dark and threatening time, George R. Stewart was writing a work of hope and encouragement.

Storm was a best seller, a Book-of-the-Month Club selection, a Modern Library Book. It was condensed in the *Weather Merit Badge Guide* for the Boy Scouts. Reprinted in more than 20 languages, the book had sold well over a million copies (according to Stewart's estimates) by the 1970s.

It is an enduring work. University of Nebraska Press's 1983 Bison Edition had an introduction by Stewart's friend Wallace Stegner. It was published again in 2003, 62 years after its first release, as a "California Legacy Book," with a foreword by *Ecotopia* author Ernest Callenbach. Callenbach noted that "when Cody's Books in Berkeley invited local authors to try to stump listeners with a mystery paragraph from a favorite work, I chose *Storm*, thinking it obscure by then. Hands shot up in recognition after a single sentence."[12]

With its suggestion that storms be named, and its ecological vision, *Storm* is one of the most important books of its time. Written one biblical generation before the first Earth Day and widely read, the novel is probably one reason why so many people today have adopted a sense of ecological awareness and a concern for the environment. But the novel's most important heritage is encouragement. In *Storm*, Stewart gave humankind a spiritual antidote to the fears of the world-destroying bomb — the ecological understanding that bomb-bearing humans are no match for the power of a storm, and the ecological reassurance that Earth will abide in spite of any bomb.

21

Storm was launched in New York City in the fall of 1941. George was on sabbatical for the fall semester so he and Ted drove to New York for the book's launch. After the publication party, they spent a few days with friends on the East Coast; then headed west for home. With a few weeks left on sabbatical they hoped to enjoy a leisurely drive home across country. But just as they started their trip, a car rushed up alongside them. According to one version of the story (from a good source) John Steinbeck and his future wife, whom the Stewarts had visited at Manhattan's Bedford Hotel after the publication party, were in the car. Steinbeck was waving a newspaper. The headlines screamed, in words like these, that "Japan Attacks Hawaii; Heavy Fighting Reported.... Nation on war footing." It was Sunday morning, December 7, 1941.[1]

The Stewarts' first thought was for their children. In Berkeley, Jack and Jill were 3,000 miles closer to Pearl Harbor and the Japanese fleet than were their parents. In a day when the speed limit was 55 and the highways went through every city and town, George hit the accelerator and the Stewarts raced across the country. They constantly checked the news, which traveled much more slowly than today. As the Stewarts drove through the Appalachians, over the plains, into the Rockies, and onto the desert, the picture grew more reassuring. The family was safe. Rumors turned out to be just that. (There would be some small attacks on the West Coast — the random shelling of an oil field near Gaviota, far to the south of San Francisco, and a few incendiary balloons far to the north — but those happened later in the war, with little effect.)

The children were fine, but the Stewarts returned to a Berkeley wrapped up, like the rest of the country, in a war fever which often approached the hysterical. (Ted remembered with special sadness the relocation of Japanese friends, innocent of any crime, to a concentration camp.) George was too old for active duty and still had lung problems, but he would serve his country. Jack Stewart joined his father on a peak in the Berkeley Hills behind the Stewart house, watching for enemy aircraft. "It was on Vollmer Peak or someplace like that near Grizzly Peak Road," recalled Jack. "We reported the airplane traffic in the area, giving the make of the plane, and its direction of flight and height. I think the only sport was in identifying the type of plane.

Stewart made a habit of posing his children or Ted and the children at various state lines, perhaps with the idea of using the photographs in a book. This photograph is of Jack, Jill, and Ted at the Georgia state line, in the 1940s.

"Dad designed a crude device that estimated the height of the airplane, essentially by triangulation using the known width of the wings. The device, as I remember, had a sliding sight of known width. Knowing the width of the wings, the size of the sight, and the distance from the person's eye to the sight, a crude estimate could be made of the height of the airplane. The plane would need to be overhead, more or less. As I remember, the device did not work very well, but it relieved the tedium. GRS was always thinking."[2]

Stewart put his thinking to good use in other ways as well. He helped organize an informal think-tank which tried to out-guess the enemy. The group included Stewart, his old friend Charlie Camp, Princeton classmate and neighbor J. H. Osmer, *San Francisco Chronicle* book editor Joseph Henry Jackson, Engineer Reid Railton, professors of French C.D. Brenner and Ronald Walpole, and C. S. Forester. (Forester, British novelist who wrote the swashbuckling "Captain Horatio Hornblower" novels and *The African Queen* was the best-known member.) The "Armchair Strategists" met once a month. Each member would bring a prediction about the war. The group would read and discuss the predictions. They evaluated the predictions' accuracy at subsequent meetings. There's some evidence it was more than a game, and the group's predictions were used by the military.

Stewart also served by substituting in the classroom. With so many young professors drafted into the service, older ones needed to fill in. In the 1942-43 academic year, Stewart accepted a position as Resident Fellow at the Lewis Center for Creative Arts at Princeton.

The trip paid some unexpected dividends. On the way to Princeton the Stewarts spent a summer in a rented house in Greensboro, Vermont. Wallace and Mary Stegner, who had become friends with the Stewarts, had a farm nearby. During that Greensboro summer, Stewart and Stegner, in long discussions about writing and the literature of the American West, swapped many ideas about their similar interests.

In 1944, his Princeton duty over, Stewart returned to active service. One of his Berkeley colleagues, Dr. Parker Trask, had been recruited by the U. S. Navy to research the conditions of ocean water for the submarine service. He encouraged the Navy to enlist Stewart in the project. After informally discussing the matter with submariners just returned from patrol, Stewart was to write up Trask's research so ordinary submarine sailors could understand it. He spent the summer working on the project in San Diego, then flew first class to Hawaii on a DC 4. At Pearl Harbor he discussed Trask's research with submariners. When he felt he knew "the needs and wishes" of the submariners, Stewart returned to San Diego on a lumbering Navy seaplane.

He remembered his naval service as a typical military experience, full of snafus. Military mismanagement disgusted him. Yet, as always, Stewart used his time well. He had the great satisfaction of discovering something new about the interaction of submarines and ocean currents — a discovery which impressed Scripps Institute of Oceanography Director Harald Ulrik Sverdrup, who told Stewart that his was indeed a new idea, and probably correct. (Since Stewart's discovery had never been tested, the Navy, in typical military snafu fashion, wouldn't let his work be published.)[3]

He also made a good friend. As Stewart was waiting at the airport in Honolulu for his return flight to the mainland, the Aerological Officer (meteorologist) of the U.S.S. *Princeton* came over and introduced Stewart to young Vic Moitoret. Moitoret, a UC alumni and graduate of the Naval Academy, who would eventually become Hydrographer of the Navy and the founder of the first organization devoted to the work of George R. Stewart, carried with him a small black notebook with a list of the ten best books he'd ever read. The notebook was dog-eared and waterlogged — Moitoret had carried it with him through the wartime sinking of at least one ship. (He was navigator on the U.S.S. *Hornet* when it was sunk in 1942 and on the U.S.S. *Princeton* when *it* was sunk in late 1944; both times he spent hours in shark-filled waters — the second time with bleeding injuries.) One of the books listed in the water-soaked notebook Moitoret carried was *Storm*.[4]

Stewart's time in San Diego also paid off in a literary way. He had begun to make notes for a novel about the ecology of a forest fire. In San Diego, when he was not working on Navy projects, Stewart worked with local United States Forest Service Rangers, doing field research for the book.

The war ended with no enemy blood on Stewart's hands and without slowing down his literary output. In April of 1945, Stewart wrote to his friend Wallace Stegner. "Names On The Land comes out tomorrow," he wrote. "I brought on Pearl Harbor with Storm, and am apparently going to bring the surrender of Germany with this book."[5] (He was right: Germany stopped fighting less than three weeks after *Names on the Land* was published.)

It was a remarkable book. And of all the books he wrote, *Names on the Land* would become George R. Stewart's personal favorite.

22

Names on the Land, the first history of a nation's place naming, has become a landmark work. Decades after the book's publication, *Smithsonian* magazine noted that it belonged on every American bookshelf. The book has been reprinted several times, most recently by the New York Review of Books Press. But as with most works of genius, it would not be born easily.

As difficult as it had been to write *Ordeal by Hunger*, or *Storm*, with their interconnecting human and ecological dramas set in complex landscapes, Stewart considered *Names* the most challenging book he'd ever written. There were a few regional dictionaries of names — the *results* of name-giving in those places — but no scholar or author had ever written a book about the national *process* of place naming. Stewart had to do his own original research on the place-naming process, across the centuries of American time and the huge spaces of the United States. "There's no model for that book at all. It is absolutely on its own," Stewart told Suzanne Riess.[1]

Stewart included a description of his sources in the book's postscript. It gives an idea of how hard his job was. He explains that to research the book he used other scholars' place-names works, explorers' journals, local histories, the W.P.A. Guides to the states, maps, government documents from Colonial times to the present, conversations with place-namers, the street-name patterns of city plans, and more. At least he had one advantage over someone writing a history of ancient place-naming. Stewart was close enough to the naming time, in the West at least, that he could talk with people who remembered how some places were named. Interviewing those people gave him insights into the way other Americans named places.

He also did his usual field research. Standing at the site of an old town in the western Sierra foothills after following old emigrant routes across the Forty-Mile Desert, he could understand why the town was named "Cool." And when he entered a green and well-watered valley in northeastern California after driving the old trail through Nevada's Black Rock Desert, Stewart knew why the emigrants named that place "Surprise Valley."

Stewart's facility with languages was an important resource in the work. He could often translate an original name himself, and thereby discover a key to the name-giving. His translations showed that place-meanings often suggested great stories. For example, Stewart described an ancient pueblo ruin called "Callemongue," or "where-they-hurled-down-stones," and wonders who hurled the stones at what invader.[2]

He looked for patterns. On the emigrants' trails, for example, names often had to do with geography, or resources, or the danger of the journey. Drinkwater Pass is just east of Stinkingwater Pass on the Oregon Trail, and there are geographic stories suggested in those two names. Searching for patterns tied to *places* like the California Trail, he soon realized that there were also patterns in American naming tied to *time*. At particular times, Americans named things in particular ways for particular reasons. So he divided the book into chapters about the naming of places, over time.

His chapter on California place-naming is a good example.[3] Stewart begins with the Spanish era, the years when a very Catholic people settled there. Often, they named places for the saint on whose day they first encountered or settled the place. Even when events in a place seemed to call for a descriptive name, the Spanish usually managed to find a fitting saint. For example, since one town had a plethora of earthquakes, the Spanish named it "Santa Ana de

Los Temblores"—Saint Ann of the Earthquakes. But the Spanish left some of the native names on the land, like Pismo, Petaluma and Nipomo.

In the mid-nineteenth century, California place names began to reflect the immigration of people from other nations, especially the "Yankees." And names of living people, Mexican and American, began joining those of saints on the maps: Sutter's Fort, for John Sutter; Benicia and Vallejo, for General Mariano Vallejo and his wife; Hollister, for town founder William Welles Hollister. Saints' names and native names remained; but since new settlers had trouble with Spanish, pronunciation changed: "Lohs Ahn-he-leze" became "Loss Ann-jeh-lus," for example. Sometimes the newcomers would translate English names into Spanish words without regard for the different grammars. So "Mountain View" might be translated as "Monte Vista" rather than the linguistically correct "Vista del Monte."

In the early- and mid-twentieth century, in what might be called a naming Counter Reformation, Californians began correcting the Yankeefied Spanish names. The debate over correct pronunciation and grammar of the original Spanish got pretty complicated. Stewart comments that *La Ciudad de La Reina de Los Angeles* could be pronounced in so many different ways that people finally gave up and began calling it "L.A." But "L.A." is an exception—the counter-reformation had its effect, so many place names in California are now pronounced in the proper Spanish way.

In California, and elsewhere in the United States, names do change. It's pretty hard to find any Nigger Mountains now (thank heaven) and Nipple Buttes are getting scarce as well. But in general, names don't change much. Names endure, far beyond a culture, in languages written or unwritten. After millennia humans still know Troy and London, Denali and the Jungfrau. Stewart believed American place names would also endure. Since Earth, from the human perspective at least, doesn't change much, ages hence, humans will likely still know the names Yosemite, Columbia, San Francisco, Montana, Santa Fe, Monticello, and Philadelphia.

Place names also record the relationships between humans and places: "Muddy Lake," "Electric Peak," "Los Gatos," and so many other places are named for some noticeable quality of an area's ecology. So Stewart included *Names on the Land* among his ecological works.

Names on the Land was published in April of 1945. Sales were good, the praise for Stewart's work high. H.L. Mencken, author of *The American Language*, wrote to Stewart: "your plan for it was ingenious and effective, and ... you executed it with great skill." Meredith F. Burrill, Director of the Board on Geographical Names, invited Stewart to share his research with the Board. H. Stanley Marcus, of Neiman-Marcus, wrote, "Your new book, 'Names on the Land' ... I found to be as delightful as it was instructive."[4]

Annie Laurie Williams, Stewart's long-time agent, commented on the book's style, calling *Names on the Land* the "King James Version."[5] It was an insight — George R. Stewart, who later told Suzanne Reiss that "the King James Bible has had a tremendous influence on me,"[6] had developed a style almost biblical in cadence and rhythm. It would help define his later novels.

In his spring 1945 letter to Stegner, Stewart gave him a heads-up about his new book. Stegner replied, "I notice that your place-names book is out, but I haven't had a chance to get one yet. For the sake of your academic reputation, I hope you didn't spell out some of the Arizona names of anatomical memory. But I shall see shortly."[7] (Stewart didn't spell out Shit House Mountain in the book — he used the initials "S.H." In the 1940s, some things were best left to the imagination. But he did list Nipple Butte and Tit Butte.)

When the book was republished by Lexikos Press, in 1980, the year of Stewart's death Stegner contributed an introductory essay. In part a eulogy for his friend, George R. Stewart, Stegner's essay is also one of the best considerations of Stewart's work. But that is as it should be. The four-decade friendship between Wallace Stegner and George Stewart and their wives was a remarkable one. It is worth a book — or at least a chapter — in its own right.

23

In the spring of 1945, Ted Stewart wrote to Mary Stegner. "Darling Mary — Ever since we heard on the end of a news broadcast that Stanford announced that Wallace Stegner of Harvard was coming, we've been so happy that you'll be near us again."[1] In May, Wallace followed up with a letter to George, "Once we get grooved in our furnished flat in Stanford, and start casting eyes out on the permanent housing situation, we'll hope to see you down in Palo Alto both frequently and lastingly."[2] He signed the letter, "Best, Wally." It was the ebullient correspondence of friends.

Their friendship began when the two men met at a writers' conference while Stewart was at Princeton, probably in the late 1930s or early 1940s.[3] (Stegner had done some graduate study at Berkeley during the 1932-33 academic year, but apparently the two didn't meet.) George Stewart and Wallace Stegner were certainly friends by 1942, cemented by the Stewart family's trip to Greensboro, Vermont, that summer. Jack Stewart remembers his father going often to visit the Stegners and the Stegners visiting the Stewarts, at least once. "It seems logical that our family also visited the Stegners, but I have no recollection of that," he says.[4] A photograph in the Anna Evenson Collection shows Jack and Jill Stewart (and several other children) on a porch in Greensboro, along with Wallace and Mary Stegner — probably taken during the Stegners' visit.[5]

Jack and Jill with the Stegners. This remarkable photograph, previously unpublished, shows Wallace and Mary Stegner with local children in Greensboro, Vermont. Jack Stewart sits with his back toward the wall; Jill is wearing the striped T-shirt. The Stewarts rented a house on Caspian Lake for the summer when George R. Stewart was on his way to teach at Princeton. This is probably taken in 1942.

The friendship blossomed after the Stegners moved to Palo Alto. The 45-mile trip from Berkeley to Palo Alto or from Palo Alto to Berkeley became a weekly family outing for the Stewarts and the Stegners. Jack was a teenager at the time and recalls "driving down when there wasn't really a freeway, just a sort of an old road. We'd come across the bridge and we'd come down this (west bay) side. I remember visiting them and the family fairly often at the house on Page Mill Road."[6] Page Stegner, Wallace and Mary Stegner's son, a

Page Stegner, Jack Stewart, circa 2008. Taken at Kepler's Books in Menlo Park, after a talk by Page Stegner about his book of the collected letters of Wallace Stegner. It was the first time Page Stegner and Jack Stewart had seen each other since their Stanford student days in the 1950s.

decade younger than Jack, has only "one memory of visiting the Stewarts' house, at the age of 10 or 11. It was a dinner party, and after appropriately being seen and not heard I was sent upstairs to read, and eventually go to sleep."[7]

Jack Stewart and Page Stegner recognized the importance of their fathers' friendship. "They were colleagues," Jack says. "They ... appreciated each other. Stegner was an intellectual, a writer, and they were both interested in western history."[8] Page Stegner adds, "I know my father was very fond of GRS, and thought highly of his work. I remember being given the Donner Party book to read, which I did (and years later used in writing my own history of the opening of the American West)—and also *Names on the Land*. I still think *Ordeal by Hunger* the best work on the Donner Party fiasco, and a terrific book on that chapter of the opening of the West."[9] (Page Stegner, himself a distinguished writer on environmental topics and the history of the American West, recently edited a collection of his father's letters which includes some of Stewart's letters to Wallace Stegner.)

For the next two decades, Stewart and Stegner helped each other on projects, met with each other's students, and kept up a bright and stimulating correspondence. Their work often brought them into the same literary territory. In 1960, for example, when they were both working on books about overland trails, Stegner wrote Stewart, "I'm interested that you may do the California Trail.... Since we're just across the Platte from each other so to speak [Stegner was writing his book on the Mormon Trail], maybe we should take the opportunity for frequent consultations."[10]

The two men influenced each other's work. Stewart's success in writing beyond the conventional fiction and poetry of most English professors clearly encouraged Stegner to follow suit. Soon, Stegner began writing his own nonfiction, including landmark works about the West such as *Beyond the Hundredth Meridian*. Stewart's ecological novels convinced Stegner, himself a "native environmentalist," to write about the environment. And Stegner's fluid style seems to have influenced Stewart's writing; *Fire*, written during the high water of the friendship, is Stewart's most romantic and lyrical book.

Why were these two men such good friends? Certainly, as university scholars and popular authors at neighboring universities, and writers of books about western history and environmentalism, they had similar interests. But there was a more essential reason: boyhoods lived on adventurous frontiers — Stewart in Southern California and Stegner in Saskatchewan — had shaped their personalities. Their childhoods were not unlike those of Mark Twain's two most famous fictional characters. Stewart was Tom Sawyer — middle class, educated, with a stable home. Stegner was Huck Finn, rougher and wilder, with a ne'er-do-well boomer of a father.[11]

Like Huck's, Stegner's rustic boyhood was the more attractive. Moving to a homestead on the frontier prairie of southwestern Saskatchewan, as described in *Wolf Willow*, the Stegners entered the archetypical frontier of myths and movies. They traveled by stagecoach, young Wallace seated on the lap of a Montana cowboy named Buck. Buck was respectful of women, and affectionate toward children, but had alcohol-soaked breath. (In the best tradition of the mythological Old West, Buck was killed in a shootout with a Mountie on the streets of nearby Shaunavon.)

The family settled in a small frontier town Stegner called "Whitemud," a rough little place with few dwellings, few trees, few rules and thousands of square miles of prairie and badlands surrounding it. Recreation was of the kind found in frontier towns: pranks against people who were "different," harassment of wildlife, disaster as entertainment. One spring, when ice jammed against the Canadian Pacific Railroad Bridge, the whole town went to watch the bridge collapse; then ran over to see the subsequent destruction of the downstream dam.

It was, Stegner wrote, a great place to be a boy.

Stegner's father was more bootlegger than farmer, so Stegner's childhood was as rough as the town. But from an early age Wallace knew he did not want to be like his father. With his mother's encouragement, he became a prolific reader.[12] Books, and education — starting with classes held above the town's pool hall — would be Stegner's way out of a life like the one that would lead his father to a tragic end.

The eclectic nature of some of the townspeople also helped. For all its frontier roughness, Whitemud had an undercurrent of enlightenment. One resident, Jack Wilkinson — described variously as a machinist, a mechanic, or a blacksmith, and in this small place likely all three — built a telescope from scratch. Then he built an observatory to house the telescope, and opened his observatory to the town.

Another Whitemud resident collected fossils for his small museum. "Corky" Jones, son of an English doctor, had visited British paleontological sites as a child. The idea of ancient animals covering the earth fascinated him. As a young man, Corky moved to Whitemud to fulfill his dream of becoming a cowboy. But he soon realized he'd moved to prime fossil country. Riding the area's ranges, he began collecting and studying the fossils. He learned so much that he became an independent scholar, corresponding with leading paleontologists about his discoveries. When he died, he left his collection, one of the finest private fossil collections in Canada, to the town.

The cowboy-scholar was still alive when Stegner revisited the town in the 1950s. During the decades since Stegner and his family had left, Jones had inspired a love of knowledge among the other residents of the small prairie place. In his memoir of the town, Stegner describes an event not unlike the birth of the University of California: the founding, by Corky Jones and others, of *The Eastend Astronomical Society* in the hope it would someday inspire another Newton.

Stegner's Huck Finn boyhood, in the enlightened small town called Whitemud, and his mother's insistence on books and education, served him well in his future life and career. He would be inspired to do what Corky Jones and others had done for the town: shine the light of knowledge into the world. That combination of love of frontiers, and of knowledge — Whitemud's gift to Stegner — also prepared him for his friendship with George R. Stewart.

George R. Stewart may have had a more stable middle-class upbringing than Wallace Stegner — the Tom Sawyer boyhood — but in Southern California's mountains he found the same passion for wilderness and frontier life that Stegner found on the prairies of Saskatchewan. And, like Stegner's, Stewart's passion would lead him to research and write about the wild lands of the West. Their Sawyer-Finn boyhoods, wandering through natural places, feeling that "ancient something" of wilderness as Stewart called it, would be one foundation for the remarkable friendship of George R. Stewart and Wallace Stegner.

24

The mid–1940s were good years for George R. Stewart and family. He and Ted had successful professional careers, and he was making good money at writing, so they no longer had to pinch pennies. George was in his most original and creative period, his "ecological" period. He had written *Storm* and *Names on the Land*— a novel and a history, each with an ecological focus. Before the decade was over, he would write *Fire*, about fire ecology, and *Earth Abides*, his legendary ecological novel.

The Stewart children's situations improved. Jill went to Smith College on a special scholarship. But there she felt herself in the shadow of the past — her grandfather Burton had been president of Smith — so after two years she transferred to the University of California. In 1946, she moved into an apartment in San Francisco's North Beach with two friends. "I never went back [home]," she said.[1] Jill became an interdisciplinary scholar, earning advanced degrees in education and art. She didn't develop tuberculosis.

Like her father, Jill had literary talent. When she sent him a poem she had written about one of her favorite family cars and the places it had taken them, he replied that he admired the lines:

> And names on many maps that grew
> From words to places that we knew.

George Stewart began taking Jack along on his research trips — to the places he was studying for his fire ecology novel, on his U.S. 40 trans-continental drives, and on expeditions to the place his father named "Sheep Rock." Those journeys would change Jack's life. "They really brought home geography.... Later, geology grew out of that," he says.[2] Jack became a distinguished geologist, and eventually the United States Geological Survey's expert on Nevada. But he kept at least some of his father's cross-discipline interests: at Jack's 80th birthday party, one of his old USGS colleagues described him as "a grand synthesizer." "Jack," said his friend, "You're hiding your light under a bushel — you're known as 'Mr. Nevada Geology.'"

There was another family milestone in the 1940s. George Stewart's surviving brother, Andrew Wilson Stewart, died on March 31, 1946. George R. Stewart was now the paterfamilias, a role neither he nor anyone else in his family had expected him to fill. But later in the decade, when he wrote *Earth Abides*, his role as paterfamilias would help him with the story.

With Jill on her own in the early 1940s and Jack off to college in the late 1940s, George and Theodosia Stewart could relax from the chaos of parenting. Of course, neither of them would relax too much. Ted became a social worker for the Family Service Bureaus in San Francisco and Oakland, and taught in the UC School of Social Work.

George, as usual, wrote.

In the mid–1940s he created another unique book. *Man: An Autobiography* is the story of humankind told in the first person. Stewart used a historical approach like the holistic ecological approach he had used in *Ordeal by Hunger* and *Storm*. In the book's first chapter, Man tells readers that his book will not detail all the wars, kingdoms, inventions, and so on of human history Instead, it will concentrate on the history common to all humans — like the discovery of fire. As always, Stewart finds encouragement in the work. For all the talk of the "end of civilization," he writes, it is not likely to happen. Humans would keep the basic and essential skills of farming, hunting, building housing, and procreating long after they forgot how to build atomic bombs or spaceships.[3] The United States or the "Global Village" may go, but villages and settlements will remain. People will hunt or fish, plant and harvest with tools, live in structures, wear clothing and use fire. The work of the 100 or so centuries it took us to get from agriculture to the Apollo program won't be easily undone.

The book was well received, and had good reviews. Yet judging by a number of indignant letters in the Stewart Papers, it was the most controversial book Stewart had written. Stewart believed the letters came from those who had read the condensed version of *Man* in *Readers Digest*—readers who apparently accepted the geological ideas of Bishop Ussher and were thus offended by the book's longer timeline. Today the book would probably be no less controversial, since it uses the term "Man" to stand for humankind. But controversial or not, the book was another financial and intellectual success.

As a boy, Stewart had decided that he didn't like the telephone. In the late nineteenth and early twentieth century, phone calls too often brought news of death or disaster. Although by the 1940s telephones, movies, and radio had become major methods of communication, and "going to the movies" the shared weekly experience of most Americans, George R. Stewart still resisted the media. But for a brief time in the mid–1940s, movies and radio would be a part of his life.

During World War II the Walt Disney Studio put a good deal of their effort into making training films for soldiers. The films did not make much money and the company found itself in hard times. Disney, looking for money-making ideas, decided there would be a large market for educational films after the war. Disney was also planning a film or films about American folklore. Stewart's books had impressed Walt Disney, and he invited Stewart to the studio to work as a consultant on the projects. Stewart went to the studio for a week, looked at the proposed educational films, and made some suggestions. He suggested that the "Americana" movie be based on unique American folklore; and that it begin with early East-Coast settlements' folk tales and move forward in time and west to follow the settling of the country.

Disney Legend Bob Broughton remembered the Americana film project as planned to encourage viewers to buy war bonds. What Bob Broughton probably did not know, since Disney was keeping this very close to his chest, is that Walt Disney was already planning what he then called "Disneylandia," an exhibit or park centered around a model of a small Midwestern town and other bits of Americana. Disney clearly knew Stewart's work and probably knew of his boyhood in a town like the one where the Disneys had their boyhoods; Stewart's ideas about American folklore would have been of great interest to Walt Disney as he thought about the Disneylandia project.[4]

Disney did not produce the Americana film, but he did make several movies based on American folklore during the next few years — *Song of the South, Pecos Bill, Johnny Appleseed, The Martins and the Coys, The Legend of Sleepy Hollow*. Disney also began to produce his remarkable True-Life Adventure films, which, although "Disney-fied," introduced moviegoers to an appreciation of the natural world in a way similar to Stewart's ecological novels. Although Stewart was never credited in a Disney film, his ideas probably had some influence on these projects. At least, he enjoyed two memorable lunches while he was at the studio — one with his old friend Buddy DeSylva, the other with Walt Disney himself. Disney followed up on the visit with a letter. "The type of work you are doing is of much interest to us," he wrote, "and I hope when you do have the time you will visit us again."[6]

Disney's would be the first studio to bring Stewart's ecological novels to the screen, producing film versions of *Storm* and *Fire* for the television program *Disneyland*. "A Storm Called Maria" is still the only film version of *Storm*. "A Fire Called Jeremiah" follows *Fire* much more closely than 1952's "Red Skies of Montana," which left out Stewart's important ecological point of view.

Anyone who has heard Bill Cosby's story of the "Giant Chicken Heart" knows how effectively radio used listeners' imaginations. Radio mysteries, leading examples of the medium, were all over the airwaves in 1946 — *I Love a Mystery, Nick Carter, The Green Hornet, The Shadow*. Some, like Mutual Broadcasting System's *The Casebook of Gregory Hood*, were quite literate. *Hood* was co-written by "Anthony Boucher," pen name of distinguished author and Berkeley resident William Anthony Parker White. Since he knew the Stewarts and respected George Stewart's work, White decided to write his friend into an episode of *Gregory Hood*.[7]

If Jack Stewart, who loved radio, had been listening to the Mutual Broadcasting System on the night of August 26, 1946, he would have encountered his father — or at least an actor playing his father — in the *Gregory Hood* episode, "The Ghost Town Mortuary."[8] A young woman is kidnapped. She leaves a one-word message: "Difficult." Private Investigator Gregory Hood invites an expert to help decipher the clue.

> GREGORY: This place is handy for the one person who I think can help us on this case.
> SANDY: And who is that person?
> GREGORY: Professor George Stewart, of the University English Department.
> MARY: Oh yes! He wrote *"Storm"* — a wonderful book.
> GREGORY: True, but what is more to our immediate point is the fact that Random House recently published his new book: *"Names on the Land."* It's a classic and definitive study of American place-naming. His virtues are many. *(with a chuckle)* Including a fine sense of entering on cue. Here he is. *(Raising his voice)* Hello, George.
> GEORGE R. STEWART: *(clearance arranged) (straight and charming)* How are you, Gregory?
> GREGORY: Fine. Let me introduce you....
> STEWART: I got your message, Greg, and it all sounds frightfully mysterious. What's your problem?
> GREGORY: I'll skip the details. Briefly, the situation is this. A girl by the name of Kay Martin disappeared yesterday.
> ALEX: I'm engaged to her, Professor Stewart.
> STEWART: And she disappeared, you say? Dear me. Go on, Greg.
> GREGORY: The only clue we have is this telegram. The young lady sent it just before she was seen to leave with an unknown man.
> STEWART: May I see the telegram, Gregory?
> GREGORY: Sure. Here. I decided the only [way] that the word *"difficult"* could make a message all by itself is if it were the name of a place.
> MARY: Gregory, that's very clever of you....
> GREGORY: I looked up *"difficult"* in the atlas, George, but I couldn't find a town of that name. So I thought you, being an expert on place names, might be able to help me. What's the verdict?
> STEWART: Your hunch was right, Gregory. There is a tiny ghost town in the Sierras called "Difficult." It had a mining boom at the turn of the century, but it's been deserted now for forty years or more.
> MARY: What an extraordinary name for a town, Professor.
> STEWART: *(chuckling)* It is odd, isn't it, Mrs. Taylor? The legend runs that when the town was originally named Washington D.C. rejected the choice and wrote to the authorities saying: "The name of your post office is difficult...."

The local inhabitants took the phrase literally and called their town Difficult.

ALEX: Oh, I remember the place now. I used to work near there on vacations. I can guide you there, Mr. Hood.

GREGORY: Fine. We can fly up there in my Beechcraft, Alex.... George, I'm very much obliged to you for your help.

STEWART: It was a pleasure, Gregory. I hope you find your girl.

GREGORY: So do we. In any case, George, there's one thing I do promise.

STEWART: What's that?

GREGORY: When next I find a town.... I'll name it after you.

The naming anecdote is adapted from *Names on the Land*. But the real town of "Difficult" is actually in Tennessee — a little far for Californian Gregory Hood to fly in his sound-effects Beechcraft.

Stewart had always written his manuscripts in pencil —*sharp* pencil. But these experiences with radio and film convinced Stewart of the benefits of technology. In the late 1940s he bought a Dictaphone. Once used to the machine, he began recording the drafts of his books, speaking them like an ancient Celtic bard. He found it helped the rhythm of his written work to speak the words before locking them down onto paper. Convinced of the value of the new media tool, he let the pencils rest.

Stewart wrote as much for the pleasure of solving intellectual and creative problems as he did for selling books. To crank out book after book on the same topic and in the same format would have tarnished the joy of the work. So he continually invented new types of books — the ecological novel, the place-name history, the history-written-like-a-novel, the novel-written-like-a-history. Yet in the late 1940s he made an exception. *Storm* had done so well that the publisher insisted on a repeat. So did readers, who sent letters suggesting another book on a similar topic — "Earthquake," "Volcano," and so on. Stewart was convinced, and decided to write a novel about another type of ecological event.

But he could not let the new book be an exact copy of the earlier ecological novel. No challenge in that. Since he had used real terrain for *Storm*, he decided this second ecological novel, *Fire*, would be set — just for the creative hell of it — in an imaginary place. But the terrain of the imagined place had to be accurate or those who knew real forest fires would scoff at the book. Fortunately, Jack Stewart, his son, had become a gifted maker of maps. He would help his father create the terrain.

In 1945, Stewart got into the research in earnest, as usual doing much of it in the field. To get the basics of fire fighting down, he spent time at the Plumas Forest School, near Quincy, California — a University of California-run school which had interested young Ansel Hall, who would later become the first National Park Service Chief Naturalist, in resource education. Later,

George R. Stewart on a fire line, probably taken around 1946. Research for *Fire*, the first novel of fire ecology.

he was "hired" as a "collaborator" by the United States Forest Service and sent out to work on the Tillamook, Antelope, and Kimshaw fires.

Stewart scholar Robert C. Lyon found a passage in Jeanne Kellar Beaty's 1953 non-fiction book, *Lookout Wife*, which shows how seriously George Stewart took his field research. Forest Ranger Gus, training new lookouts, talks about Stewart's field research. He asks the group if anyone has read *Fire*; he then describes how he helped Stewart with his research — Gus had been assigned to take Stewart to large fires in California so that he could capture the "local color." He also helped proofread the book, and explained that it was technically very accurate.

Gus was also assigned to keep an eye on the writer. When Stewart went missing for three days, and his station wagon was found abandoned, Gus and the Forest Service were pretty worried. But they found Stewart, disguised in old clothes, fighting the fire with a group of drunks who'd been hired off skid row. He was absorbing the local color.[9]

Stewart wasn't lost. He knew where he was: in the fire ecosystem, where he could get to the guts of the novel's story — following the California Enlightenment's principle of field research. Stewart was researching the group so he could write them into the novel. (In one of the strongest passages, a "habitual drunk" panics and the fire-line is broken.)

Yet Ranger Gus was right to be concerned. Field research in a forest fire can be a dangerous business. In fact, George Stewart almost paid the ultimate price. After a long and tiring night on a "very disorganized" fire, he was walking along a fire trail with the fire burning close on his right-hand side. Just ahead of him, in the fire, a dry, tall snag was burning. "I knew it was dangerous. I knew enough about things to keep an eye on it." Just then, he came to a spring-muddied place on the trail. When he tried to jump over the mud, he slipped and fell. At the same moment, the burning snag cracked and fell. Flat on his face, Stewart could not get out of the way. Fortunately, the tree hit the trail about 15 feet ahead of him. Once again, luck, Stewart's X factor, was with him.[10]

Stewart and his son Jack also did field research as fire lookouts at Sierra Butte, near Sierra City, California. Stewart described the primitive lookout as having a needle at the top and "you sit right on top of the thing."[11] He and Jack had a long climb up the lookout ladder in the morning, sat on the summit all day, then had another long climb down in the afternoon. But it was a good experience. He learned to sight the strikes and the smokes. He talked with the other lookouts and got a sense of their personalities.

Stewart liked having Jack with him. He told his interviewer, "My son [came with me]. He was seventeen then. That was very nice."[12] It was also good for the book. Mapping was critical in *Fire* and Jack Stewart was a good mapmaker. With Jack's help, George Stewart not only worked out the terrain and mapped it, he had a plaster model made of the location. (The model is now in the Bancroft — a good thing, because impressionist painter David Park, whose works are highly valued by collectors, painted the model for Stewart.) When all was said and done, the mythical terrain was so real that *Fire*'s readers still drive north from the Tahoe National Forest looking for the Ponderosa National Forest — which exists only in the novel.

One advantage of an imagined terrain was that it allowed Stewart to name the features in any way he pleased. If you study the endpapers of the first edition — maps, as in *Storm*, that show the progress of the event — you'll see creeks and landforms named for people Stewart knew. One of the names, almost hidden by an inset in the upper left hand corner, is "Jack's Creek." "Happy thought — to have a cool clear running stream forever as a memorial! And when the trout are rising, who cares what manner of man in his life was Kelly or

Jack, Sierra Butte lookout. George R. Stewart and Jack Stewart spent a time as fire lookouts in the northern Sierra, also part of Stewart's research for *Fire*.

Curran, or Hart or Jack or Potter?" wrote Stewart, in *Fire*'s litany of the creeks. It was a fine honoring of his son.[13]

    Fire closes with the ecological understanding typical of the California Enlightenment and George R. Stewart's work as the fire-opened cones drop their seeds to the ash-fertilized ground.[14] Faith in the processes of the land is part of that deep truth waiting in Stewart's work, and, as always, it brings reassurance.

    Fire received great praise. His old friend and colleague, poet-professor Josephine Miles, wrote, "I think *Fire* is a new sort of novel as I mull it over, because, far more than *Storm*, it materializes *dramatis personae* out of the powers of nature. So I remember the pine cones and the ants and the catskinner and Bo all at one level of action and character — neutral and yet important — with organization as the abstract hero."[15]

Miles had seen something important in *Fire*. The book could not be classified simply as a conventional novel or non-fiction work, because part of it was based on hard scientific fact and other parts on created dramatic prose. Stewart was writing a new kind of book, which combined science and philosophy, prose and poetry.

That is, in the form and content of *Fire*, George R. Stewart was beginning to transcend the novel.

Stewart's next book would be the highest statement of his ecological and literary ideas. Ideas like these:

• Imagine yourself poised in space....
• The land is a character in the work.
• After the fire the seeds return to earth, and the plants bloom.
• Earth abides.

He had been thinking about writing such a book for years. He'd even roughed it out on paper. He planned to structure it around two levels of writing — the author's third-person narrative of the story; and a journal, kept by the main human character, which records the land's return to a primitive state. He thought he might call the book "World Without End."

Behind this idea for a book was Stewart's intuition that the new novel should bring his ideas into some type of ordered system for understanding our place in the universe. A *Cosmos*. A faith. In its conception, its structure and its use of language, the new book would become the statement of this faith.

The book has power. More than half a century later, *Earth Abides* still haunts its readers.

25

By the late 1940s Stewart was recognized as a leading scholar, thinker, and author. Columbia University offered him a professorship. He declined. Invited to speak at an interdisciplinary exhibit, "Weather and Art," in Pomona, he accepted. In 1946, he was appointed to the Chairmanship of the Library Committee at Berkeley. (He had already helped found the Friends of the Bancroft Library.) The university cut his teaching load, certain he'd use the spare time well.[1]

The time would come in handy. Researching his new novel, Stewart sought advice from many experts about what would happen to the world if

there was a near-total die-off of humans. He called on his university colleagues — one letter in the Papers is from Carl Sauer, answering questions about
the geographic changes in a post-apocalyptic Earth — but Stewart also reached
out into the larger technical and scientific community. He asked: How long
will water flow in man-made water systems? Electric lights burn? Automobiles
work? How long before the great bridges that span San Francisco Bay rust into
the water? Would domestic animals survive? Would those animals that had
come to depend on humans — rats, ants, gulls and the others — prosper or dis-
appear?

But Stewart went beyond such scientific and technological questions. Since
he had an intuitive feeling that the post-apocalyptic world would be similar
to that of the pre–Christian Era, he studied the faith found in the Old Testament. He even taught himself Hebrew so he could translate parts of the Old
Testament into the American English of 1949.[2] The rhythms of that ancient
language would influence the word-music of the novel ... so much so that
another writer, Noel Perrin, would later call it a new work of Genesis.

Earth Abides, published by Random House in 1949, is the story of a young
graduate student named Isherwood Williams. (The skeleton of this rich and
complex story that follows will not spoil the power of this book for readers.)
During a solitary ecological expedition to the Sierra Nevada, "Ish" is bitten by
a rattlesnake. He recovers; but when he drives down from the mountains he
discovers that most humans are dead, victims of a new, unknown disease. Without humans, there are no universities or university research programs or degrees,
so his planned professorial life is impossible. His family is gone, as are all his
friends. He wonders if he should try to survive.

He returns to the family home in the Berkeley hills, trying to decide what
to do. There, Ish suddenly realizes he has a reason to live. He scribbles a note
to himself: "Want to see what to happen in world without man, and how."[3]
Ish can observe how the Earth responds to the removal of humans from the
ecosystem.

Encouraged, he decides to see if there are other survivors. In a cross-country trip from Berkeley to New York he encounters a few, but feels no desire to
stay with any of them. Fortunately, once Ish is safely back in Berkeley he meets
Em, who impresses him with her courage and her willingness to bring new life
into the post-apocalyptic world. Others join them, and a small community
grows. Children are born. Em becomes "The Mother of Nations," and humanity again begins its slow progress toward civilization.

Ish is happy with Em and the "Tribe." But he spends much of the novel
searching for a new system of belief, a faith that will give meaning in a post-
human world. In the closing scenes, as Ish lies dying, he remembers a line in
the Book of the old faith: "'They will commit me to the earth,'" he thought.

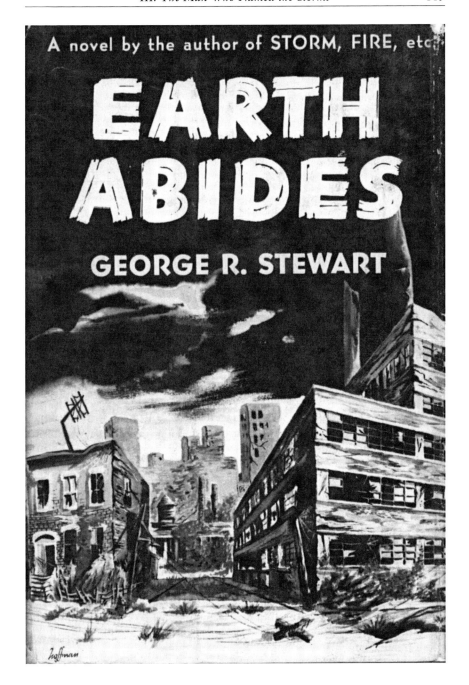

The cover of the first edition of *Earth Abides.*

"Yet I also commit them to the earth. There is nothing else by which men live. *Men go and come, but earth abides.*"[4] He has found his faith.

First published in 1949, *Earth Abides* has been printed in more than 20 languages. Do a web search for *Earth Abides*, and you will find links from America, Asia, and Europe. It is listed on pages of the right, the left, and the political center; on a survivalist page and a *Science Daily* page; on pages for Earth science, science fiction, medical science fiction, even military history. Schoolteachers and university professors list it as required reading for their courses. There are more than 300 reviews of the book on Amazon's *Earth Abides* pages, most praising it as so provocative that it changed the readers' lives. (My favorite: "I would have given this book fewer stars if I had been able to put it down.") The book sent one Englishman, Stephen Williams, on a life-changing pilgrimage. It inspired Grammy-nominated composer Philip Aaberg to write, publish, and record a "soundtrack for *Earth Abides*," and Jimi Hendrix to compose "The Third Stone from the Sun."[5] It helped convince young James Burke to become a distinguished planetary scientist. Other authors honor its influence on their works.

Yet many readers and reviewers have never heard of it. That's because *Earth Abides* is defined by most booksellers as a "genre" work and usually placed in the science fiction section of bookstores. Such placement is not necessarily a bad thing, since science fiction fans are great supporters of their genre; and *Earth Abides* can lead those readers from science fiction into a broader literature, of ecology, history, religion, and so on. (It did that for me.) But keeping the book in science-fiction sections keeps it away from lovers of great fiction. Since Carl Sandburg, James Sallis, and Wallace Stegner have called it one of the great novels of its time, *Earth Abides* should properly be placed among the other great novels in the "literature" section. Some progressive bookstores, like Shakespeare & Company in Berkeley, have begun to do that. But most bookstores have not. Not yet.

The novel almost went out of publication in the 1970s. But Alan Ligda, who made a living running one of those (now long-gone) video stores which rented fine hard-to-find films like Jean Chanois's *L'École buissonnière*, and published beautiful limited edition books at his Hermes Press and Publications, kept it in print. Ligda contacted Stewart and got permission to publish an Hermes Press edition. Ligda's edition sold well. The big publishers soon realized their error, and *Earth Abides* went back into mass distribution. But it's thanks to Alan Ligda (who, sadly, died too young) that the novel has never been out of print.[6]

As if he knew this novel would be his most enduring work, Stewart used it to honor family and friends. Em, the heroine — a strong, optimistic woman who carries the scholarly Ish through the agonies of humankind's journey into the post-apocalyptic world — is not unlike Ted Stewart. Ish and Em's descendant Jack, who will carry the symbolic hammer and the leadership of the Tribe onward, bears the same name as the Stewarts' son. The book is dedicated to Jill, the Stewarts' daughter. (George R. Stewart gave her the first copy off the press, inscribed to her.) The names of Ish's neighbors before the Fall are those of the Stewarts' closest friends and neighbors, the Harts and Osmers. "Hutsonville," the small fictional foothill town where Ish first learns of the disaster, is named for a colleague. And Stewart mentions "Dr. Sauer" in the novel, as Ish thinks over one of that great geographer's ideas.

The honoring of Sauer reveals something else about *Earth Abides*: it's a wonderful textbook. Throughout the work, Stewart discusses the geography of a post-human Earth in a way that is both dramatic and technical. He describes the effects on other animals, plants, the atmosphere, and all the components of the ecosystem. And on human culture — engineered and manufactured products, justice systems, education, religion, and so on. When Stewart focuses in on one of these topics, his writing gives a good introduction — a good *feeling*—for the discipline. The book works like a hike with a naturalist in a national park — it interprets complex scientific concepts in a setting that makes for easy understanding and appreciation of new knowledge. When readers finish the book, they have an understanding of the basics of several sciences, and a pretty good grasp of anthropology and geography — without any idea they're being educated.

Yet for all the science, the book's style and story makes it seem a religious work. That's why Professor/Writer Noel Perrin called it a new book of Genesis. It certainly has many references to the Bible: The title (and the last sentence) are from Ecclesiastes; Stewart used ancient Hebrew words for his two main human characters ("Ish" means *man*, "Em," *mother*); the novel, in part, is the story of Ish's quest for a faith by which to live and die; and Stewart's style is biblical in much of the book. Stewart pointed out to his Oral History Interviewer, Suzanne Riess that it was NOT intended to be a religious book, but even he admitted it had a certain religious quality.

Stewart's novel has had a great influence on other authors, especially those writing post-apocalyptic novels. Some authors acknowledge this by placing quiet honorings of *Earth Abides* within their own novels. S.M. Stirling names one of the minor characters in *The Sunrise Lands*— an Old Testament type — "Ish," for example.[7] Kim Stanley Robinson honors Stewart in *The Wild Shore*, a novel set in a post-apocalyptic California. Robinson writes, "I had read George Stewart's *Earth Abides* and admired it, and when I was writing my novel I decided to include references to all the after-the-fall (science fiction) novels that I admired, including PK Dick's *Dr. Bloodmoney* and Walter Miller's *A Canticle for Leibowitz*. The obvious allusion to Stewart's beautiful novel was the idea of there being a 'Last American,' meaning the last person to have been alive before the fall. My character old Tom refers to himself as the Last American, implying that he had read and is citing Stewart."[8]

In *Danse Macabre,* Stephen King acknowledges Stewart's influence on *The Stand.* A news story about a spill of chemical and biological weapons, reminded King of *Earth Abides*. Sitting one day at the typewriter, waiting (as we all do) for the muse, he typed a line about a book based on Stewart's idea that a rattler's bite might provide immunity to a plague. Two years later he had written *The Stand*.[9]

Other authors may not have written books based on Stewart's novel, but they feel its power. Keith Ferrell, author, and former editor of *OMNI Magazine*—a ground-breaking publication which mingled art, science, and fiction — considers the book to be literature of the highest order. He believes that classifying it as "science fiction" is to fail to understand the novel's great literary power.[10]

Richard Brenneman, who wrote *Fuller's Earth*, found courage in the novel during a time of terror. He was born in Abilene, Kansas, descendant of Mennonites who parked their religion so they could take up guns against slavery during the Civil War. Brenneman and his family moved west to Fort Collins, Colorado, when he was ten. A couple of years later, Fort Collins social studies teacher Pat Scheffer recognized that Brenneman was someone who, like George R. Stewart, preferred to direct his own learning. When Scheffer, whom he admired greatly, recommended *Earth Abides*, he read the book. It changed his way of thinking, and drove him to seek answers to questions he's still considering today.

The 1962 Cuban missile crisis brought the book's message home. Young Brenneman was so upset by the possibility of nuclear war that his father decided to take him on a fishing trip. They drove to an isolated campsite in his father's bare-bones pickup truck, which lacked a radio, and set up camp on a hillside above Glendo Reservoir near Cheyenne, Wyoming. The campsite, by chance, faced the missile field at Warren Air Force Base. Just after dark, he awoke to see rocket contrails and hear an explosion. He believed that the country was in a nuclear war, and it literally scared the shit out of him — he jumped outside, lowered his pajama pants, and experienced the diarrhea of terror. But then, the novel came to him. He became calm, could think clearly, and knew how he and his father would survive. Like Ish, he would have a future even in the midst of Armageddon.

As things turned out, the Air Force had been conducting exercises, and the flashes were flares. Yet, *Earth Abides* helped Brenneman survive an experience that might have damaged his mind. Thanks to Stewart's great novel, he had survived World War III.[11]

A final tribute comes from James Sallis, poet, columnist for the *Boston Globe*, author of novels (one, *Drive*, was adapted as a 2011 film), who has written what is perhaps the most beautiful bearing of witness for the novel. *Earth Abides: Stewart's dark eulogy for humankind* was first published in Sallis's column in *The Boston Globe*. Here are excerpts, which Mr. Sallis has given permission to quote:

> This is a book, mind you, that I'd place not only among the greatest science fiction, but among our very best novels.
>
> Each time I read it, I'm profoundly affected, affected in a way only the greatest art — Ulysses, Matisse or Beethoven symphonies, say — affects me. Epic in sweep, centering on the person of Isherwood Williams, *Earth Abides* proves a kind of antihistory, relating the story of humankind backwards, from ever-more-abstract civilization to stone-age primitivism.
>
> … Art's mission is to make our lives large again, to dredge us out of this terrible dailyness. I begin each reading of *Earth Abides* knowing that, once the flight's done, I'll be meeting a new man there at the end of the concourse. The guy who got on the flight's okay. I like the one who gets off a lot better.[12]

Earth Abides would bring Stewart another award, the first International Fantasy Award. *Fire, Names on the Land* and his other books also continued to receive critical acclaim and enjoy good sales. With the extra income from the books, the Stewarts could finally build their dream house. Set on Codornices Road in the Berkeley hills, the home was designed by one of Stewart's Berkeley colleagues, Professor of Design Winfield Scott "Duke" Wellington. Wellington used the lean, clean architectural lines of 1950s homes, but the house's redwood siding and its natural setting high in the Berkeley Hills echoed the Arts and Crafts style.

With a fine new home, the Stewarts became busy hosts. Friends like the Harts and Stegners came over often, and out-of-town literary dignitaries like historian Bruce Catton and poet Robert Frost stayed with the Stewarts. The Stewart grandchildren visited often. Ted threw many picnics in the backyard. It was a pleasant time, when the Stewarts could finally relax and enjoy the benefits of their decades of hard work. And yet —

In the final scenes of *Earth Abides*, fire destroys the buildings of a post-apocalyptic UC Berkeley. It was prophetic. A political fire was swirling around the campus. As Stewart had been forced into freedom by the "eleven bad years," he was now forced to *defend* freedom — the academic freedom of the university.

The poet was about to become a warrior.

IV. Of Freedom and Friendship

26 *Fiat Nox?*

We have come to a divide in the California Enlightenment, rooted in the very founding of the university. Joseph LeConte, following Hume and Berkeley's suggestion, to learn through observation, studied geology in the Sierra wilderness. He came to love the wilderness. That encouraged him to help protect the beauty of the natural world — God's book of nature, as he saw it. His scientific observations had become a life-enhancing pathway of the heart. But LeConte's brother John's work in physics led down another path: to the creation of plutonium, and the bomb. That pathway would become one of fear and suspicion. The crisis came when the United States, after using two atomic bombs to destroy the life of Hiroshima and Nagasaki, realized what had been loosed upon the world and tried to put the genie back in the bottle. The result was fear, and an attempt to dim the light of learning.

Fear breeds fear. The fear of the bomb was no exception. The same nation which had been recently advised that "the only thing we have to fear is fear itself" embraced an entire set of fears with general enthusiasm. Those who reminded the official fear mongers of FDR's advice were suspect. Any talk that raised questions about American policy or the wisdom and morality of Hiroshima was "unpatriotic," "disloyal," "communistic" or even "treasonous." Soon, citizens abandoned enlightened reason, and began to seek a protector.

The tyrant always comes in the guise of the protector. Because a fearful man or woman is easily led, certain special interests saw an opportunity. The Hearst newspapers were especially virulent. Hearst's lawyer, University Regent John Francis Neylan, led a movement to "protect security" by restricting intellectual and academic freedom on campus. The result was a "loyalty" oath which threatened enlightenment. Fiat Nox — "let there be night" — almost replaced Fiat Lux.

Yet the university that produced the Bomb also housed George R. Stewart. In the years to come, Stewart would write some of his most powerful books about the dangers of the night of fear. A new idea would enter his work, that freedom and "the land" are intertwined. That is, an ecologically sound society must be a free society. So even in this time there would be light.

The Year of the Oath started well enough. On sabbatical in Mexico, Stewart finished the final draft of *Earth Abides*, then proofread the manuscript. He returned by way of New York on his first "U.S. 40" trip, photographing road and roadsides for his book about the highway. Twice he went to the place he called "Sheep Rock," gathering ideas for another book. It was, he remembered, an especially beautiful spring.

It should have been a mellow time, a calm prelude to his retirement. But in late 1949, in the climate of nuclear fear, the Regents of the university forced a Special Oath on faculty members at the University of California. Faculty members had traditionally signed the following oath: "I do solemnly swear (or affirm, as the case may be) that I will support the Constitution of the United States and the Constitution of the State of California, and that I will faithfully discharge the duties of my office according to the best of my ability." The Regents' new oath added the phrase "that I am not a member of the Communist Party, or under any oath, or a party to any agreement, or under any commitment that is in conflict with my obligations under this oath."[1]

Regents Lawrence Giannini, Sydney Ehrman and John Francis Neylan were the leaders of the oath effort. Giannini "earned" his position as regent by accident of birth and death, replacing his late father, Bank of Italy founder A. P. Giannini. During the construction of Boulder Dam, Ehrman had been counsel to the "Six Companies," whose membership read like a who's who of the military-industrial complex. Neylan was the lawyer for the Hearsts.

The new oath came with an order: "Sign, or get out," words not easily ignored. Newer professors were in especially difficult positions. To sign meant giving up freedom many of them had just fought to defend in World War II. Yet if they did not sign, they would lose their jobs, and their families would suffer. So older professors, who thought they were protected by tenure, led the fight against the oath.

The professors based their fight on several issues. They argued the new oath: restricted intellectual and political freedom; threatened the free inquiry which is the basis of enlightened research; was imposed without consulting the faculty; and that the Special Oath conflicted with university regulation No. 5, which reads, in part:

> The function of the University is to seek and to transmit knowledge and to train students in the processes whereby truth is to be made known.... The University is founded upon faith in intelligence and knowledge and it must defend their free operation. It must rely upon truth to combat error. Its obligation is to see that the conditions under which questions are examined are those which give play to intellect rather than to passion.[2]

Faculty efforts to oppose the oath seemed to be successful. The Special Oath was removed. But then the Regents inserted the oath into the faculty contract. If you signed the contract, you signed the oath. If you didn't sign, you were neither employed nor paid. In a blow to established, older professors like Stewart, tenure was not honored. Now, all university careers — and academic freedom — were at risk.

The detailed playing out of things is not the purpose of this book. But one case, that of Dr. Edward C. Tolman, stands out. Tolman was a leader in the Behaviorist movement of Psychology, the man who gave us the concept of the "rat in a maze." (He studied cognition — "knowing" — by putting rats in mazes to see how they learned to find their way around.) Tolman's greatest contribution is the *cognitive map*, the idea that each of us, in the hippocampus of the brain, creates a personalized mental map of the common space we share with others. Cognitive mapping is now a major area of research in geography.

Tolman's was a distinguished record, with 32 years of service at Berkeley. He was a member of the National Academy of Sciences, the American Philosophical Society, Phi Beta Kappa, and Sigma Xi, as well as vice-president of the American Association for the Advancement of Science. During World War II he worked for the Office of Strategic Services as a psychologist. He published more than 80 articles in research journals.

A passionate believer in academic freedom, Tolman refused to sign the oath. There was no suspicion of his loyalty, or of any connections with the Communist Party. Yet the university fired him. His accomplishments were irrelevant. The concepts of tenure and academic freedom were irrelevant. The value of his work to the university, its students, and California was irrelevant.

Like Tolman, all faculty members now faced the guns. Would they choose to protect their careers, or defend freedom? If they decided to fight for freedom, how could they possibly win the battle, ranged as they were against wealthy newspapers and lawyers?

The answer would come through one of the tools of enlightenment to which they had dedicated their lives. They would fight the threat of what might be called "en*n*ightenment" with a book.

George R. Stewart was not one to go looking for a fight. But in this case, the fight had come to him. As the debate over the Loyalty Oath slammed into the Academic Senate at the University of California, Berkeley, some professors argued against signing. Several refused to sign. Stewart argued for signing, since that meant the faculty would still have their paychecks. "Sign, Stay, and Fight," became his slogan.[3] Then he wrote a book.

To be more precise, he coordinated the writing of a book. Stewart acknowledged the contributions of others but his was the only name listed as author. In this time of fear and the manipulation of fear, an author risked much by putting his name on such a book. Stewart compared the danger to that faced by the French Resistance in World War II. If there was to be such risk, he would take it, and keep the others clear. Stewart wrote the book quickly, so it would become part of the public debate about the oath.

Stewart's book almost didn't get published. His regular publisher, Random House, refused to publish it. Fortunately, one of the editors at Doubleday, Howard Cady, convinced his company to publish the book. Cady deserves honor here: *The Year of the Oath*, now considered a classic study of the fight to preserve our civil liberties and a testament to academic freedom, has been republished several times.

Stewart's book took the debate to colleagues in other universities and the general public. It inspired strong support. Poet Carl Sandburg, who won the Pulitzer Prize for his massive biography of Lincoln, sent a letter to Ted Stewart: "Thank George for writing The Year of the Oath. God love you both." The vice-president of the Medical Branch of the University of Texas, Chauncey Leake, wrote, "Go to it and write more!" Harlow Shapley, director of the Harvard College Observatory who more or less discovered the size and layout of our galaxy, sent his thanks. Lewis W. Terman of Stanford sent a handwritten tongue-in-cheek modern version of Swift's "Modest Proposal" in which he suggested that all youngsters be required to take an anti-communist oath.

There was also this statement of support from Princeton:

> We, the resident professors and professors emeriti of the Institute for Advanced Study, being aware that the Regents have dismissed members of your faculty contrary to the recommendations of your Committee on Privilege and Tenure and this action violates the policy of tenure, the principle of the faculty's self-determination and responsibility hitherto recognized by the University of California, unanimously wish to encourage you to unite in the sense of your traditional policies and principles against encroachment.

It was signed by John von Neumann, Robert Oppenheimer and Albert Einstein, among others. Einstein, at least, knew full well the dangers of tests of "loyalty" in various "fatherlands," "motherlands," and "homelands."[4]

Not all communications were friendly. One patriot, a Mr. John Winchester, sent the following note: "The term 'Academic Freedom' has become a mask of treason. To prove this, a lie-detector test will be given to every professor in every university."[5] Hearst lawyer John Francis Neylan, leader in the attempt to require the oath, wrote publisher Doubleday and Company, "It is common knowledge that the infiltration or embarrassment of the University of California has top priority on the agenda of the Communist forces in this country for reasons which need not be discussed here."[6]

In general, the loyalty oath was a disaster for the people of California. Some 47 eminent people declined positions at Berkeley. Formal and informal associations of theoretical physicists blacklisted the Berkeley Physics Department, which lost *every* theoretical physicist. Theoretical physics, in the West at least, gravitated to Stanford.[7] On the other hand, *The Year of the Oath* helped encourage the departure of one obstreperous regent. L. M. Giannini resigned in full glorious bluster, threatening not only freedom of speech but due process of the law: "I want to organize 20th Century vigilantes who will unearth Communists and Communism in all their sordid aspects, and I will, if necessary!"[8]

On the other side of things, those who had opposed the oath knew victory. In 1955, the California Supreme Court decided in favor of Dr. Tolman and the others who had refused to sign the oath — an oath which the court now declared illegal to begin with — and the words about Communist Party membership were removed from the faculty contract. Back pay was granted to all those who had refused to sign. And, in 1963, a new home for education and psychology on the Berkeley campus, was named "Tolman Hall" at the request of University President Clark Kerr — in honor of the distinguished scholar who had battled the illegal acts of the Regents.

Writing his small book about the oath, Stewart, like his Civil War uncle John H. Stewart, had faced the guns. Successful in battle, he left a weapon for future defenders of freedom. *The Year of the Oath* is here to guide and encourage those who fight against tyrants and for freedom. It tells readers, "We were here, and sweated, and were terrified, too. But we fought, and won, and kept the Light burning. You, yourselves, if need be, can also do this."

In 1955, George Stewart received a letter from Berkeley Chief of Police J. D. Holstrom:

> *To Whom It May Concern:*
> This is to certify that George R. Stewart has not been arrested here on any charge.
> There is nothing in Record Division files to indicate that he has been guilty of conduct subversive of good order, national security, or the structure of institutions.[9]

Thus ended the Year of the Oath. The war between enlightenment and en*night*enment continues, but this battle, at least, had been won.

With the oath crisis out of the way, Stewart could return to his ecological and historical writing. Yet in years to come his books would carry echoes of the Year of the Oath. His microcosms would often be dark ones — of societies' witchhunts, vigilance committees, and moral and social decay. Yet, he could at least write with the confidence of a lover of freedom who knew his geography. Stewart knew that in a country filled with blank spaces on its maps, freedom, even if it leaves our institutions, still resides in the land.

27

Stewart once wrote that although his scholarly life had often been a lonely one, he had enjoyed some fine meetings along the way.[1] Ordeals like that of the loyalty oath tested those pleasant meetings, but Stewart's Berkeley associates had been steadfast. He told Riess, "I worked with about seventy people on that.... I was the man they were following there at one point. You don't forget it. I don't."[2]

Stewart's colleagues were also the source of much of the scientific precision in his books. Realizing his great creative gifts were those of the poet, Stewart wisely called on colleagues in other disciplines whenever he researched a book. In a way, all his books were like *The Year of the Oath*. Stewart was the author, but he was helped in the work by his colleagues.

Words again. "College" and "colleague" meant the same — "one chosen to serve with another."[3] Stewart and his fellow scholars were colleagues by *choice*. "Choice," from another of the ancient Proto-Indo-European words, is central to our myths and epics. At the critical moment in *The Lord of the Rings*, Frodo chooses to become ring-bearer; others choose to join him; from those choices hangs that tale. At critical moments in Stewart's life, like that of the oath, he and others had chosen to join together in fellowship. From their choices hangs this tale.

His first choice in friends, Theodosia, proved best. She encouraged the books, supported him, and partnered in his work. She remembered George walking out of his office after a morning of writing to say, "You'll never guess what happened today!"[4] If she disagreed with what had happened, she told him. He always listened, and considered what she said with great care. He also knew her strength and wrote it into some of his characters.

Beyond Ted, George Stewart had several circles of collegiality. There was a literary circle, of colleagues in the Department of English and elsewhere, who shared his love of literature. A geographic circle, of those who worked across the disciplines, and who went into the field with Stewart to do research. And a final circle, that of his readers — in the millions, speaking many languages, living in many places, and spanning the decades. Together, Stewart's circles of collegiality created a group not unlike the one described by novelist Ed Abbey in *Desert Solitaire*: "The brotherhood of great souls and the comradeship of intellect, a *corpus mysticum* ... a democratic aristocracy based not on power or institutions but on isolated men ... poets, revolutionaries and independent spirits, both famous and forgotten ... whose heroism gives to human life on earth its adventure, glory, and significance."[5]

Who were these friends and colleagues, in the closest circles?

Courageous, adventurous, interested in ideas, pioneering poet-professor Dr. Josephine Miles would have gladly joined Stewart and the others sitting around the research campfires, but it was as hard for her to walk across a room as it was for Stewart to climb mountains — she had been crippled with rheumatoid arthritis since childhood. Yet her brilliance, her passion for life, and her courage led her to transcendence. She became the first tenured woman professor at the University of California, Berkeley, first female "University Professor," and the first Professor Emerita. She was a tough, smart pioneer — exactly the type of person that George Stewart admired. The admiration was mutual. Professor Miles admired George R. Stewart, and his books. She found *East of the Giants*, the story of a woman pioneering new social ground, especially encouraging.

The best evidence of the affectionate respect Stewart and Miles felt for each other is a series of poems they tossed back and forth when they were Emeriti. To read the wordplay, to see how they jumped to each other's challenges of topic and meter, is to watch the collegial dance of great minds.

On Stewart's 70th birthday, Miles wrote:

> "Seventy" is hard to rhyme,
> So I look forward to the time
> When you are eightly,
> Which will rhyme greatly

Stewart answered:

> The inducement is weighty
> To live to be eighty.
>
> But I might get to ninety,
> As the Cockney says, "My'n't'ee!"
>
> Or even a hundred
> If Someone has blundered.[6]

Another of Stewart's close departmental colleagues was Dr. James D. Hart, an heir to the MJB coffee company, who began teaching at Berkeley in 1936. In the late 1930s, the Harts bought a home on San Luis Road near the Stewarts' place and the men became fast friends. Jack Stewart recalls that "his main friend was Jim Hart. He would come over and visit. He was sort of the outgoing kind of guy."[7] Jack also told a story about how clothes made the men. George Stewart decided it was time to buy a new suit. After much thinking and shopping, he bought one that fit his self-image of how an English professor should dress. The first time he wore it to work, he ran into Jim Hart — wearing the identical suit. After they finished laughing, they christened it "The English Professors' Suit."[8]

Stewart had great respect for Hart's advice. He gave the manuscript of *Earth Abides* to Hart to review. Hart told Stewart he was disturbed by one section which he thought portrayed a Jewish couple in a stereotypical way. (Hart was Jewish and sensitive on the issue). Stewart changed the manuscript. When Hart became director of the Bancroft Library, he and Stewart worked closely

C.S Forester picnic, circa 1940. Forester was a friend and neighbor of the Stewarts. TBS loved picnics, so they often took picnic trips into the country. Woman in the back is probably Forester's wife; George R. Stewart is wearing sunglasses; Forester and Ted are in the foreground.

to expand and strengthen the collections. Stewart helped found the Friends of the Bancroft Library — a valuable resource for Hart and the Library.

Stewart and Hart's friendship lasted for decades. Stewart honored it in his work. The name Hart appears in several of Stewart's books. Hart Creek runs through the imaginary geography of *Fire*. And in *Earth Abides*, "Hart" family members are Ish's pre-apocalyptic neighbors. In turn, Hart honored Stewart's scholarship in his Introduction to *From Scotland to Silverado*.

Stewart also enjoyed a wider circle of literary colleagues beyond the Berkeley English Department. Wallace Stegner and C. S. Forester lived nearby. Others wrote or taught elsewhere, but when Berkeley asked them to come and speak they often stayed with the Stewarts. Robert Frost and Carl Sandburg, among others, would be guests of the Stewarts.

Frost was an old friend of Ted's family so it was natural that the Stewarts would put him up. Although born in San Francisco, Frost had adopted the conservatism of the New England farmer. That meant that his politics were quite different from George and Ted's. But family connections and his poetic ability made up for differences of opinion.

Robert Frost picnic at Nicasio, December 11, 1953. The woman next to Frost is probably Ted.

Carl Sandburg, on the other hand, was a radical populist — closer to the Stewarts in political philosophy, but as a school dropout different in background. Sandburg could be abrasive. Garff Wilson, chief of protocol for the university, remembered Sandburg once broke up a reception the University had thrown for him by playing his own composition, "God Damn Republicans, scum of the earth."[9] Jack Stewart, on the other hand, remembers *Frost* as the less pleasant of the two: "Frost and Sandburg were guests at the house now and then. I remember Frost … a very famous man, wrote some wonderful poems, but on a personal level he turned me off a little bit. He would dominate everything."[10]

Sandburg's visits seemed to produce better stories. Ted remembered that Sandberg, during a visit to the Stewarts, picked up the first edition of Joseph Conrad's *Heart of Darkness* autographed by Conrad and Henry Ford, saw the autographs, and asked, "Want me to autograph it?" They said yes, and he added his name. (Later authors would follow Sandburg's example and add their signatures to the book.)[11] And George Stewart recalled a great night of folk singing with Sandburg at the Stewart home. Pulitzer Prize winner H.L. Davis, ballad-collector Bertrand H. Bronson of the Department of English, Carl Sandburg, and George Stewart were sitting by the fire when Sandburg whipped out a borrowed guitar and suggested a songfest. As the night went on they passed the guitar around, each contributing new songs. It was a sublime night of singing at the communal fire, and Stewart never forgot the joy of it.

Those circles of colleagues in poetry and prose, both close and far, would help shape the literary style of Stewart's works. But it was another circle, that of Stewart's interdisciplinary scientist colleagues, that would enter literature. Stewart wrote, in *Sheep Rock*, "That time I was with Charlie. I was there again — with Jack, with Selar, with Carl and Parker and Starker, with Brig and Roy."[12] Who were these men?

Charlie was Dr. Charles Camp, who had become friends with Stewart during Stewart's research on *Ordeal by Hunger*. The friendship grew during the 1930s. Then — "Charlie, let's take a trip to northwestern Nevada," said Stewart in mid–1941. Stewart wanted to explore Noble's Cutoff of the California Trail, as described by Alonzo Delano in his 1849 journal. That meant a trip across the playas — dry desert lake beds — through the canyons of Nevada, and into Surprise Valley, California.[13]

Camp was up for it: "You never know what you're going to run into next in Nevada." So they drove the playa — off-road, mind you, in terrain still dangerous — in a 1937 Chevy. "I just marvel at the chances we took on that car," Stewart told Riess, in a joint interview with Camp. "We got down into a kind of thing like a great big ditch about ten feet wide at the bottom — steep sides on both sides of it! [Laughing] … We went out and did a little spade work … and then I took the old Chevrolet on the run, and Woop! The wheels spinning around — and got her out. Oh, we went on beyond that. We took chances all the time."

"Driving up there was like steering a boat…. We could see the … Rock across the desert. We knew that was where we were trying to get to…. And finally we decided we'd gone far enough, and we just turned, and went right across this [the Playa], just steering for the … Rock.

"I'm amazed we ever got that car back! … They were tough cars they made in those days, though.

"Without having a good man like Charlie along," Stewart said, "I would never have dared go into those places I did on that trip."

Charlie Camp added, "That's the way to travel. These people who go out with trailers and everything, never get anywhere like that." When Camp went out into the field on his own research trips, he did it from wheels up. He'd buy an old limousine — built tougher, he said — pull the heads, clean out the carbon, put new gaskets on it, and drive it trouble-free for thousands of miles. It made a good camping car since you didn't mind banging it up a bit. And when it died you didn't have much money in it.

Stewart also remembered — great word of the West — the badwater: "You know, if you taste this desert water, it's terrible [alkali water!], but if you take a gallon of wine along and put about one third wine in the water, it makes it quite palatable. And we did a lot of drinking on that."

It was a propitious trip. Along the way, Camp and Stewart discovered the place called "Sheep Rock," and Stewart would see a book in it. The place fascinated Stewart, and he wanted to learn as much about it as he could before writing about it. After the Second World War, he would return with Camp, and he would bring the others there to help him with his book.

"Carl" Sauer was the leading geographer of his time. Dr. Jeffrey Gritzner, head of the Department of Geography at The University of Montana, who was a student at the University of California, Berkeley, when Sauer was still active in the Berkeley Geography Department, remembered his brilliance.[14]

> I used to live on a porch in North Berkeley. Sauer would walk by every day, head down, arms behind him, thinking deeply. You never saw him head up, looking around, laughing. He was always deep in thought.
>
> Sauer ... believed geography must take into itself all the other disciplines if it was to be successful. So we always had professors assigned to us from other disciplines — physics, or social work. Sauer also wanted to break up the ethnocentrism of Geography. We had visiting professors from other countries. Schools of geography in different countries have very different perspectives....
>
> Sauer was, I think, the best academic in the world at that time. On the spot, he could draw in the expertise he needed to find a meaning. He was unafraid of great leaps of imagination — of inductive thinking in its highest form. Later evidence usually proved his intuition correct. [To think like Sauer] you ... extract a lot of information from things that are not obvious. To do that, you need to be a good observer, and to have a broad conceptual framework, into which to place bits of information, in context. [Sauer had] a freshness of thought.

Sauer's idea that time is geography's fourth dimension would have deep influence on Stewart when he was writing *Sheep Rock*. Sauer's belief that you needed to work across the disciplines was shared by Starker, Parker, and the others.

"Starker" was Starker Leopold, son of Wilderness Ethic pioneer Aldo Leopold. He attended both the Yale Forestry School and the Department of Zoology at Berkeley. At Berkeley Leopold developed a pioneering program in natural resource conservation. Since Leopold refused to box up knowledge, students in the program studied in several departments. They learned to see the connections in the natural world between tree and atmosphere, or garbage dump and grizzly.

Dr. "Parker" Trask, Professor of geology, was brilliant beyond the measuring. He earned a Bachelor's in math at 18, his M.A. at 21. Then he pretty much invented what might be called "statistical geology," the examination of geological qualities through scales like the Richter or the Mohs Hardness Scale. He was also an accomplished athlete and an amateur ornithologist. His knowledge of languages was extraordinary. Even those closest to him didn't know how many languages he understood. (In his final illness, Trask studied Middle English so he could read Chaucer in the original before he died.) At "Sheep Rock" camps, he described the geology with a staccato passion, but what most impressed his friends was his sensitivity and love of good fellowship, exemplified by his good cheer around the campfire at "Sheep Rock."[15]

"Jack" is George Stewart's son, Dr. John H. Stewart, who would later write the standard work on the geology of Nevada and prepare the Geological Map of Nevada.

"Brig" and "Roy," Jack remembers, were two graduate students in anthropology.

"Selar" was a mystery man until Jack Stewart managed to track him down. Selar S. Hutchings was a researcher for the Department of Agriculture whose work included several studies of salt deserts like the playa at "Sheep Rock." Interestingly, one of Hutchings's technical papers, about increasing forage for big horn sheep on mountain ranges, lists a "George Stewart" as co-author. Was the co-author our George R. Stewart? "I don't understand how GRS would be an author on this, so perhaps this is another George Stewart," says Jack.[16] Yet the paper's topic, bringing the Bighorns — the "Sheep" of "Sheep Rock" — back to the Rock, would have been important to the author of *Sheep Rock*. Stewart ends his novel with the Bighorn.

> Then, so that his friend might share, he spoke gently: "Wake up! Be quiet! Look toward the spring! There's a mountain-sheep!" ...
> The ram finished drinking. He raised his head, and tossed the great horns lightly, and stood sniffing the breeze with wide-open nostrils, although the wind was from the north and he probably did not smell the men.
> "So they've come back!" said the heavier man, softly.[17]

Others went to the Rock with Stewart. Not mentioned in the novel, but none the less important, were Jim Hart and historian Jim Holliday. Another colleague, George R. Stewart's oldest and best friend, started out more than once, only to be stopped by weather. So George Stewart dedicated the book: "To Theodosia, who was very close to it."

This circle of colleagues might be called the Fellowship of *Sheep Rock*. As the ram drank from the waters of the spring, these friends drank together at the waterhole of ideas. I imagine them sitting around the campfire, sharing spirits and good fellowship, laughing and singing after a hard day's work. Their campfire is an outpost of the enlightenments of Edinburgh and California, a modern version of England's Lunar Men or Edinburgh's Oyster Club. Over the wine (for there is wine or something like wine) each talks about his particular area of research. Then turns to another and says, "What about you, Carl? What did you discover today?" Discussions follow, and the colleagues begin to see how each one's work meshes with that of the others.

Jim Holliday, George R. Stewart, Black Rock 1953. Holliday was a distinguished historian who eventually became Director of the California Historical Society. Since *Sheep Rock* had already been published, this trip was probably for research on the California Trail. Stewart would publish *The California Trail* in the following decade.

George R. Stewart is listening carefully. He begins to get a picture of the playa, spring and rock, in time as well as space. Later, poet of the place, he will weave his colleagues' knowledge together. From the research, and the talk, and the songs around the campfire at the place called "Sheep Rock," a book will be made. It will be based on the idea that places, like knowledge, can only be understood as

> a part of long continuous space, and every place therefore leads the way into every other. Like so much else in the world, then, a place turns out to be nothing more than an abstraction fathered by the human mind, setting up artificial barriers, pretending that something ends at a hard and fast line, and that it is not in actuality running on continuously into something else.[18]

Stewart called *Sheep Rock* one of his ecological novels "in the older sense, that is, all the things that go to make up a place."[19] It is an interweaving of geological history, paleontology, paleobotany, and human prehistory and history in one isolated place, based on the scientific observations of his campfire companions who met at the waterhole of ideas. Influenced by Carl Sauer, Stewart added deep time to the work. So it is also a novel of fourth-dimensional ecology, examining change over time at one place.

Sheep Rock is also about freedom. His old friend Wallace Stegner realized that, and commented that the book was in part about how a return to wild land would affect the psychology and sociology of those who made the choice to do so.[20] Stegner understood the book was more than ecological, that Stewart was also carefully thinking about other questions: If the antidote to lost freedom is in "the land," how difficult would it be to return to the land? How many urban or suburban humans could take the harsh stress of wilderness?

Sheep Rock was responsible for a good writer's story. Saxe Commins, legendary editor at Random House (he edited Eugene O'Neill and William Faulkner, among others), was assigned to work with Stewart on his novel. In conference with Stewart in New York, Commins told Stewart that he had only one suggestion for the book: a comma in the first sentence should be removed. Even though Stewart, who believed strong first sentences were critical to the success of a book, had worked hard on the sentence, he agreed to remove the comma. But thinking it over that night in his hotel room, he decided that the comma had to stay. He called Commins first thing next morning and Commins agreed to put the comma back. It was the extent of editing on Stewart's novel.

The book stretched Stewart's idea of the ecological novel to the limit. It was a complex work, even in advance of the writing. He mapped it out, of course. In fact, there are more maps — of geography and paleogeography, of the scenes and action, of the ideas — for this book than any of his others. When he finally put everything on one map, he developed a system that used nested circles to show connections between things, people, or events at given time periods.

Like the map, *Sheep Rock* is a book of nested concentric circles. Stewart described the novel as "sort of three times round and three times round."[21] There are three sections (he named them "Parts") each with the title of a different area of "Sheep Rock": *The Spring and the Rock*, *The Beaches and the Flat*, *The Mountains and the Sky*. Each Part contains three chapters, one of which is a short story about the human history of the place. For Example, Part I includes "The Spring," and "The Rock," and a short story entitled "Of the Silver Bullet."

Complicated? There's more. The three parts, each with its three chapters of interwoven art and science, are themselves nested within a prologue, several intermediate sections that might be named "*interlogues*," and an epilogue. These sections of the novel are the observations of another character, who seems to act as a Greek Chorus. In the prologue this person describes how he found the place and decided to tell its story. In the "interlogues," set between each part, he returns to continue describing his role in the place's story.

And woven throughout all of this is the tale of poet Geoffrey Archer, human protagonist of the novel. He's there on a fellowship with plans to write a poem. He believes "Sheep Rock's" stark loneliness will inspire him. As he explores the place and works on his poem, Archer narrates the story of his life there. The poem Archer is trying to compose also appears, in bits and pieces, throughout the work. But the place defeats Archer, and he cannot finish his poem. Like another symbol Stewart uses in the book, a broken blue pitcher, the poem remains in fragments.

Yet, the poem, like a map, is important because it distills Stewart's ideas about the place. Fortunately, Tim Gorelangton, of the Special Collections Library at the University of Nevada at Reno, assembled the fragments of the poem, printing 50 copies for the friends and family of George R. Stewart.[22] Here is part of the poem:

> There is nowhere a beginning,
> Neither is there anywhere an end.
>
> There are places, soft and lush and yielding,
> Places easy to be taken,
> Like pliant and ready women.
> Men come and live there, and possess them.
>
> There are other places.
> And I have seen one of them, not in dreams.
> The light is not tender upon them,
> Even at early morning.
> They yield to no wooer.
> A man may take such a place, not possess it....
>
> No, here is black rock and red mountain,
> And edged salt-grass,
> And everywhere, eager salt —
> Red rock, black rock, bubbling spring —
> They were the same before,
> Before men came,
> And went.
> Now I walk here.
>
> Yes, if you dug, and screened the sand,
> You would not even find their bones —
> (The eager salt has taken them.)
> Only here and there the earth
> Richer, a little, in phosphorus.
> Yes.
> They have come and gone, and now I walk
> here —
> A rotting house,

> Some blue-on-white shards of a shattered
> pitcher,
> A silver bullet, a blue-corroded cartridge....
> This little world, this microcosm.

Not pretty. But accurate. Stewart told Riess that the place "used to scare me to death."[23] Like a seaside beach in a great and dangerous storm or a mountain forest in a vast and deadly fire, "Sheep Rock" was the land with all safety and comfort stripped away. But the storm and the fire pass; in human terms "Sheep Rock" was (and is) eternally harsh. Yet again and again Stewart went across the playa to the Rock and Spring to feel the raw power of place. To capture it, find truth in it, and put in a novel.

This was more than literature, or research. Stewart was on a personal quest. He was still seeking an idea that would give meaning and purpose to life. He believed the idea — the truth or belief or faith — would be found not in interactions between humans, or humans and their gods, but in humans' relationships with the land. Sauer's concept of deep time made Stewart rethink the comforting belief that Earth abides. Once, "Sheep Rock" had been a lakeshore, lush and verdant. In our time it had become a sometimes-scorching, sometimes-freezing desert. It would change again. In *Earth Abides*, he thought he'd found the truth: "Men go and come, but earth abides." His saunters to "Sheep Rock" made him realize that that truth was inadequate. Earth does *not* abide. As the novel's poet Geoffrey Archer says, writing to a friend, "Now I know that the earth, too, passes."[24]

But if Earth does not abide, what can we believe in? What is *the* truth? Archer — for whom we can read George R. Stewart — builds the answer in part around the phrase often quoted by Stewart's old professor, Gayley.

> I have learned where I fit in. I too have become part of the place, which itself is part of the earth, and of the whole....
> "after me cometh a builder — tell him, I too have known."...
> I have looked upon the chips of obsidian and the lost shoeheels of Sheep Rock, and I have gained a little insight.[25]

Archer, and Stewart, have found a revised ecological faith: our lives get their meaning from the knowledge gained from our passages through place, from our observations during the passage, and from the small signs we leave behind — the structures or the books or the descendents — for future explorers to ponder on their saunters.

Sheep Rock would be Stewart's last effort to find a faith based on ecology. He would write other books around the theme of ecology, but this book was the climax, the pinnacle of his ecological work, the end of his long saunter toward a belief system built on ecological ideas.

As if to make the point, the author steps forth in the epilogue, to reveal himself.

I, George Stewart, did this work....

I have looked into the blue and green depths of the spring, and have climbed the rock, and gazed out across the desert. That first night, the grim fascination of the place rose within me, and I thought of this book.

That time I was with Charlie. I was there again — with Jack, with Selar, with Carl and Parker and Starker, with Brig and Roy. I said to myself, "I shall know more about this place than anyone knows of any place in the world." So I took the others there, and one looked at the beaches and the hills, and another at the grass and the shrubs, and another at the stone-work among the hummocks, and so it went, until at last each had shared with me what he knew. Besides, I read the books.

But if you ask me, "What is true, and what is not? Is there really such a place?" I can only say, "It is all mingled! What does it matter? In the end, is what-is-seen any truer than what-is-imagined?" Yet, if you should look hard enough, you might find a black rock and a spring — and of the other things too, more than you might suspect.

So here, I write of myself, for I also was there, and I am of it.[26]

Alexander von Humboldt had written his multi-volume work, *Kosmos,* to summarize truths he discovered about relationships between humans and "the land." Stewart was trying to do something similar in one novel. In fact, in *Sheep Rock* he went beyond the novel, to create a new literary form. So the book is not an easy read. All conventional approaches to traditional forms of literature have to be left behind, because this is not poetry or fiction or biography or non-fiction. It's all of those things, put together in a new way. As Stewart said, "three times round and three times round." The reader had better know how to shift intellectual gears without synchromesh, how to double-clutch his or her way through it. It's a pleasant read, not an easy read.

But does the book *work*?

George R. Stewart never renewed the copyright on *Sheep Rock*. There is no explanation for that in the Papers. Jack Stewart thinks George Stewart simply forgot to renew it, since the copyright expired while his father was ill. But Ken Carpenter, who built the second largest collection of George R. Stewart materials at the University of Nevada at Reno, thought Stewart believed the book was a failure and let the copyright lapse.

Carpenter himself believed the book didn't work. He told Stewart scholar Stephen Williams

> If you'll look at his Oral History, you'll find that he mentions the novel *Sheep Rock* as often or more often than any other novel.... It's a flawed novel, but it's very interesting. Now throughout it all, there's this broken pitcher that (the protagonist) is trying to put back together. And that's exactly what he's trying to do with *Sheep Rock*. The geology, the fauna, the history to try to get some idea of just what Sheep Rock is like.... But just as he failed to put together the pitcher he fails to give a complete view of that country....
>
> And as a matter of fact, if you look at his whole writing career, there's frag-

ments here and fragments there, from *The City* to *Storm* to *Fire*, trying to fit things together. So I really think *Sheep Rock* is very, very central to George Stewart's work.[27]

Others felt Stewart succeeded. His old friend, Poet-Professor Josephine Miles, wrote:

In the poem of the meaning of objects, the words are George Stewart's:

"Today (at Sheep Rock) I came upon the broken fragments of what seems to be an old-fashioned blue-on-white pitcher, the kind that stood on a washstand. Right beside it was lying one of those soaplike shaped pieces of rock which I had thought at first were merely natural formations, but have now come to realize are stones used by very primitive people, ages ago, to grind seeds. The pitcher can scarcely be more than a hundred years old. The grinding stone may be, for all I know, ten thousand. And on the other side of fragments of the pitcher lay a tin can, so recent that the paper cover had not yet disappeared, although the once bright-red tomatoes in the picture had faded to a dingy yellow. Thus here all the past seems to be preserved at once. And the only arranging — that is, simplifying — element is that of place.

Is it nothing to you, all ye that pass by?"

This question of lamentations is not for George Stewart.
For this place, Berkeley, as for Sheep Rock,
He has made many nothings into meanings by which we may learn
Not only symbol, but principle.
Not only the place, but the way.[28]

Who's right? Carpenter or Miles? It depends on what Stewart set out to do. Restore the pitcher — that is, completely describe one place? Josephine Miles believed (and I'd agree) that Stewart's intent in the novel was not to complete the pitcher, or completely describe the place. Miles understood that "Sheep Rock" is a microcosm, showing readers that a place, like a broken pitcher, can be understood only when its fragments are seen as part of a greater, interconnected whole. We may never find all the fragments of a place (or a pitcher), but the more we find the more we understand. And since human life is a function of place, self-understanding comes from the understanding of our places, and that comes from putting the fragments together.

In *Sheep Rock*, Stewart created another great literary symbol — the broken pitcher. As Ish's Hammer is the symbol of what endures in human society, the pitcher symbolizes the challenge humans often face, of putting the pieces of an incomplete puzzle, a mystery, together — in science, or art, or their daily lives — so they can visualize and understand the whole. The pitcher also completes Stewart's symbolism. As a hammer is a male symbol, a pitcher is the female symbol. It balances the hammer's hard upthrusting utility with its apparent fragility, and its mystery.

Stewart at Black Rock. This is probably taken in the late '40s. Stewart was always ahead of his time. Here, during one of his research trips, he even demonstrates — years before anyone else — a late 20th century way of wearing a billed cap!

As the novel ends, the poet and his family drive through the desert to the closest town, leaving Sheep Rock. Mirages shimmer. Archer tells readers that it was "as if they were driving out of an enchantment."[29] Stewart was also leaving an enchantment, that of the ecological novels. Archer/Stewart writes, "When only a few days of the vacation were left, you knew suddenly. There would remain those higher peaks that you had never climbed and those farther streams — beautiful and full of leaping trout — that you would never fish."[30] George Stewart had fished as many of the ecological streams as he could. The others would have to wait, for the next wondering wanderer.

At the end of *Sheep Rock* George R. Stewart writes.

So here, I write of myself, for I also was there, and I am of it. I followed the old road of the covered-wagons, I traced the lines of the beaches, I felt the stab of the sun, I shivered in the night-wind from the north. I took it all into my mind as a furnace takes lumps of ore.

I too am of it. I am that one who stood apart a little, speaking with godlike authority — for that is the right of the one who sees the work before it is, and shapes it to take the form of his vision, though never wholly. Yes, this is my little world, which godlike I created, and now abandon to uncaring time.

And he who will brave the desert and come after me to the spring, he may find my traces, where I wandered wondering, and thus wandering wondered, and he too may take to himself a little of me as I in my time took to myself a little of those who had been there before me.

Thus, like the artist who paints himself into the corner of the picture, I make my mark at the end. **Opus perfeci.**[31]

Opus Perfeci: "I finished the work."
But *was* his work completed, his long intellectual saunter ended?

28

George R. Stewart turned 55 as he was writing *Sheep Rock*—time for him to begin thinking of retirement. He had certainly earned the right to relax. And he needed to relax—his pneumonia-damaged lung was acting up again. But Stewart kept working, and working hard.

In 1951, the Stewarts took a six-month sabbatical trip from Britain to Greece. When they returned, Stewart was offered the Fulbright Professorship in Athens. He accepted, for a half-year term. Back in Athens Stewart gave a series of lectures on "American Ways of Life," then worked the lectures into a book. He used his spare time to research another novel. He told interviewer Riess, "I practice Superfetation.... Superfetation is what a rabbit does. She starts one litter before she finishes the last."[1]

But he was older, and sometimes he felt it. So Stewart turned to a project that could be called a vacation on paper. It would be a collection of photographs and short essays that used a transcontinental highway as a self-guiding geographic interpretive trail for a "Cross-Section of the United States of America." The book would also be about the road itself, and roads, and the experience of driving, described at a high point of the United States' highway system. That is, it would be a popular book about "odology," the study of roads.

Again, Stewart would break new literary ground—so new he had to change publishers. Random House did not "buy" the concept. The rejection, following Random House's refusal to publish *The Year of the Oath*, was the final straw. Stewart began looking for a new publisher. Fortunately, Wallace and Mary Stegner had become the West Coast editors for Houghton Mifflin and saw an opportunity to sign Stewart up for the publishing house.

The new book was no problem. Stegner himself had suggested it. Stewart once mentioned to Stegner that he wanted to do a book of photographs and literary essays about the national forests. In a 1947 letter, Stegner encouraged him: "I can conceive of a picture book on the national forests which would involve all your knowledge of geography, history, meteorology, forestry, fire fighting, and related sciences, and that I think ought to be a hell of a good book."[2] But after thinking it over, Stegner suggested Stewart instead write a book about a highway: "I ... want to get down on record the fact that when I proposed that Highway 40 book the other day I was not just making idle talk.... In most people's hands it would be just another regional-folkways-geographical job, but I think you'd make it something special."[3] He also mentioned that Houghton-Mifflin was offering a very handsome $5000 advance for the book (about $42,000 in 2011 dollars). Stewart eventually accepted the offer, changed publishers, and went to work on the book.

Stegner's suggestion was one reason Stewart chose U.S. 40. But there were others. Transcontinental and central, the highway follows the old trails that Stewart loved so much — the National Road in the East, the California Trail in the West, and others. And in its eastern sections at least, it was the road Stewart had hitchhiked in that post-pneumonia spring of 1919.

As usual, George Stewart took to the field to research the book. Although he'd been over the road before, he now drove the entire route, twice, with a scholar's eye. Ted joined him on one trip, Jack on another, and George benefited from their observations and ideas. George and Jack also photographed locations typical of the regions crossed by the highway for use in the book.

Wallace Stegner had encouraged the book, but when it was done it was George R. Stewart's work. In fact, Stegner was somewhat disappointed by it. He wrote Houghton Mifflin to say, "I saw scraps and pieces of [the U.S. 40 manuscript]; it looked rather matter-of-fact and unglamorous to me, and I told George so, but he thinks it ought to be that way."[4] Unglamorous, perhaps, in its straightforward way of displaying photos and essays, yet it has become a classic. It was the first book of its kind, a thoroughly cross-disciplinary look at the geography of the United States of America of 1950 as seen from a highway, U.S. 40. And, as was so often the case with Stewart's work, it inspired others.

Published by Houghton Mifflin in 1953, the book opens with a series of introductory essays about the idea of roads, the history of U.S. 40, and the experience of driving it in mid–20th-century America. The heart of the book, divided into sections named for historic trails which U.S. 40 followed, includes photographs of and essays about places along U.S. 40. Drawings and maps by Master Cartographer Edwin Raisz embellish the pages. Stewart concludes with a final photo essay of place-name signs found along the road.

Wallace Stegner may have had doubts about the book, but it was successful. It was, and is, a wonderful book for the armchair traveler. It's also a fine book to carry along on road trips over the highway. Some readers did so, using the book as a road guide. My second-hand copy of *U.S. 40* carries notes from the Wingards of Pasadena, California, who, when they visited a place Stewart described, penciled in the date. So we know they drove through Kansas City on June 10, 1956, and crossed Colorado's Berthoud and Rabbit Ears Passes on the 13th.

In 1957, Stewart followed *U.S. 40* with *North America 1*, a two-volume work that follows the route of a proposed highway from Alaska to Panama. *North America 1, Looking North* follows the Caribou, Hart, Alaska, and Steese Highways to Circle, Alaska; North *America 1, Looking South*, the "Pan-American Highway" from Mexico to southern Costa Rica. Although the highway has not yet been completed, the books preserve fine examples of 1950s highway landscapes in the northern and southern parts of North America.

Some might find it strange that the father of the ecological novel was also father of the highway book. But Stewart believed in freedom as well as ecology; and, as he wrote in the essay "On Motoring" in *U.S. 40*, people "like to drive because driving is, actually and symbolically, a perfect mechanism for escape."[5] Nor was he opposed to good highways, those which follow the contours of the land and open landscapes to the traveler. Interstates too often steamroll over the natural landscape, separating the traveler from its human and ecological communities, but in general the old U.S. Highways take travelers *into* the land's ecosystems and communities and thus can be considered ecologically "good." Or so George R. Stewart believed, and wrote, in his widely read road books.

U.S. 40's influence is still felt. Travelers again drive the old U. S. highways and, following Stewart's lead, some write about them. William Least Heat Moon, for example, does so in *Blue Highways*, the wonderful tale of his saunter along the U. S. highways looking for small towns with interesting names — Difficult, Nameless, Dimebox, Igo and Ono — and the neighborly folks who live in such places. When I met Least Heat Moon, I said, "You were influenced by George R. Stewart." He looked up, surprised. "Yes. Profoundly. In fact, I tried to find a copy of *Fire* when I was writing *PrairyErth*." I offered to send him a copy. In a card of thanks, for the book, Least Heat Moon wrote, "You're only the second person I've met who knows how important Geo.S. is."[6]

If Least Heat Moon's book was the first book inspired by U. S. 40, Thomas R. Vale and Geraldine R. Vale's *U.S. 40 Today*, published in 1983 and now considered a classic work about geography and roads, is the first work that could be called the "direct descendant" of a George R. Stewart book. The Vales followed Stewart's route, photographing most of the locations on the old road photographed by George and Jack Stewart to show change in that American landscape in the 30 years between his book and theirs.[7]

Stewart's road books and old U. S. 40 went electronic in 1995. That year, Frank Brusca created an award-winning National Road/U.S. 40 website — an electronic waterhole for U.S. 40 scholars and travelers. When I emailed Brusca about Stewart's book's possible influences on his work, he replied, agreeing that he was profoundly influenced by Stewart. Brusca first read *U.S. 40* when he was nine, and it shaped his life in the same way *Earth Abides* has shaped others'.[8] He believes that no other book of its kind has had the effect of *U.S. 40*.

Brusca suggested contacting German director Hartmut Bitomsky, who'd done a film about the old highway, inspired by Stewart's book.

Of all the works based on *U.S. 40*, Bitomsky's *U.S. 40 West* is most widely known. Widely known in Germany, that is, where it plays to huge audiences. Brusca says that its annual television showing of the film is watched faithfully by millions. As things turned out, Bitomsky was working in Santa Clarita, California, not far from where I live, which made an email interview easy to do.

I asked Bitomsky, "Why did a German director make a film about an old U. S. Highway?" He answered that, in the late 1970s, he received a commission from a German TV network to produce a documentary about the American West, to be shown during a festival of Western movies. He originally planned to do his film about the roads which opened the West — trails through the Appalachians, rivers, railroads, and emigrant trails to California and Oregon. But when German actor, writer and scholar Hanns Zischler gave Bitomsky a copy of Stewart's *U.S. 40*, Bitomsky had a revelation: he would revisit the old highway, movie camera and tape recorder in hand, and make a movie about it.

"Why is the film so popular in Germany?" I asked. Bitomsky replied that a film about a place of vast, largely untouched spaces, where a civilization could confront ancient problems as if they were new ones, has a tremendous appeal for Europeans.

When I asked Bitomsky if he'd read any other books by Stewart, he listed *Names on the Land*, *Fire*, *Bret Harte*, and *The California Trail*. But *U.S. 40* was the most important book for him. He found Stewart's documentary approach a revelation, since there is no tradition of such literature in Europe. He considered the author's examination of America through eyes both loving and critical to be a good example of American documentary literature. *U.S. 40*'s realistic photography and factual essays, and Stewart's detailed curiosity about what he saw along the old road were especially fascinating for the filmmaker. Bitomsky was also impressed with the fact that Stewart's book did not spring from the author's desk, but came from that firsthand knowledge that only field research can bring.[9]

Bitomsky plans an English-subtitled DVD version of his popular film, to be released sometime in the early 2010s.

U.S. 40 continues to inspire the creative mind. In 2000's *Roads: Driving America's Great Highways*, Pulitzer Prize-winner Larry McMurtry praised the book and George R. Stewart. Disney's animated film *Cars* (2006) teaches viewers that old highways and highways towns are American treasures to be visited and appreciated. In 2008, German filmmakers Florian Schewe and Vojtech Pokorny produced the film *Amiland*, based on Bitomsky's film.[10]

Also in 2008, in another fine highway book, William Least Heat Moon again honored Stewart's book. *Roads to Quoz* includes several chapters about U.S. 40. Least Heat Moon describes his travels over the old highway, inspired by its *Quoz*— defined by the author as "anything strange, incongruous, or peculiar ... the unknown, the mysterious."[11] In this case, the quoz is an ancient stone mileage marker he had seen decades earlier. Over the years he discovered that the stone is one of several remaining mileposts on the National Road, the first major infrastructure project of the United States, and the grandparent of U.S. 40.

Least Heat Moon's research led to a meeting with another road scholar inspired by the same milepost: Frank Brusca. Brusca and Least Heat Moon traveled together, researching the book. In the book, Least Heat Moon recounts the exploration of the National Road sections of U. S. 40 for several chapters.[12] Passing Stewart's odological torch onward to new generations, Least Heat Moon begins the U.S. 40 section of his book with a quote from Stewart's *U.S. 40* essay, "On Motoring."[13]

George R. Stewart is often characterized as an "environmentalist" author. But as *U.S. 40* shows, he was much more than that. He was an inventor of books, who (in the best sense of the Scottish Enlightenment) had an interest in many diverse subjects. He could write about humans' dependence on the ecosystem in *Storm*, *Fire*, and *Earth Abides*. He could write about the history of place-names in *Names On The Land*. But he could also write books which celebrated the highway and the automobile, books which might be considered anti-environmental by some.

In writing *U.S. 40*, his unglamorous and matter-of-fact book about a highway and the country through which it passes, George R. Stewart had blazed another intellectual trail — in this case along an historic highway which followed the geography of older trails. As always, Stewart's vision inspired others — artists and scholars like Least Heat Moon, the Vales, Larry McMurtry, Disney and a generation of German filmmakers like Hartmut Bitomsky. He also inspired all who read the book and use it to guide them along the old road — thus learning the value of those old, gentle highways that lead INTO rather than over American places.

29

Through the 1950s Stewart often considered the theme of freedom. *The Years of the City* is a novel about how freedom is lost; *Pickett's Charge*, a history of what it takes to keep it.

On the surface a novel about the fictional ancient Greek City State Phrax, *The Years of the City* is actually a fable for his time, and ours. Book III, a dark and cautionary tale that is the crux of the novel, describes the city state in the decades after its citizens have defeated an attacking "Horde." Phrax society decays, old families weaken, the children and grandchildren of hard-working pioneer citizens become lazy. The peoples' values shift from the old values of respect for God and nature, hard work and sacrifice, and toward lazy narcissism.

Unwilling to work or fight, the people of Phrax become dilettantes, endlessly debating meaningless issues of poetry and philosophy. Soon, poverty and hunger rage throughout the city. But citizens no longer have the character to rebuild the city's institutions — or resist a takeover.

A demagogue named Melas — interestingly, a contractor — sees an opportunity. He invents an enemy. Soon, acts of blasphemy and terrorism spread throughout Phrax — acts, in fact, carried out by Melas's henchmen. Fear of the unseen "enemy" and "terrorist" acts convinces the city's old families to appoint Melas tyrant. He becomes rich through taxation, given willingly by residents afraid of foreign "enemies" or local "terrorists." Soon, illegal foreign wars are being fought for the financial and political benefit of the contractor-tyrant.

In a few critical years citizens of Phrax have given themselves over to the ancient Greek version of the big box store, the sexual freedom movement, the unconstitutional war, the checkpoint, and the permanent army. The "Law of the Belly" has replaced the "Laws of the City." Phrax has lost its backbone, its conscience, and its enlightened democracy and replaced it with a military-industrial-contractor state.

Finally, others attack and the city dies, passing into history. It has lived its life, with some great moments; but it has also seen its lands and its people grow infertile and unproductive. It no longer has the resources or spirit to keep it going.

Although it lacked the sharp ecological focus of *Fire*, *Storm*, *Earth Abides*, and *Sheep Rock*, Stewart included the book in his list of ecological novels. In a dictatorship like that of Melas, especially when it's embraced by first families, people cannot debate the merits of conservation, let alone vote for it. And a human community with no sense of conservation will not last long. So the story of Phrax is also a reminder that the wealth of human communities is based on healthy air, water, and farmland; and that, in turn, is based on healthy and enlightened discussion of those things. The "land" decides the fate of Phrax, but freedom determines the fate of the land — a dramatic illustration of Stewart's idea that freedom and the "land" are intertwined.

Years of the City did not sell well. Stewart blamed the book's length, but it seems more likely that its dark mood discouraged readers. For the first time, Stewart was unable to take a non-judgmental approach to a work. He finds no good in Melas. Melas is evil. For readers used to Stewart's optimism, it made *The Years of the City* a hard book to read.

The story's nature, as a fable for its time, may have been another reason for the book's poor sales. The nation had (and has) involved itself in undeclared wars, ignoring the Constitution. Concerns over abuses by defense and other contractors filled the news. Newspapers often carried stories about assaults on American civil liberties. So perhaps the book was too close to home for comfortable reading.

Stewart did not follow the path of the decadent fictional citizens of Phrax when it came to liberty. He returned to the fight for academic freedom in 1953 to support a young professor at the University of Nevada at Reno. He offered his experience in the Berkeley campaign. But the professor, discouraged, chose to leave Reno.

That same year the University of California granted an honorary degree to Regent Sydney Ehrman, who had been outspoken in support of the loyalty oath. Stewart refused to attend the University's Charter Day Ceremony. In a statement to the university community he wrote:

> I do not wish to walk in the same procession with the majority of those Regents, whose beliefs and actions I abhor, and especially by walking behind them to accept symbolically the position of inferiority....
>
> I earned my doctorate by hard work and honest scholarship.... I do not believe that the professors that once granted me that degree.... would wish me to wear my academic regalia under such circumstances.[1]

When exams were censored, Stewart challenged the university. Every undergraduate applicant to Berkeley is required to pass the Subject A Exam in English composition. In 1960, a controversial essay question was added to the exam: "What are the dangers to a democracy of a national police organization, like the FBI, which operates secretly and is unresponsive to public criticism?" The FBI complained, and the university pulled the question.[2] University President Clark Kerr even wrote a letter of apology to J. Edgar Hoover.

Stewart was furious. Kerr wrote to Stewart, trying to placate him. Stewart was not placated, and wrote, prophetically as it has turned out:

> In a democratic society ... government, or any of its agencies, are the servants of the people, and not the masters. From this it follows logically that all public officials or public bodies should be subject to criticism from their employers, the public. Not excepted from this are the University of California and the Federal Bureau of Investigation of the United States Justice Department....
>
> We believe that one of the strengths of the University of California is that it has managed to stay out of the realm generally designated as "politics." Actions such as the recent regrets expressed by the Regents [to Hoover], while perhaps pacifying one group or some groups, may well be a precedent for other groups to make similar, and perhaps more damaging, demands on the University....
>
> The axe has fallen once. Who knows where and when it may fall again?[3]

Although by nature non-political, Stewart now turned to political action. He helped found the Berkeley chapter of the American Civil Liberties Union, soon serving as a national director of the organization. Then, in 1961, convinced that university governance needed major reform, Stewart sent some ideas to California business leader Joseph Bransten (the "B" in MJB Coffee). Bransten answered in a friendly way, writing that one of his friends on the Board of Regents agreed with Stewart. The Regents eventually added student and faculty representatives to the board, so that on paper, at least, it represented a broader part of California society than it had during the Year of the Oath.

But the war for freedom had, and has, not ended. Those who wanted to restrict academic freedom at Berkeley and elsewhere simply moved from anti-communism to new tactics, finding other ways to politicize hiring and teaching.

In *Pickett's Charge*, his last book of the first decade of the Oath, Stewart asked a question which grew out of the time.

> In a sense, even the charge may stand for all of human life. Some time in the years, if not daily, must not each of us hear the command to rise and go forward, and cross the field, and go up against the guns?[4]

At the climax of the Battle of Gettysburg, Confederate soldiers from Virginia, under the command of General George Pickett, led an attack over open ground toward Union positions on Cemetery Ridge. The Confederates lined up in ranks and marched across a long field and up a hill toward the Union position. They had no protection from Union cannons and rifles massed at the top of the hill. (Union soldiers had a stone fence to protect them.) The Confederates managed to get over the wall and break through Union lines. Only last-minute reinforcements by the Union stopped the Confederates from winning the battle, and probably the war. It was the "High Water Mark of the Confederacy."

Stewart visited the place several times. As he walked the field, he began to understand that Pickett's Charge represented a microcosm of human courage and duty. In the few minutes it took to walk across the field and up the hill, soldiers went through an ordeal that would define their lives. Those minutes could stand for any time that humans needed the courage to go up against the guns — or the cave bear, or the vacuum of space, or those who would deny academic freedom.

Stewart saw a book in it. Once again, to write about that macrocosm of duty, courage, and ordeal, George R. Stewart invented another literary form — the micro-history. His book would not wander over the foreplay and aftermath of the battle, or its vast context. It would focus on the charge itself. So *Pickett's Charge* is not about the Battle of Gettysburg. It is about 15 hours that were the most important ones in the lives of those involved.

For some men, those 15 hours were the last moments of life. For others, those 15 hours *were* their lives. From then on they lived with the charge, and its consequences. They were damaged by it or celebrated it or both, but it never left them. Nor did the results of the battle ever leave them or their families, down to this day.

(If you don't believe that, go, as I once did, to Gettysburg. On Little Round Top, I met another man, a truck driver, who had brought his son with him to show him the field of battle. As we talked, we learned that our ancestors fought at Gettysburg — on opposite sides. We shook hands as we parted, comrades of the place and its event.)

As usual, Stewart's research was thorough. He reviewed everything from the massive 200-volume "Records of the War of the Rebellion" to an account kept by a citizen of Gettysburg. He reviewed the records of the regiments that fought there, a suit brought by Pennsylvania veterans about the placement of the Pennsylvania Monument, 400 individual accounts of the battle, and other sources. In the best tradition of the California Enlightenment, he also used his field experience of the Gettysburg landscape to figure out some of the probabilities or improbabilities of various accounts.

As he did the research, Stewart discovered something that made the project even more compelling. "It's amazing when you think what's in the books about that charge, and how much of it's wrong.... You begin to think, 'Well, if the whole Civil War is as bad as that, we don't know anything about it.' And you begin to think, 'What if *all* history's as bad as that?'"[5] Even the most commonplace data was questionable:

Times? Times given varied by as much as four hours, since no "Standard Time" had been established in the U.S.A.

Confederates involved? The histories say 15,000, based on a comment by General Longstreet, but Stewart's count from official army records showed 10,500.

Pickett's letters to his wife? Stewart found them to be full of mistakes. He was convinced that she wrote and published the letters herself.

So the book was also a challenge to return to primary sources — including, as always, the field — to write the real history of the Charge.

Then, as he began to write, the old X factor came into play. Stewart himself faced the guns. His lung acted up again. "I almost died. And I think that makes a difference in a man, too. You have a feeling you've got to keep the chips sort of picked up a bit."[6] Once again, it was a fortunate illness, helping him understand what the soldiers felt as they walked up that long hill. It elevated the work from a simple retelling of the story of a battle, to an epic human tale about facing the guns of death and yet continuing up the hill to the last bit of lead and powder or the last minute of life. Like Stewart, those soldiers must have been wondering, as they walked with death, if they had picked up their chips.

Pickett's Charge was published in the autumn of 1959. But as the decade of the 1950s ended, assaults on liberty continued. Would Stewart's efforts, his going against the guns to defend freedom, succeed? Or, like Pickett's Charge, would it simply be a noble but failed effort?

V. Emeritus

30

The Stewarts' first grandchild, Anna Catherine Evenson, was born in 1954. It was a joyful event, but it also was a sign, telling George and Ted that their time on earth was growing short. Stewart ignored the milestone as best he could, but by the beginning of the 1960s, he could feel his creative well beginning to run dry.

And the old couple faced illnesses, more and more often: a stay in the hospital for Theodosia; prostate and bladder operations for Stewart. Pneumonia, Stewart's nemesis, had almost taken him in 1958 while he was writing *Pickett's Charge*. After several hospital stays, and removal of one lobe of his lung, he recovered. But he was convinced. It was time.

At 2:40 P.M. on May 25, 1962, George R. Stewart ended his lecture in English 106E and stepped away from the lectern for the last time. A full 43 years after a young man wearing a porkpie hat and Harry Potter glasses hitchhiked up the old Pacific Highway to enter the University of California, 39 years after he was hired as an instructor in English, and 38 years after he had brought his enthusiastic young bride to Berkeley by automobile, Professor George R. Stewart had retired.

It was a time of celebration. On May 21, 1962, the Stewarts went to a retirement dinner. On June 30, to a retirement party. On July 6, George went fishing for almost a month, at Downieville, Packer Lake, and Silver Lake in California. On July 31, 1962, he began receiving Social Security.

It was also a time of regrets. Naturalist Joel Hedgpeth, who had been inspired by Stewart's teaching, sent a letter congratulating Stewart on his retirement, but lamented his leave-taking: "I feel that still another landmark is about to be removed from the Berkeley scene." Hedgpeth added, "My hopes are that your retirement will not be too retiring."[1]

Hedgpeth knew his correspondent well. Stewart immediately went back to work. The Citroen needed a battery — and the Volvo also, not long after. He oiled the redwood siding. He trimmed the trees (as he had trimmed the

Baby Anna, Jill, George R. Stewart in 1954. Jill married Morris Evenson, leader of San Francisco's Painters' Union. Anna (now the keeper of the George R. Stewart photograph collection) was the couple's first child, and the Stewarts' first grandchild.

orange trees in the family grove so many years earlier). He built brick flower-beds, of which he was very proud.

And, of course, he wrote. There were tales yet to be told.

The California Trail was finished and published in that first year of his retirement. Subtitled "An Epic with Many Heroes," the book reminds readers that the greatest heroism in this epic was the simple plodding onward of those uncommon common folk, moving ahead, day by day, through ever more difficult country until the goal had been reached. Stewart quotes emigrant John Benson, 1849, who recorded in his journal that for the emigrants, the wagon train was their entire world.[2]

But there was more than the daily plodding. There were the unprecedented sights and experiences of a new world. Rivers that did not run into the sea. Vast plains without a blade of grass. Springs hot enough to cook eggs. Mountains four times higher than any they knew, rising out of the plains. Vast spaces of land and sky on the Great Plains and in the deserts. These people from forested lands were traveling through country as foreign to them as Mars, and as dangerous.

Every day, even in the best of conditions and on the best wagon trains, there were alarms and emergencies that tested courage. Rattlers bit, wheels broke, storms scared stock, family members sickened and died, tempers flared into fights. The people dealt with those things, and moved westward, but their heroism stays in the mind. Sometimes, the heroism was transcendent — like that of little eight-year-old Patty Reed, encouraging her mother to carry on without her if necessary, when her mother left Donner Lake to seek help.[3]

Most of the time such experiences along the Trail forged a community, almost a family, from these individualistic Americans. When some wagons turned for Oregon and others for California, and the time for parting came, Stewart reminds readers how poignant the moment was. He quotes emigrant Bill Trubody, who remembered people calling out heartfelt farewells to each other as the wagons separated onto the two trails.[4]

After all the plodding, and the dangers and the adventures, after the heroism and the poignancy, when they made it through, to Sacramento and the great valleys of California, the people could tell the great story, of wonders seen, and dangers defeated. And they could feel a little pride because they had brought the family through.

They had made it. They were heroes, and they would wear the title of "emigrant" like a badge of honor for as long as they lived.

Stewart's old friend Wallace Stegner considered the book a masterwork, indispensable to anyone interested in the overland movement, the best single-volume history of the California overland immigration. Yet for the first time, Stewart repeated himself in the book. "Sheep Rock" and its pitcher appear in the Epilogue. And he closed the book with a line already used, in *Fire*. It was a perfect ending line for *The California Trail*—but not original. Was it the repeating of himself that an old man does? Or a completing?

It was probably a completing. Stewart had more to write, but he was beginning to close the circle of his works by recalling milestones along the way.

With its powerful scenes of the judgment and punishment of the outlaw Charlie, *Earth Abides* may have been the inspiration for Stewart's book about the San Francisco vigilantes. The novel showed that Stewart had been thinking about vigilantism for some time. Stewart himself said the university's loyalty oath fight also influenced it, probably since his arch-foe on the Board of

Regents, Giannini, had threatened vigilante action against those he considered Communists.

Because of Giannini's threat, readers might expect *Committee of Vigilance: Revolution in San Francisco 1851* to be critical of the Vigilantes. But Stewart's study of the events of the 100 days of the Vigilance Committee of 1851 in San Francisco was done in his usual objective manner. It is an honest book, written about reality, not myth. The "Wild West," Stewart noted, was not the hallowed myth of Western movies but a disgraceful, violent raping of the country's natural resources and genocidal slaughtering of the native peoples. Yet in the book's history of citizens who take the law into their own hands, Stewart does not judge harshly. He concludes that the committee's use of capital punishment was justified, and applied with courage and moderation. He writes — cautiously, and probably with an eye to Regent Giannini — that the later meaning of the word "vigilante" should not be blamed on the earlier Vigilance Committee.[5] In Stewart's eyes, at least, the 1851 San Francisco Committee of Vigilance was an example of Americans' ability to mete out justice when formal institutions fail, not the type of vigilante justice that Giannini advocated.

The subtitle indicates that he was also thinking about the events of the 1960s — mass movements for civil rights and other noble causes. In a way, they, too, skirted the law and were certainly considered revolutionary by those who opposed them. Yet, like 1851's revolutionary actions, the movements were, in general, well-organized attempts to make certain that justice prevailed in American society.

At the end of the 1960s Stewart turned again to ecology. Former Dean of the College of Engineering at the University of California at Los Angeles L.M.K. Boelter sent Stewart a letter suggesting he write a novel about air pollution. Not long after, Stewart had a conversation with George Maslach, dean of the College of Engineering at Berkeley, who suggested a book about the problems of waste and pollution. Stewart decided to take the advice. This time, instead of writing a philosophical adventure novel about humans' relationship with "the land," Stewart took a practical look at ecological problems and ways of doing something about them. Once again, Stewart's *Not So Rich as You Think* would be a new kind of book.

It is one of the first books of its kind. And although many other books about pollution and waste have been written since, this one is still unique. It has all the usual chapters found in such books, about sewage, junk, litter, agricultural refuse, factory effluence, and so on. But it adds a chapter unprecedented for its time. "The Ultimates" was the first popular description of the greenhouse effect, the first widespread warning of global warming.

Stewart also included an unusual chapter, "Waste Without Weight," the only of its kind, so far as I know, in a book about ecology. Stewart describes another type of waste product from the corporate state—the wasting of the human spirit caused by corporations' and bureaus' tendency to move employees and their families at frequent intervals. The moves mean that the families never have a sense of home, of community, of place. And even though the move-for-promotion may be well intentioned, it, like the effluent that comes from factories, will have its effects. The result, writes Stewart, may include nervous breakdown or juvenile delinquency.[6]

Always the prophet, Stewart was warning readers about a national decline in social capital more than 40 years ago. "Social capital," a term popularized by Professor Robert Putnam of Harvard in *Bowling Alone*, is the sum of all those informal human get-togethers which keep societies healthy—sharing meals around the table, going to church, attending community meetings, talking with neighbors, bowling in leagues rather than alone. Regions which have high social capital—like the rural northern states—also have the longest life expectancy, the best health, the lowest rate of crime, and so on. But after 50 years of a national emphasis on *economic* capital and the "bottom line," American social capital is, in general, pretty low. Stewart suggests that we cannot separate the wasting of social capital from the wasting of "ecological capital." A sense of community encourages people to protect their homes. But a society in which people get moved around lacks any sense of community so its "science of the household"—its *ecology*—suffers. Thus, when social capital is low, the ecosystem is open to destruction.

Not So Rich as You Think earned Stewart another honor, the Sidney Hillman Award. But it was also the end of an epoch in the work of George R. Stewart. As *Sheep Rock* was the last of his great ecological novels, this book was his last ecological work. He would write more place-name books, which consider the relationship between humans and the land. But his great ecological cycle, his books about "all the things that go to make up a place," was finished.

31

Ted earned her Master's in Social Welfare in 1952. In 1955 she became a member of the faculty of the university's School of Social Welfare. She continued working for several years after George retired. "Noted for her excellence in developing young social workers,"[1] she would remain on the faculty until she retired, in 1966.

The house on Codornices Road became a haven for the Stewart grandchildren. Bancroft Librarian Baiba Strads, who babysat the children, remembers the time fondly.

I was in awe at how beautiful everything [in the house] was.

I have an image of GRS sitting in an easy chair, reading, but pausing to smile and greet me. I remember him as a quiet, pleasant, warm man. Theodosia handled my employment in a straightforward, businesslike way, from directing what activities to engage in with the kids, to writing out my paycheck. I was a shy, quiet teenager and took note of her being "less warm," but not uncomfortably so, during my times there.

The few times I was there I had the same two kids (I believe). One was definitely a boy; both were under 9 years of age. I would play with the children there, take them for walks, or take them to the park.

I wore prescription glasses just for driving. One time I left my glasses on [when I went into the Stewarts' house]. The little boy immediately noticed and yelled at me "Take those off!" I guess he wanted the "same me" he was used to from previous visits, looking exactly the same![2]

The house on Codornices also became a bed-and-breakfast for great minds. Historian and author Bruce Catton stayed with the Stewarts when he came to Berkeley. Carl Sandburg and Robert Frost were houseguests, although never together — they disliked each other. Imogene Cunningham, a founder of the f/64 Group, photographed Robert Frost at George and Theodosia Stewart's house.

After Ted retired the Stewarts had more time to travel, entertain, and work on projects both personal and professional. George became a passionate fly-fisherman; so George and Ted's retreats from the world were often fishing places: Northern California's Hat Creek, for example, and the Allers' Boulder River Ranch near Big Timber, Montana. The Allers owned the rights to what has been called the best section of fishing stream in Montana — and that's saying something. For a reasonable price, guests had their own cabin, meals, and a horse for the week or two they stayed. Guests who had spent enough vacations at the Allers' qualified to stay during the best fishing season. George and Ted qualified, so he spent many happy hours practicing that muscular Presbyterianism described by Norman Maclean as having "no clear line between religion and fly fishing." Stewart even saw a book in it: *Fly-Fishing Around the Pacific*. He began a series of fishing expeditions to places like Australia, South America, and Scotland. His grandson, Eric Evenson, went along on the South American trip and remembered it as one of the great experiences of his life; his granddaughter Anna Evenson went on another, to Bettyhill, Scotland. But Stewart never finished the book.

Retirement also meant more socializing with neighbors like the Harts or friends like Charlie Camp. Stewart, the shy scholar, wrote, "I've become quite a swinger of parties lately."[3] He even composed a song about it — "A Roistering Song for Sexagenarians."

> To our lasses who think our lads not viable,
> Dry, over-aged, and not even try-able,

George R. Stewart, Ted, Anna, John O Groats in the summer of 1966. This was a research trip to Scotland for Stewart's never-published book about fly-fishing. He took his grandchildren along on some of the trips.

Oh, if your boy-friend's only a talker,
Then put your trust in Johnny Walker.
Alka, alka, alcohol![4]

But he was constantly reminded of his age. When he boarded the 38 Geary Muni bus one day, for example, a young woman got up to give him her seat. Stewart could have slipped away into the grim mental grayness of so many elderly. That was not his nature, but he needed something to keep him active and interested. So he turned to his clubs.

George Stewart had discovered the social pleasures of clubs when he was elected to a Princeton dining club, and clubs' intellectual possibilities when he joined Princeton's Whig-Clio Club. Later, at Berkeley he became a passionate member of Ted's Drama Section Club. He told Suzanne Riess, "It's a very remarkable group. It's been going for over forty years now … it's really lots of fun. That was one of the best things we ever had…. We've put on a lot of plays in that time."[5]

George Stewart was also a member of the Berkeley Faculty Club for many years. Elected secretary-treasurer in 1960 and president in 1963, Stewart helped bring the club back to life after a misplaced renovation caused some financial hard times. Stewart explained, "After lunch there would be a big gathering of people in that room which is now the Howard Room. They'd be playing cards and cursing and reading magazines and playing chess, and the next room was full of billiard players. There was a real gathering of spirits there, after lunch. [But] When they remodeled the club they got that room all shifted around, and the only lounge is upstairs. The thing just went absolutely dead."[6] Stewart began recruiting younger members so the Faculty Club would no longer be known as a club for old men. He also added the stained glass windows that represented the alma maters of the Berkeley faculty — unveiling the last one, the Princeton Window, in 1963.

George Stewart and Charlie Camp were great club mates. They remembered meeting at a club in the early 1930s, although they differed as to which club it had been. (Stewart thought it was the Faculty Club, Camp the Folio Club.) Wherever it took place, the meeting was prescient. Charlie and George would be in several clubs together. In fact, they became good friends during a long drive to a Sierra Nevada function of one of the clubs, E Clampus Vitus.

E Clampus Vitus — ECV — was Camp's and Stewart's "fun club." It had been founded as a humorous nineteenth century response to sometimes-pompous Gold Rush Era clubs. Historian Carl Wheat called ECV "the comic strip on the page of California history."[7] The original group's motto was *Credo Quia Absurdium*, which seems, more or less, to mean, "Take nothing seriously unless it is absurd." In the 1930s, Charlie Camp, Wheat and others brought the club back to life as an organization to honor California's informal history — like the locations of brothels in gold-mining towns. (Another co-founder,

George Ezra Dane, is now believed to be the one who dreamed up the Drake's Plate of Brasse hoax, the "discovery" near San Francisco Bay of a brass plate which supposedly carried a message from Sir Francis Drake. The plate was considered authentic until metallurgical tests proved it was made of twentieth century metal.)

George R. Stewart enjoyed the ECV. But more satisfying to a scholar like Stewart were the small intellectual dinner clubs to which he belonged, direct descendants of the eighteenth century Edinburgh Oyster Club that so shaped the modern world. "These clubs are all the same type," Stewart told Riess. "They represent—I won't say the non-intellectual, but the man who's not in an intellectual business—they represent his attempt to express himself intellectually, and I think it's very good.... I think that's what these groups represent, more than the social. The social is very pleasant that way, but it's not social primarily."[8]

Stewart belonged to several such clubs.

The Kosmos Club, probably named for Alexander von Humboldt's *Kosmos*, met at the Berkeley Faculty Club. Membership included both scientists and humanists, so its talks and discussions, like those of the Oyster Club, crossed the disciplines. It was a perfect place for Stewart to see the world as others in other disciplines see it, or to meet someone who could tell him where he could find precise knowledge of something like fire behavior or storm development.

Another of Stewart's intellectual dinner clubs was (and is) known simply as "The Club." There are only 12 members—the number that can sit comfortably around a dinner table. "The Club" has no officers; the member in charge of a meeting arranges for food, sends out reminders, and hosts the event at his home. Dinner is at seven, papers are read at eight, discussion follows. Guests, including female guests, sometimes attend meetings. "There is fortunately no record, however, of ladies who have listened from adjoining rooms during the paper reading and discussion period and have later strongly commented to their spouses," writes club archivist William Waste.[9] Spouses listening in might well have had strong comments to make. Consider one of George Stewart's papers, "The Four Letter Words," even today a little earthy: "You will be pleased to know," Stewart wrote, "that 'fart' meant 5,000 years ago exactly what it means today."[10]

Stewart also joined the Chit-Chat Club. The club was described by member Frank Sloss as "a small discussion group, limited to twenty-five members. [It is] over a century old. It meets the second Monday of each month at the University Club in San Francisco for cocktails and dinner, after which a member reads an essay, as it is officially called, written by him on any subject whatever. His name and the title of his paper have been announced in advance, but it is permissible—indeed almost customary—to choose a title that will not reveal the subject. After the reading, each member present is called on for a comment. There is a strong tradition of courtesy, so the essayist can count on receiving compliments, whether deserved or not, but beyond that he never knows what to expect, for the comments tend to fly off at unpredictable tangents. At any rate, when all have spoken, he may make whatever rejoinder he pleases, and so the evening ends. It is a highly civilized exercise … my monthly escape into the eighteenth century."[11] The Club has had a distinguished membership of lawyers, and professors from Berkeley and Stanford — including legendary UC Chemistry Professor Joel Hildebrand and Stewart's old friend Charlie Camp.

With their broad-ranging discussions of ideas around fire or dinner table, and refusals to box ideas up into rigid disciplines, the Kosmos and Chit-Chat Clubs and The Club were fitting places for a man of liberal ideas like George R. Stewart.

But then Stewart joined a club that was not at all a place for liberal ideas. The Bohemian Club — the place where the bomb was planned — includes or has included just about every leader of the "Military-Industrial Complex" — George W. Bush, George Schultz of Bechtel, Henry Kissinger, oath-advocating Regent John Francis Neylan, and others of similar views. Stewart's membership still raises eyebrows among those who knew him or who study his life.[12]

Jack Stewart says, "I was a little surprised that my Dad joined. It's very conservative … not really his politics at all. I don't know that it was too intellectual. That would interest him. They had these plays … that would interest him.

"There were two groups — the rich, and … what I'd call 'artisans' — musicians, playwrights, entertainers, writers. My Dad was obviously there as a writer — to entertain the others.

"I went maybe two times. Didn't mix much — they were very right wing. There was a tradition — you urinated against a [giant Sequoia] tree. It was a little different, to say the least.

"It wasn't his politics. It was certainly not my Mother's!" (Jack laughed.)

George Stewart told Suzanne Riess he joined for the convenience and the conviviality. The San Francisco headquarters of the club was close to the Stewarts' retirement home, and he had known some of the other members for decades. In fact, it was an old Princeton classmate, Chauncey Leake, who invited Stewart to join. In a letter to Stewart, Leake listed other members, like antiquarian bookseller Warren Howell, who Stewart would know. To be accepted into such a distinguished group, Leake suggested, would be a great honor.

Jack is still unconvinced. "I don't know why he joined. Maybe for the recognition. But I guess we'll never know."[13]

In 1968, the university celebrated its centennial. Ted and George Stewart had been active members of the university community for nearly half of its

100 years. In the Drama Section Club and the Faculty Club, on field research trips with George's colleagues, and during the ordeal of the Oath, the Stewarts had helped build the social capital of the university. George's books, famous and influential worldwide, added to the reputation of the university and the Department of English. Ted was a distinguished faculty member at the university's School of Social Welfare. George had become active in library affairs, helping found the Friends of the Bancroft Library and serving on the Library Committee. The two veterans could expect to be called upon to contribute to the centennial celebration.

George Stewart was asked to consider editing a large collection of centennial essays by alumni, alumnae, and faculty. But then the university decided Irving Stone should edit the book. Stewart did contribute an essay, now acknowledged as one of the best in Stone's *There Was Light*.

The English Department decided to prepare a centennial history, and, much to his surprise, asked Stewart to do it. "This invitation was somewhat moving," he wrote in the book's introduction. "I had not been a down-the-line man in the Department. One of my colleagues ... once told me ... that I had made a career out of being crotchety."[14] He accepted the honor, and produced another fine book.

The Department of English of the University of California on the Berkeley Campus, published in 1968, is no dry administrative history. As always, Stewart saw his subject as a microcosm. So after writing a lively, honest history of his own department, Stewart added two chapters — his consideration of that ancient word, "good," as it applies to all Departments of English. What makes a good department? What is a good curriculum?

Stewart believed curriculum battles were actually battles about the essence of an English department. "Without it we are nothing," he wrote. "In pursuing our research, our writing, and our private lives, we scatter far, but we draw together around the curriculum, as around a hearth." (A lovely image in an administrative history!)[15]

What *is* the essence of an English department? Stewart considered the question at the end of his book. Although English professors teach others how to write, Stewart believed that departments of English must be about more than composition. Teaching a language and the meaning of its words, the professor conserves and passes on the ancient meanings of deep time. By teaching the literature that preserves and transmits our oldest human ideas, the English professor conserves and transmits the values of humankind. Since literature can be widespread in its values and its content, an English professor must, by definition, have a liberal — a "generous and tolerant" — attitude toward books. He or she must not censor literature. Stewart once described the typical English professor as "a political liberal and an educational conservative."[16] Although he didn't write that phrase into this book, it's a good summation of this last chapter.

Stewart finished writing *The Department of English* in that sweet month of pilgrimages. "So I end," he wrote,

and the bright sun of an April morning shines in, warmly....

Few people, I think, will read this small book, and even who those will be, I scarcely know. Generally the image of my reader has been one of my colleagues, and this must mean one of my younger colleagues, since only three are older, and they will never be more numerous. So this is, in its way, a testament.

I have been writing under the figure of a palace, of foundations and wings and pinnacles. Perhaps I was moved to use such a figure, because I had in my mind a poem that Gayley liked to read ... its key line was:

After me cometh a Builder. Tell him, I too have known.[17]

Thus, in ending his work for the Department of English at the University of California, Berkeley, Stewart reached back to its beginning. As his lifelong saunter through the English language drew to a close he passed Gayley's gift on, to future professors. They, too, would become pilgrims into the words that bind us all. Fittingly, Stewart passed the gift onward in the month of pilgrimages — that month immortalized by the first great poet of the English language, Chaucer.

Being selected to write the history was a great honor. But there would be others. The University had created a new organization for the Centennial, the Society of Berkeley Fellows — an "honorific society of one hundred distinguished friends of the Berkeley Campus."[18] Some 300 names were suggested. After spirited debate the advisory committee sent 125 names to the chancellor, who made the final selection. The first One Hundred Fellows, announced during the Centennial, included second Director of the National Park Service Horace Albright, Secretary of Health, Education, and Welfare and founder of Common Cause John W. Gardener, actor Gregory Peck, and James H. Doolittle, who led a daring raid over Tokyo during World War II. The Fellows also included Theodosia Burton Stewart, founder of the University Section Club; and Professor George R. Stewart, the man who named the storms.

There were other honors. George R. Stewart was "given" Donner Pass at the dedication of the new Donner Lake state museum — a proper gift, as Wallace Stegner said, since by writing books like *Ordeal by Hunger* and *Storm* Stewart had "made" Donner Pass. *The California Trail* was cited by California Supreme Court Justice Stanley Mosk in an opinion about the California Coastal Zone Act. And the University of California appointed Stewart Professor Emeritus because of his long and distinguished service to students and the larger university community.

Welcome as the honors were, age was creeping up. There came a time when either one or the other of the old couple was always sick. George would get sick and Theodosia would care for him. Then Theodosia would get sick, and George would care for her. Soon, there was no avoiding the question. What would happen if they both took sick at the same time?

They decided to move to a retirement community which had good medical care. The first choice, on Oakland's Lake Merritt, had a waiting list, so a friend suggested the Sequoias in San Francisco. The Sequoias, run by the Presbyterian Church, had an opening. Ted and George were accepted.

The Stewarts sold the house on Codornices Road, and most of their collection of books, artifacts, and memorabilia. Since much of Stewart's work focused on northern Nevada, Reno seemed the ideal place for a Stewart Collection. University of Nevada Special Collections Librarian Ken Carpenter, who had been the first Rare Books Librarian at Berkeley, knew the importance of Stewart's work. He arranged for the University of Nevada at Reno to buy much of Stewart's accumulation of published material. Currently under the care of Librarian Donnelyn Curtis, the George R. Stewart Collection at UNR is the second-largest collection of George R. Stewart material in the world. (Appropriately, you enter the UNR Special Collections room through a reproduction of Lorenzo Ghiberti's 15th-century doors, the "Gates of Paradise.") The Stewarts gave the rest to family, the Bancroft Library, or other libraries. Stewart's collection on the history of place names went to the American Names Society Library in upstate New York.

In 1970, collections and possessions distributed, the Stewarts moved one last time, heading west to San Francisco. Once settled in at the Sequoias they began looking for a place where they could hike and picnic. Somewhere like Cass Lake, the campsites they shared on their honeymoon trip, or the area around Dutch Flat. Easy to get to, yet not over-crowded. Urbane, but with the grand sense of wilderness they both loved. And it should be a fine place for picnics.

Daughter Jill, who had lived in San Francisco for decades, made a suggestion. Following her directions the Stewarts found a small state park on the ocean, just over the line in San Mateo County. The park was compact and easily explored. Yet it opened a window into wildernesses of ocean and mountain as majestic or delicate as anything George and Ted Stewart had known.

By coincidence Thornton State Beach was also the place where, inspired by George R. Stewart's books, I was working as a state park ranger. So here I re-enter the story.

32

In the years after those first readings of *Earth Abides* I finished my education, worked as a shipping-receiving clerk, drove a truck, married, became

a father, taught school, divorced, and joined the old California State Park Service — always, thanks to the book, on my Stewart saunter. I soon learned that
once you're on a saunter, even an involuntary one, there's no getting away from
it. You may try to avoid it, because there are other duties in your life and you
think those are more important than some wander toward wisdom. But when
you least expect it, you make a decision or turn a corner and find that you're
still on the pilgrim's trail.

In my case, I was still fishing for that deepest truth about Stewart and his
work. Over the years, the quest even got a name: *GeoS*. It's cumbersome to
say or write "the ultimate truth of a set of ideas evolved over eight decades of
the twentieth century by professor and author George R. Stewart." Since Stewart's name can be abbreviated "Geo.S." and in ancient Greek *Ge* meant "Earth,"
I named the object of my quest "*GeoS*."

As things turned out, it wouldn't be a simple quest. It would be a journey
like the one suggested by Dr. Helen Stadermann in my college days: "You can
rush from San Francisco to Los Angeles on 101. Or you can take the scenic
route, driving up every interesting side road you find. In this class we will
explore as many side roads as we can." The search for *GeoS* would be a saunter,
via the scenic route.

There were discouragements aplenty, yet at the moments of greatest dis-
couragement there would always come a great encouragement. And there were
pleasant meetings, and campfires, and new side-roads galore to explore along
the way. From all this I learned a wisdom first taught by John Steinbeck: that
we don't take the journey; the journey takes us. So after a time, I let the saun-
tering lead where it would, and where it will.

Along the way I became a teacher, teaching, as Stewart taught, that the
human story is a function of the ecosystem and that Earth is one small place
in the universe. To fill in the summers, I worked as a ranger. In the ranger
days, I wandered one small place on Earth, often wondering about my quest.

In that small place, Thornton State Beach, I helped build a trail.

Suddenly the squall ceased and the sky cleared. I opened the door of the
ranger office and stepped outside, into spring.

It was one of those extraordinary Thornton Beach days when spring covers
the California coast, filling the senses. Clouds towered over the ocean. Small
diamonds of rain sparkled on the plants. Scent of sagewort, touch of the wind,
calls of wild birds. Yellow sourgrass, floral harbinger of spring, carpeted the
ground. I picked a blade of sourgrass and chewed it, savoring the first taste of
spring.

It was a day for the old poet, who wrote:

> Whan that Aprille with his shoures soote
> The droghte of march hath perced to the roote,

And bathed every veyne in swich licour
Of which vertu engendred is the flour;
Whan Zephirus eek with his sweete breeth
Inspired hath in every holt and heath
Tendre croppes, and the yonge sonne
Hath in the ram his halve cours yronne,
And smale foweles maken melodye
That slepen al the nyght with open ye
(so priketh hem nature in hir corages);
Thanne longen folk to goon on pilgrimages.

The smale foweles of Thornton Beach, warmed by the sun, were certainly maken melodye, the quail calling in celebration of new territories. The wind's sweet breath, filled with the green scent of new growth, blew through the north valley. And, as always in the spring, I felt that April longing for pilgrimages.

It was, in fact, February. But on the California coast, where we're months ahead of snow country, February is our April. I was not at all confused by this, and easily accepted the February spring day as the day when April thoughts begin.

Midweek, it was pretty quiet. Kailas Shugendo, the park's bluegrass-playing Buddhist regulars, dropped in to serenade the park. Then left the place to me, and me to the place. Since most of the weekly cleanup had been done and there were no other visitors, I could pretty much make my own day.

I decided to take a walk between squalls. Following John Muir's advice — saunter, don't hike (stomp, stomp, stomp) through wildernesses — I sauntered around our new trail-in-progress. This was called "patrolling" and was a critical part of ranger work.

I started in the Valley, heading north. Thornton Valley is a rotational slump block valley. Once, the cliff that shades the Valley stretched a few hundred yards farther west. At some ancient time it broke along a fairly straight line and the inland part slumped. (Face west. Hold your arm in front of you with the forearm level: That's the original bluff. The ocean is to the west of your hand. Drop your elbow down about 35 degrees; the area between your forearm and upper arm is the rotational slump block valley.) Now, the cliffs on the coastal side act as natural flying buttresses, holding up the western side of Thornton Valley as if it were the wall of a cathedral.

During the un-numbered years since the slump, a healthy community of California native plants, known by the unlovely name "coastal scrub," established itself in the Valley. The flora, especially in spring, is lovely. There are sourgrass, beach sagewort, yarrow, seaside daisies, yellow bush lupine; even tiny wild strawberries, bursting with sweetness. Elizabeth May McClintock, distinguished California botanist, once said that our stand of coastal scrub was the finest in the San Francisco area.

A diverse community of animal life lives there. Migrating ducks, California quail, Loggerhead Shrikes, and other land birds fly by or run through openings in the network of plants. Redtail hawks fly overhead, watching for foolhardy ground squirrels who've wandered too far from their burrows. There is an occasional opossum and even a feral pheasant family escaped from the nearby private golf club. And, although I never saw one, there are the damned feral cats, working hard to decimate the natural wildlife.

I walked through the tiny, greening valley, inhaling its sage-like scent, listening to melodies. Then turned west with the trail and made the short climb to the bluff.

The bluff was always the highlight of a patrol. From the summit Rangers could read the park. We checked weather conditions by looking at clouds and ocean and feeling the breezes. We then looked north and south along our stretch of beach to see if anything — yachts, whales, bottles with messages, oil-soaked birds — had washed ashore overnight. In the right season, on clear days, we saw striper runs in the ocean and knew fishermen would soon flock into the park.

I looked south. "Glider Bluff," named because model glider enthusiasts flew radio-controlled models in an uplift created by the prevailing westerlies hitting the cliff below the bluff, was close — about a hundred yards — but there were no glider pilots this day.

Mussel Rock, a most prominent local feature, was about two miles south. The Rock was a "horse," the geologist's term for a rock displaced along a fault line. Our fault was the great San Andreas, which came ashore from the sea at Mussel Rock, heading inland toward the lake for which it was named.

(No fisherman on the Rock — too stormy — and no boats close to shore.)

Ours was a celebrated geology. William Glen of the United States Geological Survey wrote his Masters' thesis about that geology, and the University of California published it. The California Division of Mines published a geologic guide which included Thornton Beach, for use by teachers, rangers, and wanderers. John McPhee's *Assembling California* begins and ends at Mussel Rock. So as far as we were concerned, Thornton Beach's geology was as good as anyone's.

I stopped my reading of the landscape for a while to think geologically. Like Stewart in *Sheep Rock*, I wanted to add some time to this space. Since older fossils from more ancient epochs are exposed near Mussel Rock, a walk toward the Rock is a walk back in time. Some fossils — shark, whale, clams, sand dollars — reveal that this had once been the bottom of an ocean; others, that, in a different age this had been a terrestrial ecosystem with camels, saber-toothed cats, and mammoths.

Ending my saunter into deep time, I looked west. Just below the bluff was the beach, a community of life called "the coastal strand." There were no plants on the beach itself; but some plant life huddled in protected areas behind small dunes at the bluff's base. Evidence of ocean life littered the sand, especially after a storm. Today, gulls circled above, sanderlings raced the surf, and whimbrels, oystercatchers and curlews prospected for food on the sand.

Since more than a million people lived within a few miles of the park, Thornton State Beach was classified as an "urban park." Today, with the storm passing and the sun out, the ocean seemed pacific. But I knew better. On that beach you entered a wilderness as vast as any on Earth, and it was not urban down there. The rules were different, and strict to the point of unforgiving. People who ignored them — who got drunk and then went fishing in storm swells, for example — washed up on the beach a day or 40 later. Once, a Maria of a winter storm hit Thornton State Beach. The next day, rangers discovered that seven miles of beach had been lowered seven feet, and driftwood logs three feet thick had been tossed 75 feet up the ocean-facing bluffs.

Yet, in spite of its wildness, Thornton State Beach was a very *urbane* park. On a lovely spring day or a good fishing day we had visitors who were as interesting as those in any park in the state. In fact, in some ways Thornton State Beach was a miniature version of the Edinburgh of the mid–18th century Scottish Enlightenment. There were local families, of course, like the Byrnes and Kennedys (who came down daily in a small robin's-egg blue Volkswagen Beetle, rushed to the beach to swim, then somehow wedged themselves into the car and headed for home, smiling and waving vigorously). But there were also visitors who would have fit right in at old Edinburgh's Oyster Club. Former tennis star Mary Odenthal often stopped by the office to discuss the works of Thomas Merton, or the fossil mammoth she'd helped discover. Professor James Perlman of San Francisco State University would come by to talk about his book on the history of science. Gifted artist Rene Weaver, who painted watercolors in the style of the California school, walked the long beach with his wife Clare to encourage his phlebitis-ridden legs back into health.[1] I enjoyed all the visits, especially on wet days that bound us to office and paper, and these people became friends.

Two of our regular visitors, products of and contributors to the California Enlightenment, were *Fiat Lux* visitors and so deserve some attention here: H. Wilder Bentley the Elder and Chiura Obata.

Bentley, whose grandfather built one of the first cottages in the Berkeley Hills and whose father and uncle helped found the California Packing Corporation (Del Monte brand), was a calligrapher, poet, artist, and master printer.[2] He and his wife Ellen established the Archetype Press near the Berkeley campus in the mid–1930s. The Press published *Sierra Nevada: The John Muir Trail*, the first printed book of Ansel Adams' photographs, in 1938 — a work still considered among the finest art books of its time. (Adams had previously printed a portfolio of photographs and published his famous how-to book, *The Camera*.) The book also helped promote the idea of wilderness preservation by making a successful case for adding Kings Canyon to the National Park System.

In the late 1950s Bentley became a professor at San Francisco State College, teaching there until he retired in 1971. Since San Francisco State was near Thornton Beach, and since Bentley had known the place for decades — he had first seen the beach when he rode the Ocean Shore Railroad south in 1910 or so and remembered a small village of native people living near a spring in the valley next to Mussel Rock — it was not surprising that he would choose the park as the place to go fishing with his old friend and mentor, the gifted artist Chiura Obata.[3]

As a young man in the early twentieth century, Obata traveled through California drawing, sketching, and painting watercolors. Returning to Japan, Obata supervised the production of a series of Japanese woodblock prints, some requiring more than a hundred carefully registered impressions, from his watercolors. Obata printed 100 copies of each of his prints of California in his "World Landscape Series." The prints, some of which can be seen online, capture California in the early 20th century as it was seen by the great Japanese artist.

A gifted teacher, Obata became a professor of art at UC Berkeley. Wilder Bentley the Younger, Wilder Bentley's son, who took lessons from Obata, remembers, "What he taught was to have faith in your own abilities, carry something out from beginning to end without vacillation, stand up to adversity without complaint, be generous with your time to other people but don't let them waste it and to correct people without resorting to destructive criticism."[4] After a long career at Berkeley — interrupted by internment at Tanforan and Topaz during World War II for the crime of being Japanese — Obata retired.

Obata had suffered a stroke, but he loved to fish. So in the season of the striped bass Professor Bentley often brought Obata to the park. He helped Obata down the long, steep trail to the beach, helped him use the heavy surf-casting equipment, and then guided him back up the trail on those foggy days when Striper fishing seems to be at its best.

Bentley and Obata usually stopped by the ranger office for a visit. As they warmed up over a cup of coffee, we talked about the events of the day, or of their lives. Obata was a quiet man, so Bentley did most of the talking. The stories helped us build up a history of the park's area; but in the best traditions of the old Oyster Club, Obata, Bentley and the rangers also discussed literature, politics, ecology, education, and art.

Thinking about the old artist friends, I began considering Thornton Beach with an artist's eyes. On a partly cloudy day, looking out over the Pacific and the Golden Gate coastline from Thornton Beach is like looking at the Grand Canyon. The colors are different, and there's more water than rock visible from the Thornton Bluff, but there is the same sense of majesty and variety. And, just as at the Grand Canyon the scene has a motion to it. Cloud patterns change, ocean patterns follow clouds. It's a slowly swirling chiaroscuro on an expanse of water and headlands that covers a vast area.

If it's a clear day, Point Reyes is visible 35 miles to the northwest, its light flashing. Mount Tamalpais, "The Sleeping Lady," thrusts up about halfway to Point Reyes. Some 30 miles west the Farallon Light flashes over the Farallon Islands. Montara Mountain is about ten miles south, Pedro Point at its western foot: all together more than 40 miles north-to-south, 30 miles east-to-west. It was a viewscape of 1,200 square miles of ocean and headlands, a scenic area that was little larger than Yosemite National Park.

Thornton State Beach itself was only 40 acres or so. But with its world-class geology, its enlightened minds and its mind-expanding artist's view, Thornton State Beach was place enough for anyone. On a day like this day of the clearing spring storm, we knew ourselves to be rangers as good as any. As I stood there, taking in the view, a phrase came to mind. One used by Yosemite's old Curry Company to describe guests' valuables: *of small compass and unusual value.* That certainly described Thornton Beach — small, but as valuable as any park that ever existed.

The only flaw in the picture was behind me, to the east: the drainpipe, large and ugly, slithering down the hill behind the office. Highway people put it there to drain runoff water from Highway One. As I swung around from the grand view to the west and saw that slithering pipe I thought, "If that S.O.B. ever lets go, Thornton Beach will pay a heavy price."

The thought broke the mood. But that was okay — I couldn't patrol forever. The people of the State of California and the chief ranger expected some labor.

I went back to the office to pick up some tools, then returned to the bluff to work on our new trail. In a couple of hours of cutting and raking with the McLeod, I moved the trail a few more feet toward completion. But the passing storm had a squall or two left, and one was moving toward me. I kept an eye on it and when it got close enough, I grabbed the McLeod and raced back toward the office. The first drops hit the building as the office door closed behind me.

I fired up the coffee pot. Had a cup. Then, while the squall lashed the windows, I started to work on a report about the park's natural and human history. It was a listing of the resources — the geology, the flora, the fauna, and the human community — of Thornton State Beach.

A cup and five pages later, the rain ended. The sky cleared. Now, as the day was getting on, the storm had passed for good.

A beige Dodge Dart drove into the park. All the cars that day, except the Buddhists', had been turnarounds, but this one parked. When the driver got out and headed toward the office, I recognized him as one of our regular visitors.

As he walked over, I appraised him. In his seventies. Distinguished, in a lanky way. Tall and lean, with the easy, graceful stride of someone used to long hikes. But I also noticed he had some difficulty getting out of the car. And he limped, slightly, as he walked over.

Since it was the time of year when people bought their annual park passes, I guessed he was here to buy one, and took the passes out.

I opened the door. "C'mon in. Can I help you?"

"I'd like to buy a new annual pass," he said.

"Sure. " I said. "A good value, isn't it?"

"We use ours all the time. Especially here. This park is one of our favorite places," he said.

"Yes — I've seen you and your wife here many times," I said.

New rules — it was the Reagan era — required those buying a pass to sign it in our presence. I took out the pass and a pen, and handed them to him.

He wrote his name. I glanced at the signature:

George R. Stewart.

Astonished, I looked at him. "You're not *the* George R. Stewart, are you?"

He looked up. "Which one is that?"

"The author? The one who wrote *Fire* and *Storm* and *Earth Abides?*"

"Yes. I guess I am that one," he said. "There's a Mount George Stewart in the Sierra, named for a ranger. I thought you might mean the George Stewart the mountain's named for. But that's George W. Stewart and I'm George R. Stewart."

"I meant the author. Your books —*Earth Abides, Storm, Fire*— I've read them all. They changed my life. Gave me a love for — an *understanding* of— nature. That got me to thinking I should become a ranger. Why, I'm a ranger because of you — a ranger *here* because of you — and you're a visitor in my park!" I was pretty excited.

He was a little taken aback. But he managed to say, "Thanks." Then, "Would you like to meet my wife?"

"Sure. This paper work can wait."

We walked over to the car. George R. Stewart introduced me to his wife, Ted. Then he told her that I'd read his books.

"How *wonderful!*" Ted exclaimed. "George and I have been coming here for *years*. We *love* Thornton Beach! How *nice* to meet a ranger who likes George's books. I'm so *glad* you've enjoyed George's books!" (Ted, as I was learning, always spoke emphatically.)

We talked for a while. Then I went back to the office. The Stewarts drove out, waving as they left.

I finished writing the report.

Then I sauntered back up to the bluff. Looking out over 1,200 square miles of the earth and its oceans, I thought about this day — this fine day —

this *exceptional* day—for a long time. The day spring covered the California coast at Thornton State Beach, and Ted and George Stewart and I, by coincidence (or was it a coincidence?), had entered each other's lives.

The old poet wrote, "Whan that Aprille with his shoures soote ... when Zephirus eek with his sweete breeth.... And smale foweles maken melodye.... Thanne longen folk to goon on pilgrimages," and I had thought to take my longing out on a walk around the park. Now I felt the call of pilgrimage, of saunter, toward *GeoS*.

The trail was Ranger Nicholas J. Lee's idea. Lee, sailor and ranger (and poet), wanted Thornton State Beach shipshape, so he'd begun a park renewal program. Buildings were painted, asphalt repaired, erosion-control grasses planted. A new trail was a centerpiece of his program. Designed to keep visitors off hillside-eroding "social trails," it would also open up our small ecosystems for visitors. A soil engineer, member of Kailas Shugendo, volunteered to draw up plans for the trail. Headquarters approved the plans and we went to work.

To build a trail is true ranger work. First you think about it. Then plan its alignment. Then build it. Every day you extend it a little. As you do the physical labor of trail-building, watching the colors of light play over the Pacific, your mind is also at work, thinking about the human and natural history of the land you're working through, and how to interpret that to visitors. So as you build the trail, you also construct a cognitive map of the land through which it passes. When the storms wash over the trail, you head for the office to put that map on paper. Fleshed out by research and writing, it will become a trail guide.

Trail building brings a park's human community together. At Thornton State Beach the trail building became a trail-raising. Kailas Shugendo helped. The Boy Scouts helped. On busy days, people brought food for the laborers. With all the help, the trail was finished sooner than we'd expected. About six months after I'd met George and Ted Stewart, the Scouts had completed the last major section. But we had one small problem. No one, not the rangers nor the volunteers, could come up with a name for that trail.

Ranger Steve Gazzano had an idea.

One day, a few of us—Bill Chamberlin, Nick and I, at least, maybe John Lucia—were in the office, talking names. The ones we thought up were pretty lame: "San Andreas Vista." "The Sunset Trail."

Steve came in. Always on the move, he rushed past us into the workroom, grabbed some supplies, and rushed back, heading for the front door. He stopped; listened; then said, "Why don't you name the trail for that author guy everybody keeps talking about. What's his name? Stewart."

We looked at each other. Then we all started to talk at once.

"The 'George R. Stewart Nature Trail.' A perfect name!"

"But you aren't supposed to name things after living people, are you?"

"This is Thornton Beach. Headquarters is 35 miles away, on the other side of Devil's Slide. We live under the rule of benign neglect. We can do anything we want up here that's not blatantly illegal."

So it was decided.

The Area Manager said, "There are two ways to do this project. We can go through channels and hope they'll approve it; by the time they do, if they do, Stewart will likely be dead. Or we can build the trail, write and print the guide and then tell them we've done it." It was an easy choice.

In record time, with the help of the Chief Ranger, who made and placed the numbered posts, and the Area Manager, who had the trail guide printed, our trail was ready. The Area Manager added one final touch to the trail: a beautiful trail sign hand-routed out of a huge piece of redwood burl driftwood.

We dedicated the George R. Stewart Trail in the spring. Kailas Shugendo played a little Buddhist Bluegrass to welcome the small crowd of family and friends. We handed the new *Trail Guide* out to the assembled guests. There were a few short speeches by rangers.

Then George R. Stewart, author of *Names on the Land* spoke about the first place named for him.

> When the boys here first told me they wanted to name the trail for me I was very much pleased, but ... I knew there was a matter of principle — and it's not a bad principle either — that you should not name things for people who are still living.... I don't know quite how this went through.... The only thing I can think of is ... a man in Sacramento said, "Well, they're getting closer [to Stewart's passing] all the time, so we won't bother about this.
>
> I want to say I'm tremendously happy to have this trail named for me. Mrs. Stewart and I have come down here quite often. I think that was one of the reasons why they thought about it ... [we often bring] visitors to the park, here, and in spite of a bad knee, I still manage to walk around the Trail ... to see the flowers when they're all out, as I hope they soon will be ... and in spite of the fact that it's a late spring, there seem to be a lovely lot of flowers. I hope you all come and walk around this trail.[5]

George and Ted cut the ribbon over the entrance. Then the old couple led the first hike over the new trail.

In the years to come, the Stewarts often hiked the trail. It became a part of their annual Thanksgiving ritual. Every year, they held a Thanksgiving potluck in the north picnic area, near the beginning of the trail. Then after the feast the family would join Ted and George on a saunter around the trail — walking through the fragrant coastal scrub, climbing up the bluff to take in the spectacular view, and continuing, some of them, down the trail to the fossil-rich, life-rich beach. Since "election day rains" usually greened up our hill-

George and Ted Stewart cut the ribbon to open the George R. Stewart Trail, April 1974.

sides a bit, the Stewarts' Thanksgiving hike showed them the first hint of the Californian spring.

For Stewart, place names were the most important human connection with the land. The George R. Stewart Trail at Thornton State Beach was the first place named for him. In the early 1980s, Wallace Stegner, in his essay about George R. Stewart, "George R. Stewart and the American Land," describes the naming of the trail as one of the highest honors Stewart received.[6] Self-effacing, he would never have asked for such an honor. But the rangers of Thornton Beach, thanks to Ranger Steve Gazzano, had put George R. Stewart's name on the land.

33

In spite of restful times at Thornton State Beach, George R. Stewart was not able to avoid the battles over academic freedom. Although no longer involved in the day-to-day of university affairs Stewart felt its events swirl through his life. When the Era of Movements swept over the campus he was forced to rethink some of his ideas about freedom. That would lead him to write a last novel, never published, finished at about the same time the trail was dedicated.

The Era of Movements began soon after Stewart retired, in 1964, when the university again tried to restrict academic freedom.[1] For years an area on Telegraph Avenue near Sather Gate had been a place where people of all political stripes could speak or set up tables and hand out literature. The university acquired the property but kept the tradition. Then, in 1964, moderate Republican William Scranton came to the campus to recruit student support for the upcoming Republican National Convention in San Francisco. Students for Scranton set up tables in the free speech area, near Sproul Hall. Under pressure from those who opposed Scranton, the university changed its policy, and forbade all political advocacy on campus. Students — including the conservative Young Republicans — protested the ban on speech. The university tried to crack down on the dissenters. Clark Kerr, supposedly liberal president of the university, even suggested the dissent was Communist-inspired. But this was a passionate era, with a new kind of student-citizen, and they would not yield.

By 1964 many students were adults working to put themselves through the university. Many were married. As spouses, employees, and sometimes parents, 1960s students had stresses unknown by those of earlier times. They were struggling to find money to pay for their education — trying to do good academic work *and* good work-for-income at the same time. These students were also the first to face a grim depersonalization of the college experience. They became numbers. No longer admitted to the university by pleasant young women in pleasant campus settings, they waited in endless lines to register, were sent on endless chases to get answers to simple questions, and sat in huge classrooms where they watched the professor "lecture" over television monitors.

And by the 1960s, many of the students could vote. The university might not view them as adult citizens, with the right to hear all political points of view, but they *were* American citizens, and voters, and in the best American tradition they would protect their citizens' rights.

So, in violation of the administration's and Regents' new policy — but in keeping with their rights as citizens — students placed now-outlawed tables near Sproul Hall and began to distribute literature. One of the students was arrested and locked in the back of a police car which had been driven onto the campus. Angered, other students surrounded the police car. One, with university permission, climbed up onto the car and began to speak. Others followed. The Free Speech Movement had begun.

The somewhat unruly assemblies for the petition of grievances (and what assembly for the petition of grievances is not unruly?) continued for weeks. The conflict escalated. As it came to a climax, the student who had spoken from the police car stood before a crowd and spoke again. He said,

> There is a time when the operation of the machine becomes so odious, makes you so sick at heart, that you can't take part; and you've got to put your bodies upon the gears and upon the wheels, upon the levers, upon all the apparatus and you've got to make it stop. And you've got to indicate to the people who run it,

to the people who own it, that unless you're free, the machine will be prevented from working at all.[1]

Jon Carroll, later a columnist for the *San Francisco Examiner*, was there. Carroll wrote that the speaker had a glowing eloquence.[2] The speaker's name was Mario Savio.

Many Americans remember Mario Savio as an un–American rabble-rouser who led radicals to attack the university. Yet nothing could be further from the truth. For one thing, he was only one of many citizen-students working to gain the same rights on campus that they had off campus. And Savio was not by nature a stump-speaking leader. He was, in fact, a quiet student who was much more interested in science than politics. One of his scientific colleagues later described Savio as a pilgrim, a seeker after truth, and a "brilliant" genius.

As a youngster, Savio was a finalist for the Westinghouse science talent search. His interest was in the transmission of sound through seawater. When he found that the Navy sonar tables had an error, he spent two weeks in his room fixing it. Savio graduated from New York City's elite public high school, Van Buren High, at the head of his class. He entered Berkeley in 1963.

Son of an immigrant Italian workingman, who often heard stories about the virulent discrimination against Italian-Americans from his father, Savio was passionate about civil rights. In the summer of 1964, during the Civil Rights Movement, Savio helped register black sharecroppers in the south. Their courage impressed him; their possible fate, after the northern students left, haunted him. When Savio returned to Berkeley, he discovered that the freedom people were dying for in the South was being denied on his own campus. It was in this storm of events that Mario Savio got up and spoke his eloquent words.

Ironically, Savio was the *conservative* in this event. He and others in the movement were simply asking the university to keep — to *conserve*— traditions that had existed since its founding. But Savio was severely, and sometimes illegally punished — expulsion, jail, a series of menial jobs, and a decade or so of being under often-illegal F.B.I. surveillance.

Eventually, he returned to school at San Francisco State University. There, he worked with planet-finder Geoff Marcy, discovered a theorem now called the "Savio Theorem," and graduated summa cum laude in Physics. Savio began teaching innovative interdisciplinary courses at Sonoma State University. He was moving his family into the first house he could afford to buy when he died, prematurely at age 53, of a weakened heart.

Savio had gone up against the guns and paid the price. But in doing so he helped other students, professors — and the rest of us — keep the freedom to hear different ideas.

Soon after the beginning of the Free Speech Movement at the University, Savio wrote down some of his ideas about education. He wrote,

Schools have become training camps ... factories to produce technicians rather than places to live student lives. And this perversion develops great resentment on the part of the students. Resentment against being subjected to standard production techniques of speedup and regimentation; against a tendency to quantify education — virtually a contradiction in terms. Education is measured in units, in numbers of lectures attended, in numbers of pages devoted to papers, number of pages read....

The undergraduate has become the new dispossessed; the heart has been taken from his education — no less so for science students — for the humanities are no longer accorded the central role they deserve in the university....

In a healthy university an undergraduate would have time to do "nothing." To read what he wants to read, maybe to sit on a hill behind the campus all alone or with a friend, to "waste time" alone, dreaming in the Eucalyptus Grove. But the university, after the manner of a pesky social director, sees to it the student's time is kept filled with anti-intellectual harassment: those three credits in each three unit course, those meaningless units themselves. The notion that one can somehow reduce Introductory Quantum Mechanics and Philosophy of Kant to some kind of lowest common denominator (three units apiece) is totally irrational, and reflects the irrationality of a society which tries to girdle the natural rhythms of growth and learning by reduction to quantitative terms, much as it attempts to market the natural impulses of sex.

From my experience, I should say the result is at best a kind of intellectual cacophony. There are little attractions in various places, philosophy in one corner, physics in another, maybe a bit of mathematics every now and again, some political science — nothing bearing any relationship to anything else.[3]

A member of the Scottish Enlightenment, or the great scientist Alexander von Humboldt, or George R. Stewart might well have written that passage. In fact, Stewart once said something similar: "The great trouble now is that there hasn't been enough synthesis of all these different knowledges. The extent of knowledge has increased so much that it's very hard to get any kind of general view. I think that's the problem for the future, sometime, to synthesize these things, so you're able to get some kind of view of life."[4]

The movements and their ideas affected George R. Stewart. Stewart was quiet and creative, a lover of nature and books, passionate about freedom. His works were liberal in tone. Yet near the end of his life, at about the same time that he joined the Bohemian Club, Stewart wrote a novel that seems out of character. One that seems to swim against the tide of his liberal thought. Had something happened to change his ideas? Or had the world changed?

The world *was* changing. In what would turn out to be a prescient letter about a proposed ban on smoking in one area of the Sequoias, Stewart wrote, "The prospect for the future is bleak ... if such restrictions begin. Will not smoking, next, be barred from the other public rooms? Since my neighbor's cigar can actually be smelled in my apartment, what is the guarantee that the restriction will not be extend [sic] to private apartments? Moreover, will tyranny … not be extended, undemocratically, to other matters than smoking?"[5] Today, people might argue that restricting someone's right to smoke was a good thing, but Stewart realized that if the government began to restrict one freedom, it would soon restrict others. There would be an enforced use of seatbelts, enforced searches at airports, enforced stops at interstate highway checkpoints, enforced restriction of free discussion of certain issues — always, of course, with the argument that it's done for the protection of citizens and the security of the homeland.

Stewart was also concerned by campus events. After a fairly democratic start, the movements began to attack academic freedom. Their goals became demands, the demands "non-negotiable." At Berkeley, one group demanded a College of Ethnic Studies without any university control over hiring, promotion of students, or expenditures. Another insisted on the use of race and gender as grounds for University admission, employment and promotion.

Stewart knew there was a need for social change. He had written approvingly of marriage across racial lines, of strong women leading men, of the need to organize and take action to get justice. Yet like many others, he wondered: should change, even just and necessary change, happen through "non-negotiable demands," strikes and sit-ins, the violence of the spray-painted slogan and the thrown rock? And if hiring, admission, promotion, or grading were done on a basis other than academic quality, would competency decline? If so, would not the university decline?

Friends fueled his concern. Wallace Stegner retired when the situation on the Stanford campus became violent; then wrote *All the Little Live Things* to show his disgust for the excesses of the time. In 1969, Jim Hart sent the Stewarts a letter which described Berkeley's campus situation in gloomy terms.

> A fellow's good humor gets fairly well exhausted by what's going on the campus.... It began more or less two weeks ago … with the escalation … of the old demands for an Afro-American Studies Department … as part of an entirely autonomous "Third World College" with self determination of faculty, students, budgets, etc., etc. This whole matter was not put in the nature of demands … until after a militant group of two or three hundred began a strike. The reasons for the strike were announced after the fact and were never formally communicated to the Chancellor, although I guess he can read picket signs and hear chants as well as the next fellow.
>
> There have been some pretty ugly affairs.... On top of the open violence … came an all-too-successful burning of Wheeler Aud. [sic] It was completely gutted one night … in a holocaust of flame.... On top of that came two forays last week of gangs going through the first floor of the hall, breaking many of the windows in the doors of classrooms, spraying glass over students in class.[6]

Burning Wheeler was bad enough; roving gangs using the tactics of fascist brownshirts was worse. But there was a greater concern. In Stewart's novel *The Years of The City*, contractor-tyrant Melas creates an apparent crisis when he organizes phony "terrorist" groups who carry out "terrorist attacks." Could that have been a foreshadowing of the real world of the late twentieth century? That is, were these truly student movements? Or were they manipulations, choreographed behind the scenes by dark and sinister forces?

Reading or listening to the news in 1967, George Stewart might well have believed he had foreseen the future when he wrote the tale of Melas. On February 21, 1967, the *New York Times* broke several stories of Melas-like manipulation of American progressive institutions and movements by the CIA. The paper carried detailed reports of CIA involvement with the AFL-CIO and the influential Hobby Foundation. Since the Hobby Foundation had connections with the publishers of the *Washington Post*, CIA involvement raised the danger of news censorship. In another of that edition's stories one movement's "progressive" leader was quoted as *praising* the CIA's behind-the-scenes work in her supposedly democratic group.[7]

There was CIA influence close to home, too. Stewart may well have seen a memo sent out by Berkeley Vice-President (and secret CIA consultant) Earl C. Bolton, since it was widely circulated throughout academia. In the memo, Bolton encouraged dishonesty among members of the academic community working with the CIA: "The real initiative might be with the Agency but the apparent ... launching of the research should, wherever possible, emanate from the campus." And Bolton put secrecy above academic freedom when he wrote, "[University researchers working at the CIA] would of course have to recognize the agency's right to review the finished document for accidental leaks."[8]

The FBI was also active on the campus. Papers acquired by the *San Francisco Chronicle* after a 17-year Freedom of Information Act battle prove that Hardin Jones, assistant director of the University Radiation Lab, was a paid FBI informant. The papers also reveal that Jones set up what can only be described as a network of spies on campus.[9]

CIA and FBI manipulation of the university, non-negotiable demands for "diversity" rather than quality, even the destruction of park-like areas on campus for the construction of new buildings in the appropriately named Neo-Brutalist style — there was a sense the university had lost its way. People from all parts of the political spectrum felt the university was descending from its lofty perch as a place for enlightened scholarship into a sub-basement of fear and ignorance — where ideas could neither be pursued nor exchanged without interference by secret state police forces like the FBI and the CIA, or by "student" movements that were not what they appeared to be.

Elderly and perhaps with some of the conservatism of age, Stewart turned to the one tool with which he could hope to sound an alarm against the danger of the time. He wrote a book. "I had the idea," Stewart said, "... about the dramatic problem that would come if some senior member of an English department took up one of the Shakespeare heresies ... I wanted to take up the Marlowe phase of it." He called his book "The Shakespeare Crisis."[10]

Stewart's novel, set at the same mythical campus as *Doctor's Oral*, begins with a debate between two professors over the possibility that Christopher Marlowe authored Shakespeare's works. An unethical cub reporter who attends the debates inflates the controversy, describing it as a personal vendetta between the professors. With each story she writes, she escalates the conflict, turning the professors' discussion into a heated battle between light and dark. Her news stories get the attention of a shady character named Hal, who makes his living selling term papers. Hal is also a Melas, secret head of a local organization of protest groups who starts protests because he enjoys the chaos they create.

Hal sets up a meeting attended by "a real cross-section ... at least one of you for every case — color, sex — three sexes, maybe more."[11] He fires up the protesters:

> Some of you have put a lot of energy, at times, into seeing that someone does not enjoy his Freedom of Speech, that is, in breaking up a meeting. Just the same, Freedom of Speech is a good issue, pulls in a lot of the Faculty, and the liberals, gets support of the press....
> You decide, on your own, that some position is immoral or obscene, or vicious — or, you can just say "racist" — and then, of course, advocacy of that position becomes all those things too, and you are justified, morally and conscientiously ... in breaking up the meeting entirely.... [For example], South Africa. You'll decide that it's Fascist and racist and vicious — as it is all right — and then if a speaker from South Africa tries to speak on the campus, you'll keep him from doing it.[12]

Aided by one of the Regents' wives, the local police, and the cub journalist, Hal brings the crisis to a boil. The protestors storm the University Library. "Burn the books!" they cry. Once again, as in *Earth Abides*, the Library is threatened by fire. But the fire of ignorance does not win. The Librarians refuse to yield: "Holding the point was the book-binder, armed with an antique flatiron that he used for a book-presser. Beside him the Chief of Gifts, planted firmly, stood brandishing her stapler.... A crippled cataloguer stood to one side waving her cane, and howling, 'Out, you...!'"[13] (Here, Stewart used a word by far the strongest he ever wrote into a book. It would not have been in the published book — Ted would never have permitted it. But it was an honest reflection of his feelings toward the Melases of this world.)

The protestors are vanquished, and disperse. Librarians, keepers of the light, have saved the light of learning, and the crisis is over. But not without its price. One professor is so humiliated by the controversy that he takes his own life.

The wealthy regent's wife agrees to pay for all damages, and to keep her mouth shut in the future. But she refuses to accept any personal responsibility for events. Hal slinks away, into the darkness.

At the end of the book, librarians, professors, and others meet to discuss the crisis. One old professor — obviously Stewart — rises, and speaks.

> In those eighty years that I remember, the world has not moved ... in a way that I, as an old man, now find wholly agreeable. The trust in reason, and the sway of the intellect, seem to have weakened....
>
> Like an old-fashioned preacher, I now present an anecdote that might be called an emblem. When I took my modest walk, as I do twice daily on the campus, I saw recently a word, POWER, illegally sprayed on a wall. Then, a day or two later, it had been partially scrubbed away, and reduced to POW, the traditional word having been transformed into a kind of semi-word, as if in replica of our times, moving from reason to un-reason.... Then, this morning — again walking — I saw it still further reduced to OW, a mere instinctual cry of human confusion or distress, animal-like, lacking in what we once called reason. So have my times gone!...
>
> There was a famous saying ... in my day ... "The lamps are going out all over Europe."
>
> Yet one of them never went out, though it flickered at times. And that was the lamp of learning, which we sometimes envisage as a torch.... And always — or, at least, in our times — the universities (as we in these walls must always remember) are entrusted with that torch.

Those are the cautionary words of someone who knew the value of academic freedom, and who saw it slipping away, the time of light becoming a new age of darkness.[14]

"The Shakespeare Crisis" was never published. Ted and other members of the Stewart family felt its criticism of the movements was overdone. They found its tone disturbing. And they felt the writing was not up to George Stewart's usual standard. There was even talk of destroying the manuscript after George's death, but Ted finally agreed to add the manuscript to the George R. Stewart Papers.

There, in the full context of his writing, it can be seen in perspective. It is not his best work, and it's outside his usual views. But it is an honest expression of his lifelong concern for the threats to academic freedom, and all freedoms, and his worries about the manipulations of our society by the Melases of this time.

34

Nearing his eighties, Stewart sensed the shortening of years. Ecological novels and books about freedom were set aside so he could finish his work on names. By the time he laid down his pencil and turned off his Dictaphone for the last time, he'd written three more books about names and naming: *American Place-Names, American Given Names,* and *Names on the Globe.*

Place-Names is a dictionary of the meanings of place names. Like Samuel Johnson's *Dictionary,* the book has the author's opinionated stamp upon it. In the book's introduction Stewart cautioned readers that since the dictionary was created by one individual, it would have a touch of individuality.[1]

Reading the definitions which Stewart so carefully collected, travelers learn why George Stewart loved American names. Consider the following: "Possum Glory" is a place frequented by possums; the railroad company's "Coaling Station," became "Coaling Station A," when other stations were added; then "Coalinga," California. "Accident" was named when surveyors accidentally marked off some land. "Pizzlewig Creek," for a woman of questionable virtue (Pizzle is slang for penis or intercourse). And "Pirate Cove" because of the place's reputation. There are 550 pages of such good American names in *American Place-Names.*

Publication by Oxford University Press acknowledged the book was a work by a scholar of the highest rank. Yet, as always, Stewart wrote the dictionary with a general audience in mind. Scholars may consult it, but anyone on an American saunter will find the book a good traveling companion. At almost every milepost, American travelers can use the book to find the meaning of local place names. In the same way that *U.S. 40* helped guide the Wingards of Pasadena on their trip, *American Place Names* can be a guidebook through the names of America for those who wander.

American Given Names was a dictionary of names given by American parents to their children. But, as usual with Stewart, the book transcends its form. He uses it to raise some broader questions. Noticing that there has been an abandonment of traditional names, he wonders whether that's a sign of creativity — or of cultural disintegration.[2] It is the old professor of *The Shakespeare Crisis* speaking, worried about civilization. But Stewart was not judgmental. He was merely considering the question, leaving it to future scholars to find an answer. *American Given Names* would be Stewart's last book. He finished the book in August 1978, two years before he died.

Although published before *American Given Names, Names on the Globe* is George R. Stewart's last major work. *Names on the Globe* is not *Names on the Land,* broadened, but a deeper look into the way humans name places.

Stewart begins by defining *place*. Then he considers why places are *named*— to distinguish them one from another for human convenience.[3] Since humans can distinguish places one from another in various ways, the ways they come up with place names will vary. In the book, Stewart describes ten ways-of-naming he's identified; *descriptive, associative,* and *folk-etymology,* for example. Since description gives important information about places, many names are descriptive: Mud Lake, High Mountain, Arroyo Grande, Sweetwater, Badwater. Associative names associate a place with something else — a dream or a danger — in the area: Gold Creek, Bad Route Road. Folk-etymology names develop when two or more languages are found in one place and translation of place names distorts meaning. Colorado's Rio Purgatorio, for example, was translated into French as "Purgatoire"; that name morphed through folk etymology into an English name which sounds similar but which has a completely different meaning: "Picket-Wire."

Place-names, Stewart writes, are also a key to culture. They often tell as much about namers and their times as about places named; so he spends some time on namers. "Sweetwater" says someone enjoyed the good water he or she found there. "Gold Creek," that another person was as interested in gold as good water. "Spooky Nook" records the shivers people felt when they passed one small, wild place.

At the end of the book, in a chapter entitled "Place-Names and Poetry," Stewart returns to the main idea of his 1930 article about science and poetry: that other disciplines are rich sources of words for poets — geography, for example. Geographers, who choose the names to place on maps, have as fine a sense of history and word-music as they do of description. So maps are covered with names that are descriptive and commemorative, and which carry a lovely music. Stewart believed that those names which combine sweetness of sound, romantic appeal and evocation of memory are the most useful of all names for poets.

Stewart closed the book with a question, as any good teacher must do. Discussing an apparently simple name, Cowbridge, he points out that the name is, in fact, complex. It leads to a set of questions. For example: was it named, he wonders, for a cow that crossed the bridge, or one that refused to do so?[4]

Stewart knew *Names on the Globe* would be his last major work, so he used the "Author's Note" to tie up some loose ends. He explained his lack of self-promotion by mentioning that he wanted his text to speak for itself, and added that he always wrote with integrity.[5]

Then, at the end of things, Stewart honored his first, his oldest, his best friend and colleague, Theodosia, who, he said, should be known as Encourager of Books.[6]

Now the work was complete. *Opus perfeci.*

VI. *Opus Perfeci*

35

There's a handwritten note in the George Rippey Stewart Papers: "Fatigue ... Body stiffness ... Shuffling walk ... Muscular slowness (left hand) ... Tremor ... Passing out ... Bad breath ... Constipation ... Expressionless face ... Lack of appetite...." There's another note in Stewart's Datebook. "Dr. Parson says it's Parkinson's."[1] Like the terrible diseases which spread across the world in the years of his youth, Stewart's Parkinson's Disease was not curable.

Stewart could no longer write. He tried to write one more book, a biography of Marion LeRoy Burton, but even with the help of Ted and her sister Jane he finished only 40 pages — often repeating himself, and scrawling in an almost unreadable hand.

A sense of finality was everywhere. Old friendships mysteriously ended. Jim Hart's wife died of cancer, and the Stewarts seemed unsympathetic. Wally and Mary Stegner disappeared from the correspondence, and are not mentioned in Stewart's Oral History.

In June 1980, he held his first great-grandchild, infant Heather, for a photo. It would be his final act. Afterward, the Parkinson's washed over him. The brilliant man, who first wrote the Whole Earth vision into books — the man who named the storms — could not even talk. It was as if he were once again the frustrated child who swallowed a penny, but could tell no one. Ted felt anger flooding out of him, but he could not tell her why he was angry.

George R. Stewart passed away on August 22, 1980.

A few weeks later, on a lovely day, a memorial service was held in the Great Hall of a Faculty Club at the University of California, Berkeley. It was a gathering of rangers of the mind, praising their lost leader. Professor John Raleigh celebrated George R. Stewart's courage during the Year of the Oath. Professor Travis Bogard read the epilogue from *Sheep Rock*, with its litany of colleagues. Then Professor Bogard closed the ceremony with the statement of faith from Ecclesiastes and *Earth Abides*: "Men go and come, but earth abides."

George and Ted Stewart's Christmas card for 1975.

It grew silent. The campanile began to play Stewart's beloved songs of the Westward Movement. "Sweet Betsy from Pike," "She'll Be Coming 'Round the Mountain," and others rang across the glades and grounds of the University of California, Berkeley, and beyond the university, into the Berkeley air. The music washed over the places of *Earth Abides* (the library, "San Lupo Drive," the park with the rocks), over 100 Codornices Road (where he and Frost and others had talked, and he and Sandburg and others had sung, around the ancient circle of fire). On that lovely day, the music of the westering blanketed the geography of George R. Stewart, Ish, and *GeoS*.

The service ended. People walked outside, into the Faculty Glade, to meet and mingle. Those of us who were older and knew George R. Stewart shared memories, often smiling at some warm recollection. The children, new generations of Stewarts and Evensons, laughed and played, celebrating the joy of life on a summer's day.

As George Stewart grew older, he often wondered if he'd lived a good life. To answer the question, of course, he wrote a book. "In a sense, *Good Lives* was an attempt to sum up my life," He told Suzanne Riess. He told his son Jack, "That's a book that an old man writes."[2]

In his study of six men — Joab of the Bible, Francisco Eduardo Tresguerras of Mexico, Heinrich Schleiman, Prince Henry the Navigator, John Bidwell of California, and William the Marshall — Stewart found the beginnings of an answer. Each man's life suggested six qualities of character: clear goals, commitment to those goals, the acceptance of responsibility for his acts, courage, and, at the end of life, fulfillment and an integration of spirit. For Stewart, those qualities of character, goal, commitment, responsibility, courage, fulfillment, and spiritual integration defined "The good life."

Did that definition fit his life?

Although his goals evolved, they were always founded on two things. "The land," as a character in the drama of human life, a way to memorialize human history through names, and a place to seek freedom. And his obligations to his family, as he understood those, to provide a good home and opportunities. He clearly met his responsibilities. His was a life of service — military service, service to the university and the larger world of enlightened thought, to academic freedom. His writing brought money into the family and sent ideas out into the world. He saw the sweeping spread of the understanding of his idea that the land is character in the work, and of wilderness protection. He lived to see the first photographs to show what he had visualized, the view of Earth from near and far space. And his descendants have themselves lived successful lives.

Stewart, more than most, achieved his personal and his scholarly goals. As the end approached, he could feel a great sense of fulfillment about that.

Was Stewart's an integrated spirit? I thought about this one Thanksgiving Day, working at Thornton Beach, as I watched George R. Stewart share a Thanksgiving picnic with his family.

Throughout his life, his concept of "the land," of nature's ecosystems, was central to everything he did. He developed himself on journeys through grand landscapes, where he *felt* the land's ancient power. His honeymoon was an adventurous trip across the prairies and through the great western mountains. He and Ted involved nature in the upbringing of their children. His works, on names, recycling, highways, and his ecological novels and his books about freedom, were all founded on the idea of "the land." Through his commitment to public service and education, not always an easy commitment, he passed his epiphanies and his wisdom on, teaching the rest of us that the land is a key to human character, and the human experience. He was willing to face the guns to protect and share these ideas. So, by his own definition, it seemed that Stewart had lived an integrated life.

I glanced again out of the office, north, to the picnic area where the Stewarts were gathered. Thanksgiving dinner was over. George and his old friend Theodosia had started to hike through the small but lovely ecosystems of Thornton Beach on the George R. Stewart Trail. As I watched them it seemed to me that George Stewart had integrated flesh and soul as much as any person I'd ever known. He had lived a good life.

Years later, I asked Jack Stewart for his thoughts about it.

"He never talked about that. I don't know if he'd say he had a good life or not."

"Do *you* think he had a good life?"

"Yes. I think so," said Jack.

And we left it at that.[3]

Theodosia Burton Stewart lived on for several years, the hearty, ebullient head of an extended clan of Stewarts and Evensons. I often visited her at the Sequoias on Geary Boulevard, where Ted was kind enough to share many stories of her life with George — stories which helped make this book. Sometimes I'd bring my sons along. Always warm and hospitable, Ted made them welcome. We enjoyed the visits, memorable for the company and the view from her 25th-story penthouse. (Once, I remember, Ted, Bill, Ken and I watched the Cherry Blossom Festival in Japantown, the performers like twirling like tiny marionettes to a music we could not hear.)

Then, in 1989, three months after the Loma Prieta Earthquake, Theodosia Burton Stewart passed away. In his inscription for her copy of *Storm* — first ecological novel, first Whole Earth novel, the story of a storm named Maria — George R. Stewart had written:

> *To Theodosia....*
> *whose name also ends in -ia*
> *who was always along, and*
> *who drove the pass, at night,*
> *alone, and in the storm.*

It is the finest of epitaphs.

The Man Who Named the Storms and his Encourager of Books were gone.

So were Thornton State Beach and the George R. Stewart Trail.

Just 16 months after George R. Stewart died, a century-sized Maria of a storm hit California. A full 11 inches, half of San Francisco's annual rainfall, fell in one day. Flooding was widespread. An estimated 18,000 landslides happened in one night. At Thornton State Beach, the volume of water rushing through the highway drainage system overloaded the capacity of the drains. The drainpipe on the hillside behind the park office blew apart. Water flooded out of the pipe, washing the hillside down and toward the ocean. Mud filled the office, burying the place where rangers had met to decide the naming of the trail. Mud filled the file cabinets. It destroyed the park journals, with their records of the visits of George R. Stewart and Ted Stewart and family to Thornton State Beach.

Mud and water continued, heading west, into the lower drains, and blew them out. The ramp and the stairs to the beach collapsed. Mud backed up into the North Valley, filling restrooms and burying the picnic tables where the Stewarts had their annual Thanksgivings. It covered the George R. Stewart Trail sign. It buried the trail. It buried the parking lot where the Stewarts (and

Chiura Obata, and Wilder Bentley the Elder, and the Kennedys and the Byrnes, and all the visitors) had parked — under several feet of mud.

By the end of the day, it was hard to see anything of Thornton State Beach except (Earth abides) the landforms.

A few months later, the California State Department of Parks decided to abandon Thornton State Beach. They bulldozed the remaining structures, and hauled the debris away. Thornton State Beach had passed into history.

When I heard the news, I put my pen down for a while and thought of the last time I had seen George R. Stewart, at that family Thanksgiving in the north picnic area. After the meal, George and Ted walked the trail. His illness made it painful, but Ted helped him. Ted and George would walk for a short way, then stop to catch their breath and smell the new green (growing as it does in California after "election day rains"). When George was rested, they'd walk a little farther. On they walked, the two old friends — up, and over the ridge. Then they vanished from sight, withdrawing into the sky.

36

"George R. Stewart Peak": Peak, elevation 2,252 m (7,389 ft.), 0.8 km (0.5 mi.) NE of Donner Pass and 2.4 km (1.5 mi.) W of Donner Lake; Nevada Co., Calif.; sec. 16, T 17 N, R 15 E, Mount Diablo Mer.; 39°19'26" N, 120°19'07" W.

http://geonames.usgs.gov/pls/gnis
website of the USGS Board of Geographic Names

George R. Stewart wrote the first ecological novels, the first Whole Earth books, the first name-history books, the first road-study books, the best twentieth century book about academic freedom. The ideas in his books are now widespread, their ecological insights helping humans understand their place in the ecosystem. To name a mountain after him would — physically and symbolically — be an appropriate honor. If not a godhood, it would be an appropriate apotheosis.

Jack Stewart led the effort, encouraging several distinguished people to write letters to the Board of Geographic Names in support of the idea. The most memorable letter came from George Stewart's old friend Wally Stegner:

> I have seldom heard a proposal (or rumor) that I greet with greater enthusiasm.... Your father ... practically invented Donner Pass.... A country which has wasted a lot of peaks on Secretaries of the Interior, Secretaries of War, Directors of the Naval Observatory and other Washington figures would ennoble itself by naming whatever peak is left after George R. Stewart, because his books may actually last, considering the way we chew up the environment, longer than the peaks themselves.[1]

Jack was successful. In 1984, the Board of Geographic Names named the mountain for George R. Stewart and again his name was on the land — this time, on a more enduring landform than the small, sandy piece of Earth known as the George R. Stewart Trail. Although the peak, over the long geological time of Earth, would change, it, in "comparison at least with the passing of man's generations — remained without changing."[2]

George R. Stewart Peak is in good company. McGlashan Point, named for the man who wrote the first book about the Donner Party, is less than a half mile to the southeast. Two and a half miles southwest is Mt. Disney, named for Stewart's admirer and colleague, the first person to make Stewart's ecological novels into films. Donner Pass is nearby. The California Trail, the transcontinental railroad, Ish's route, U.S. 40, and the Pacific Crest Trail pass wander through the high Sierra just below George R. Stewart Peak.

The naming of the mountain was not the only posthumous honoring of Stewart.

There were also accolades from other writers. Ivan Doig's novel *English Creek*, one of the books in his Montana Centennial trilogy, carries a passage about how we name places. The Mother's Fourth of July speech seemed to reflect *Names On the Land*, so when I met Doig I asked if I'd seen Stewart's influence in his novels. "Yes," he said, and praised Stewart's work. Larry McMurtry, Pulitzer Prize winner best known for *Lonesome Dove* and *The Last Picture Show*, also praises Stewart in *Roads: Driving America's Great Highways*. As he drives I-70, he writes a short paragraph about Stewart, whom he calls greatly under-appreciated. McMurtry mentions that the only work he knows about that praises Stewart is an essay by Wallace Stegner which is found in *Where the Bluebird Sings by the Lemonade Springs*.[3]

Stegner's essay, "George R. Stewart and the American Land," and Dr. John Caldwell's "George R. Stewart" were in close competition to be the first literary honoring of Stewart. Although it was pretty much a dead heat, Caldwell seems to have won — his fine little book was published in 1981, while Stegner's essay made its first appearance as the introduction to the 1982 Lexikos Press reissue of *Names On The Land*. But Stegner's essay has had a much wider readership since it was reprinted in *Where the Bluebird Sings to the Lemonade Springs*.

Stegner writes as literary colleague, and friend. In the essay, he admits to reading the Stewart works on his shelves often, feeling their inspiration, even borrowing from them. Stegner describes Stewart's books as challenging works which force readers to consider many things — storms, names, the ecosystem — which they've always taken for granted and to rethink their attitudes. Stegner also points out the importance of Stewart as a writer and — with a comment directed at those in the Eastern literary establishment who dismiss Stewart as a regional writer — suggests that the failure to grant national literary recognition to Stewart is their loss, not his.[4]

In 2006, the first biography of Stewart was published. Dr. Fred Waage's *Crucial Role of the Environment in the Writings of George Stewart (1895–1980): A Life of America's Chief Literary Ecologist*, considers Stewart's life and work from the viewpoint of both environmentalism and literature. It is invaluable to those studying Stewart's work.

Others less well known also praised Stewart and his work in their own ways. Alan Kaplan, park naturalist at Tilden Regional Park, led "George R. Stewart Memorial" hikes up Vollmer Peak on the anniversary of Stewart's death, discussing place-names and other GRS concepts to visitors, until he retired. Vic Moitoret, the young officer who'd had two aircraft carriers shot out from under him before he met Stewart on the way from Hawaii to San Diego, founded the George R. Stewart Fan Club at his Silver City, New Mexico, home, in the late 1970s. Seattle area Humanities teacher Bob Lyon founded The Friends of George R. Stewart.

Lyon's idea was to have his group meet at the conferences of the Western Literature Association; and the group did so, at least once. Members included publisher Alan Ligda (he who kept *Earth Abides* in print), Frank H. Sloss of the Chit-Chat Club, author Ferol Egan, essayist Bruce Nelson, Librarian and author John Caldwell (who had written that first book on George R. Stewart) and bookseller Roy Squires. The group also gathered to discuss and celebrate his work whenever the opportunity to do so presented itself. As she had done for decades, Ted Stewart became a kind of social director for those celebrating her husband's work, introducing Moitoret to Lyon by mail. The men became friends, and Moitoret participated in "Friends" events as he could.

One such event was the visit of "The Pilgrim," Steve Williams.

As down-to-earth a fellow as you'll ever meet, Steve, of Lancashire, England, was raised in a working-class Liverpool family. But he had talent — he attended the Liverpool Institute of Art with fellow Liverpudlians Lennon and McCartney, and became a good painter. After graduation Williams got a job with a supplier of high-quality printers' inks, married Carol, and began to raise a family. The couple now has two children, Steve Jr. and Jenny, and grandchildren.

Steve Williams was a very conventional Englishman — until he picked up *Earth Abides*. He read it, put it away. But a few years later, he picked the book up again and gave it another read. Then again. Again. And again. By now, he's given it well over a hundred reads. "I pick it up one day, just to read a page or two, and the next thing I knew I've read it again."[5]

In the spring of 1985, with the support of his wife, Carol, Steve followed the call of the book. He boarded a plane for the first time, left Britain for only

Steve Williams, affectionately dubbed "The Pilgrim," stands with Ted Stewart, holding Ish's Hammer, March 1986.

the second time, and flew thousands of miles over the Canadian tundra, the Basin and Range country and the Sierra Nevada to San Francisco. (His first words to me in San Francisco were, "All that wilderness!") He spent a busy week in the Bay Area, researching the Stewart Papers at the Bancroft, attending a series of get-togethers organized by Bob Lyon, sharing a lunch or two with Ted, and meeting others involved in the Stewart story. Steve interviewed many of the people on tape, donating the recordings to the Bancroft Library as his gift to future scholars. (Like Ted's stories, Steve's interviews helped make this book.)

But one thing was missing from Steve's itinerary — a trip through Stewart country. So a friend and I invited Steve to join us on a run to Carson City. We drove over Donner Pass just after the huge rotary plows had opened the highway on that first day of spring, then wound down old U.S. 40 to the monument at Donner Lake so Steve could see for himself the awful depth of the snow in that year of the Donners' ordeal. That night we went through Reno, lit to glory with lights. Steve's only comment was, "My God."

The next morning there was another comment from Steve, as he looked at the dun, dry sagebrush valley, the great eastern front of the Sierra Nevada near Carson City, and the road signs reading "open range": "Ne-*vah*-dah!"

When he got back to England, he began writing. *The Year of the Pilgrim* is Steve's long letter about his pilgrimage to *GeoS* country, and his new understandings of George R. Stewart.

> During my brief trip to California … I read Stewart's original notes on *Earth Abides*, met many of his family, colleagues and friends, visited some of the houses featured in the book — not least the house on "San Lupo" Drive — and stood on the rock formation upon which Ish and Em recorded the years….
>
> *George R. Stewart Peak* is … near Donner Pass…. Almost on cue, as Don and I stood there, a snow plough with chains on its tyres clanked past and over toward the lake; a snow blower was arching plumes of snow sucked from the road, over the meadow, recreating a scene from *Storm*….
>
> Stewart has a way of opening your mind.[6]

In 2005, the first George R. Stewart Symposium was presented, at the annual gathering of CONTACT. Described as "a unique interdisciplinary conference which brings together some of the foremost international social and space scientists, science fiction writers and artists to exchange ideas," CONTACT includes NASA scientists, authors, artists, musicians, filmmakers, philosophers, anthropologists, social psychologists, high school and college teachers and students. It's a watering hole for minds, like the "Sheep Rock" campfires, and a modern version of Edinburgh's Oyster Club. Since it was considering "Science and Literature," CONTACT 2005 seemed a good place to talk about George R. Stewart and *GeoS*.

Stewart's books and the Hammer of Ish. This is an original sketch by Stewart scholar and artist Stephen Williams, also known as "The Pilgrim." Williams went to the Liverpool Institute of Art with John Lennon and Paul McCartney, became a Stewart fan, then a Stewart scholar. He traveled to Berkeley and the Donner Pass country to study Stewart; he then returned home to write and paint about Stewart's work.

Four people spoke at the symposium: two scientists, a teacher, and a composer, each of them deeply influenced by Stewart.

Dr. James D. Burke was Project Manager for the Ranger lunar missions which gave us our first close-up photographs of the Moon. When he was 12, Burke's family moved to a cabin in the California transverse ranges, not far from the place young Stewart first felt the touch of the ancient on his long-ago mountain hike. In the mountains, Burke discovered *Storm* and it changed his life: "All the senses were enlarged by the book. (Remember, I was living in the forest at this time.) Love of driving snow; Love of rough wood and bark; Love of the taste of watercress. Love of forest scent, of the smell of hot sunshine on the pine bark, of wind in pine." Dr. Burke explained how the novel's descriptions of highway workers, power plant operators, telephone linemen and others, gave him a love for work and achievement, much "celebrated in the book." Stewart's interdisciplinary approach also influenced young Burke and "connections became the stuff of a lifetime."

Dr. Burke still calls on Stewart's work for inspiration: "I still go to broken when I recall the scene near the end of *Earth Abides*, where the ancient tribal leader rests wearily against the wall of that great library while he thinks of the million books in it that now won't be read. I quoted that in a paper for an international lunar conference, where I advocated the building of a great archive in the Moon to save our treasures and our wisdom in case we get hit. That paper and others in the same vein are surely a Stewart legacy."[7]

Jovial Bob Lyon followed Dr. Burke, talking briefly about George Stewart's dry sense of humor, and giving copies of Stewart's "A Roistering Song for Sexagenarians" to the sexagenarians in the audience.

Dr. John H. Stewart — for whom that clear, cool stream, "Jack's Creek," in *Fire* is named — talked about his father as a teacher. "I was [at "Sheep Rock"] with my father on two trips. I witnessed his style of research and learned how to approach scientific study. The trips had a profound effect on me. What I learned the most was the sense of the scientific method, an understanding of how science is put together, starting with the gathering of facts. I learned about imagination, and was able to use it as a geologist."[8]

The last speaker stood up, walked over to the Steinway that was parked in front of the stage, sat down, and began to play. When the music ended, Grammy-nominated composer Philip Aaberg stood, faced us, and said,

This is what happened to me....

The thing that happened to me when I read this book was that it removed me from being caught up in what was going on. [The Vietnam War.] It took me out into space.

It was difficult for me in those days to do what I was supposed to be doing, which was making music. I had one professor who said, "You just need to think beautiful thoughts." At the time I thought that was the worst advice I could have possibly gotten, but this book enabled me to do that.

Fire and *Storm* and *Earth Abides* and *Sheep Rock* in particular are the ones that have that same effect on me. They pick me up; they zoom me ... out from the Earth.

He played another of his compositions, then continued his talk: "Stegner and George R. Stewart were great friends. Stegner's been one of the huge influences on my life because *Wolf Willow* could have been written about my hometown. Stegner's book encouraged me to write about what I knew, which was Deep Montana."

Commissioned by National Geographic to write a score for a film about one of the earth's lines of longitude, Aaberg decided to create music inspired by Stewart's greatest novel. It wasn't easy to compose a "Soundtrack for *Earth Abides*," Aaberg told the audience, but he found a clue in Stegner: "Stegner was writing about the meadowlark. If you've been out in Montana, if you stand out on the high plains, you know exactly what he's talking about. Stegner wrote that the meadowlark is at the center of the circle of his music. When the meadowlark moves, his geometry moves with him. So the meadowlark is always at the center of a circle." Aaberg carried the idea of the circle beyond art, to science, and to life. "Science can expand our circles. Just imagine what we could do by getting into schools and expanding the kids' perspectives, expanding their circle from their school room to their community — past their religion, past their world, into the universe." Those circles, like the great round circle of the Earth itself, were the key: Aaberg used Pythagoras' Circle of Fifths to compose his soundtrack for *Earth Abides*.

His talk finished, Philip Aaberg sat at the Steinway again and played "A Soundtrack for *Earth Abides*."[9]

Listening to Aaberg's composition, I had a thought — to follow Philip Aaberg's example and head for the place Stegner wrote about in *Wolf Willow*. If Stegner, the great friend and admirer of George Stewart, could help Aaberg find a way to compose *Earth Abides*, maybe he could help me on my saunter. Help me find *GeoS*. So I turned the old Toyota Chinook north and east and went to Canada, hoping to complete my quest for the deepest truth or meaning about Stewart's work and ideas. Before I set down the pen for the last time, I wanted to find that meaning.

37

The Chinook and I headed to Eastend, Saskatchewan, where I would spend some time as a visiting writer. An enlightened little community, Eastend would be the perfect place to continue — and maybe conclude — my quest. Hopefully, while I was there, I'd get closer to the elusive *GeoS*, that deep truth about Stewart and his work

Eastend is the town Wallace Stegner called "Whitemud" in *The Big Rock Candy Mountain* and *Wolf Willow*. In his writings, Stegner saw enough promise in the town to predict it would someday develop a civilized interest in the arts and sciences — given a millennium. He was right to believe in the town, but wrong in his timetable. Eastend has already become the center of its own small enlightenment. Artists, authors and scientists from other parts of Canada (and the States) are moving into the town. Local folks are setting up galleries, potteries, studios. A coffee shop floats from location to location, but prospers. Until recently, Eastend even had a bookstore with 16,000 books in it.

The town would do justice to the Smithsonian. The magnificent T.Rex Discovery Centre, built after the 600 or so local citizens raised two million dollars in a couple of months, houses a museum and laboratory to preserve and interpret Earth's most massive T-Rex skeleton and the only T-Rex coprolite ever discovered. The town's Arts Council renovated Stegner's boyhood house as a Canadian Heritage Property. Wilkinson's Observatory, after renovation by Sig Giverhaug and friends, is again in operation. Three world class institutions — in an isolated rural town of 600.

Why here, in this small farm town, located, as a town slogan puts it, in "the middle of nowhere?" Dinosaur hunter Tim Tokaryk, whose title is "Head of Palaeontology, Royal Saskatchewan Museum Fossil Research Station" but who reminds me of Indiana Jones, says, "I've seen a lot of small towns with ideas. But never before one that put out the hard, sustained work to make the idea happen." And, "I've spent a lot of time in small, rural towns. In each of those towns I was always the oddball, the eclectic. Here, everybody's eclectic."[1]

Eclectic means "choosing … what appears to be the best from diverse sources."[2] That certainly describes the Scottish Enlightenment, the California Enlightenment, and the work of George R. Stewart. It also fits Corky Jones, the man who brought enlightenment to Wallace Stegner's boyhood town. Jones taught the town to value the eclectic, and now it's a town of eclectics. How could there *not* be an Eastend Enlightenment?

I knew nothing about Eastend until, out wandering one day, I happened upon the place. Amazed to see a T-Rex Laboratory in such a small town, I decided to stop for a while. I parked, went for a walk, and discovered the Wallace Stegner Boyhood Home. I had encountered Wallace Stegner, briefly, through the Stewarts, and knew about the friendship Stegner and Stewart shared and the influence they had on each other. So I understood that this coincidental encounter (or was it a coincidence?) was another important stop on my *GeoS* pilgrimage.

Years later I found Stegner House again, on the web. It's now a residence for artists and writers managed by Ethel Wills of the local Art Council. The house seemed the perfect place to work on the chapters about Stegner's friendship with Stewart, so I applied. I was accepted. So after a journey of visits with family and friends and a final blessing from the Aabergs I was in Eastend again.

One afternoon it began to storm thunderously. I didn't want to use the computer with lightning flashing nearby, so I went down to the parlor to read. I took Stegner's book of essays, *Where the Bluebird Sings to the Lemonade Springs*, with me. I hadn't read many of the essays — in fact, I'd only read the one about his friend George R. Stewart — but this seemed a good time to give the book a thorough read. The storm clearly intended to stick around for a while, so I settled into the couch, turned to the front of the book, and began to read. The essays were about place; and the first two were about the place I was in. "Finding the Place" described Eastend. "Letter, Much Too Late" was a hymn of praise to his mother and Eastend. As rain lashed the windows of the Stegner living room, I read, and was soon immersed in Stegner's description of the small town and his mother's feelings toward it.[3]

Sometimes we are so drawn toward a goal that we forget important things. I had been so focused on writing my book that I had forgotten where I was writing it. But reading this passage, I remembered: I was in *her* house, reading about her house. I was sitting on a couch in the room where (Wallace Stegner tells us) she read "everything she could get her hands on," where she gave young Wallace the gift of books and started him down the less-traveled road to the writing of his own books.

Suddenly, I felt her presence. Hilda Paulson Stegner, mother, grandmother, and grandmother-in-law of great writers, was in the house as surely as I was. Too moved to read for a time, I put the book down and watched and listened to the storm. The rain was coming down hard, the thunder booming, the lightning crackling.

That storm was settled in. I settled in, too, and decided to read all the essays. This was clearly a book to consider, and this was the place to consider it.

I sauntered into other territories of the book unknown to me, found an essay titled "The Sense of Place," and started to read. Stegner began by quoting Wendell Berry, who wrote that there is high human value in sticking to a place. Then George Stewart wandered in, as Stegner considered Stewart's idea that no place exists until it has been named and the name worn smooth with use. Stegner sauntered on, writing himself toward another of Wendell Berry's ideas — that to know *who* you are, you must know *where* you are.[4]

Thunder pulled my mind away for a moment. It quieted and I read Stegner's next line, *that no place can be a place until it has found a poet.*

I wish I could say lightning flashed at that moment. It didn't. But it was the moment of discovery, of seeing the light illuminate the end of the trail. It was the "Fiat Lux!" moment.

I had found the deep truth of *GeoS*: Earth could finally be a place, because it had its poet — George R. Stewart.

Like a wide-ranging scout, Stewart had gone across the deserts and over the passes and into the lush valleys of ideas before the rest of us. Then he returned to show us the way. His description of this planet from orbit, in *Storm* and *Ordeal by Hunger*, and his view of the tiny earth-dot as seen from Venus, showed humans the Earth as it truly is: one small place. With his detailed interweaving of the life, land, air and water that made up the stories of *Storm*, *Fire*, *Sheep Rock*, and *Earth Abides* he showed how complex and wonderful — and how easily disturbed — is Earth.

Writing about Earth from within the web of life, and from deep space — but always writing about it as both *place* and a "character in the work," George R. Stewart had become the first poet of the place named Earth. And in his writings the poet-scholar was preparing us — enough of us, if not all of us — for a great change. The greatest change in human understanding. An event far more powerful than any bomb or Melas.

It happened while he still lived. On Christmas Eve, in 1968, Borman, Anders, and Lovell, three representatives of humankind, saw the earth rise over the dead moon. Being good travelers, they photographed what they saw and brought the pictures back with them. Some 20 years earlier British astronomer Fred Hoyle had written, "Once a photograph of the Earth, taken from outside, is available ... a new idea as powerful as any in history will be let loose."[5] Hoyle was right. Humans were so overwhelmed by the photographs that the English language itself changed. Thanks to George R. Stewart, who prepared us, and the photograph, which showed us, "the earth" became "*Earth*." A place.

It was an epiphany for humankind.

Less than a year after the photograph was taken, two humans stood on another world and looked back at Earth. They were there to do scientific and engineering research, and win the space race. But Neil Armstrong knew they had a much more important mission. He told biographer James R. Hansen that he believed going to the moon would begin a new enlightenment, since humans would now recognize how small and precious is our small place in the universe.[6] Neil Armstrong — born and raised in another deeply American town less than 300 hundred miles west of Stewart's Indiana, descended from another Scottish family, and like Stewart a wanderer who loved geography and maps — understood that the great purpose of his first step was the same as that of George R. Stewart's works: to enlighten humankind about Earth, our small place in the inconceivably vast universe.

A few years after Apollo, NASA scholar Jesco Von Puttkamer wrote an essay for the now-defunct *NASA Magazine*. In "Spaceflight and the New

Enlightenment" he argued that, since you cannot send dozens of people on early flights to Mars, spaceflight is, by necessity, the work of cross-discipline thinkers and workers. Each astronaut must have more than one specialization — engineering and medicine, or geology and social psychology, or gardening and biology. Von Puttkamer also wrote that it is at the meeting place of disciplines that change happens, not within the disciplines themselves. So when a group of cross-discipline explorers travels together to Mars, they will almost surely help create another Enlightenment.

Apollo Astronaut John Young, answering a question, carried the idea even further. I had the chance to ask Commander Young what courses of study he'd recommend to those preparing to go to Mars. "Math," he answered. "Science, engineering and medicine."

He paused for a minute. Then said,

"Poetry. When we were on the moon, all we could say was 'Gosh.' or 'Magnificent.' They need to study poetry so they can express the beauty and wonder of the experience."[7]

So we have come full circle in this story, from Enlightenment to enlightenment. From Edinburgh, through the California Enlightenment and the books of Earth-Poet George R. Stewart, to the Sea of Tranquility and the new enlightenment of spaceflight.

Like the circles, of prairie Meadowlark and music and science and ideas that Philip Aaberg described, like the circles of the orbits that carry us to new worlds, the wheel of enlightenment turns. Wherever we go from here there shall be poets, and there will be the light of knowledge.

What more is there to say about the life, the work, or the influence of George R. Stewart? In *Sheep Rock*, he writes, "We may imagine it all as a pitcher broken into a billion pieces. We have found a few hundred, and have fitted together some dozens, but we cannot even imagine what the whole will be like."[8] Perhaps not. But we have found many pieces. We have some idea of the whole. And if you read and re-read the books and mine the archives and go off the roads and visit the places, *if you should look hard enough, you might find … more than you might suspect.*

Epilogue

How to end the book?

With a climb up George R. Stewart Peak, to look over the high Sierra Nevada country that—as Stegner put it—Stewart "made?" Up there, on the summit, thinking about something Wendell Berry once wrote? "Often my fairest hopes have rested on bad mistakes. I am an ignorant pilgrim, crossing a dark valley. And yet for a long time, looking back, I have been unable to shake off the feeling that I have been led—make of that what you will."[1]

Or with the synchronicity of a visit to Sewickley, Pennsylvania, and the realization that I was accidentally there on the centennial of George R. Stewart's birth—which resulted in the pouring out of a little single malt in celebration?

Or a trip to "Sheep Rock" to complete the geography of this work, enabled by Ranger Phil Butler, and bracketed by rangers and ranger events, like a mountain lion that crossed the path of the Chinook and an historic donner-und-blitzen of a storm?

All these things happened and any would be a good ending. But after thinking it over I decide to end this saunter as it began: in a library.

Keepers of the Light

One day, not long ago, I went to the University of California, Berkeley, to do some research in the Bancroft Library.

As I walked into the campus I thought (as I always do) that it is like entering an enchantment. The noisy city vanishes in a hush. The farther into the campus, the more peaceful the feeling becomes. It is clearly a place for recreation.

But there was also some darkness to my thoughts, because enlightenment seems threatened in this place of Fiat Lux. The university recently suggested, for example, that all incoming freshmen should send in a DNA sample rather than read the traditionally assigned book. And buildings are named for those who could be Melases (because they engineered excuses to go to bloody war for personal profit) but nothing is named for George R. Stewart. Most surprising of all (if the web listing of its courses is correct) the Department of English offers no courses about the man who wrote the novel that has been listed as high as number eight on the Amazon list of twentieth century United States fictional literature.

But I let the beauty of the place sweep those thoughts away.

Walking east on Campanile Way, I paused for a moment between the library and Wheeler Hall, imagining George R. Stewart in his office on the third floor in the northeast corner thinking about books he wants to write. Then I went into the Bancroft, center of Enlightenment, and started to work.

After a few hours I found my mind wandering. I began thinking, as I often do, about the meaning of words, especially those words which are the foundation of the university.

Powerful words, *fiat* and *lux*. Like *teach, educate,* and *lead* they are among the most ancient words we use. They come, across the millennia, from the ancient mother language. Millennia ago, the words were "bheu," *to grow, to be.* And "leuk," *brightness* or *light. To Be,* and *Light.* Long before the bomb — and "bomb," like "training," is a recent word — there was *being* and there was *light.* How encouraging that is![2]

As encouraging, this: ideas, the tools of enlightenment, are safe, held in this great library and other libraries around the Earth. No matter what happens, librarians, like those ancient Irish monks perched on their craggy islands at the end of the known Earth, will find a way to keep the light alive. As long as there are libraries, and librarians — and there are enough of both, not even counting the millions of private libraries like the Vales'— there shall be light. Librarians are the Keepers of the Light. And I would safely wager that as I write these words, somewhere a librarian is handing a book to a young boy or girl, with the words, "Here. I think you'll like this book."

Later, work done for the day, I left the Bancroft and walked into the campanile plaza. It was the beginning of a new school year, so student organizations had set up recruiting tables. One, which carried a banner emblazoned with the name of the club — "Fiat Lux: Berkeley Students In Search of Enlightenment"— brought me to a standstill. I went over to talk with the student, Nicolas Lux Fawzi, managing the desk. (Yes, "Lux" is his middle name.)

"We want to put the motto of the university into action," he said. "We want to learn what other people are interested in — other disciplines, departments, grad, undergrad. We meet to have discussions ... but we also do fun things like going hiking."[3]

Discussions across the disciplines. Field hikes. *Enlightenment.* You cannot keep a good idea down. Encouraged, I left Nicolas Lux Fawzi, whistling a song of the Westering.

Then Shakespeare's Sonnet LXV came to mind:

> ... unless this miracle have might,
> That in black ink my love may still shine bright.

The university would benefit from the naming of a building for Stewart, but *he* does not need it. His black ink, the words of his books, will keep his ideas in our memory.

I turned the corner of old South Hall, headed between the Library and Wheeler Hall; then stopped and took one last look at Lux Fawzi's table:

"Fiat Lux"

Walking west, I realized *that* was the monument: What better memorial for George R. Stewart, or his colleagues in the work, than to pass on the making of light to those who make the future?

After me cometh a builder....

The story of humans is the story of ideas that shine light into dark corners.

— Dr. Jill Tarter, former director, SETI Institute,
and holder of the Bernard M. Oliver Chair
(as quoted on Mike and Denise Okuda's Log)[4]

Chief Sources

Manuscripts and collections of Stewart material

AB   George R. Stewart's unpublished autobiography. A copy is in the George Rippey Stewart Papers BANC MSS CH-13, Series 5, Carton 9, Folders 80–91. ("GRS 1")

GRS   The George Rippey Stewart Papers. In the Bancroft Library, the University of California, Berkeley. The papers are in two collections. The main collection (17+ linear feet of material) is BANC MSS C-H 13. In the Endnotes, I have designated this collection as GRS 1. This collection contains his manuscripts and research notes. It covers the years 1914–1984.

    The George Rippey Stewart Papers: Additions, BANC MSS 70788c, covers the years 1750 to 1984.

    Researchers should be aware that much of the collection is stored off-campus, and must be requested in advance of use. An online request form is found at http://bancroft.berkeley.edu/cgi-bin/storreq.cgi.

    Keys to the collections of Papers are online. The key to the major collection, BANC MSS C-H 13, is located at http://oac.cdlib.org/findaid/ark:/13030/kt9n39r1hp.

    The Key to the additions, 70788c, is located at http://oac.cdlib.org/findaid/ark:/13030/kt7s2027gr.

OH   George R. Stewart's Oral History, *A Little of Myself*. 1972. Susanne B. Riess, Interviewer. Now online: http://www.archive.org/details/alittleofmyself00stewrich.

PC   That part of the Stewart family photograph (and other) collection maintained by Stewart's granddaughter Anna Evenson. Primarily historic family photographs, also includes school annuals, etc.

WS   Stegner, Wallace Earle, The Wallace Earle Stegner Papers. MS 676, Manuscripts Division, Special Collections. University of Utah.

Published and unpublished writings of George R. Stewart

NOTE: These are listed below in the chronological order of writing or publication, not alphabetical order:

GRSD   George R. Stewart's unpublished diary of a 1919 hitchhiking trip. (Original, in Dr. John Stewart's possession, is not paginated.)

BIKE   Journal kept by George R. Stewart during his bicycle trip to Europe.

GRSC   "Color in Science and Poetry," *Scientific Monthly*.

GRSO   *Ordeal by Hunger*

EAST   *East of the Giants*

STORM   *Storm*

NAMES   *Names on the Land*
MAN   *Man: An Autobiography*
FIRE   *Fire*
EA   *Earth Abides*
OATH   *The Year of the Oath*
SR   *Sheep Rock*
40   *U. S. 40*
PICK   *Pickett's Charge*
TRAIL   *The California Trail: An Epic with Many Heroes*
COMM *Committee of Vigilance*
RICH   *Not So Rich As You Think.*
DEPT   *The Department of English.*
CRISIS "The Shakespeare Crisis"
GIVEN *American Given Names*
PLACE *American Place-Names.*
GLOBE *Names on the Globe.*
GIVEN *American Given Names.*

Other sources

AH   Arthur Herman, *How the Scots Invented the Modern World* (New York: Three Rivers Press, 2001).

ALBR   Albright's history of the founding of the national park service.

DICT   Peter Davies, ed., *The American Heritage Dictionary of the English Language* (New York: Dell, 1970).

DB   Duncan A. Bruce, *The Mark of the Scots* (New York: Kensington, 1996).

FISH   Gary Fishgall, *Pieces of Time* (New York: Scribner's, 1993). James Stewart biography.

GP   "It is a Wonderful Life," *Guideposts*, December 2005.

HARV   Miles Harvey, *The Island of Lost Maps* (New York: Random House, 2000).

IM   *In Memoriam* website at the University of California.

JB   James Buchan, *Crowded with Genius — the Scottish Enlightenment* (New York: HarperCollins, 2003).

JE   Interview, discussions, and correspondence with Jill Stewart Evenson.

JS   Interview, discussions, and correspondence with Dr. John (Jack) Stewart.

JM   John McPhee, *Basin and Range* (New York: Farrar, Straus, and Giroux, 1980).

JU   Jenny Uglow, *The Lunar Men* (New York: Farrar, Straus, and Giroux, 2002).

LYON   Correspondence with and papers by Stewart scholar Robert C. Lyon.

RLS   Robert Louis Stevenson, "The Scot Abroad," in *The Silverado Squatters*, ed. James D. Hart (Cambridge, MA: Harvard University Press, 1966).

SHAN   Shankland's biography of Stephen Mather.

THEO   Author's conversations with Theodosia Burton Stewart, in the 1970s and 1980s.

WEIN2 Richard Weingroff's history of the Lincoln Highway http://www.fhwa.dot.gov/infrastructure/lincoln.htm.

WEIN   Weingroff's history of the National Old Trails Road http://www.fhwa.dot.gov/infrastructure/trails.htm.

WILA   Audio recordings made by Stewart Scholar Stephen Williams during his 1986 visit to California. They are now in the Bancroft Library.

Notes

There are citations for quotations or materials from sources other than a chapter's principal references. Wherever possible, I have indicated which collection of the George R. Stewart contains the item cited.

Please note that in citations from Stewart's unpublished autobiography I have adopted his method of pagination. Thus, "1—10" means Chapter 1, page 10.

Used carefully, the internet provides a much greater amount of information than is otherwise available to the independent scholar. So I have used many websites to help with the research on this book, following certain self-imposed rules. I assume, for example, that websites of major universities and libraries contain carefully researched and therefore trustworthy information. I assume the same about sites of individuals of high reputation — like that of Donald B. McIntyre, Distinguished Fellow of the University of Edinburgh, or road historian Dr. Frank Brusca, whose web articles I've cited here. I've used the information on other individuals' sites or "collective" sites like *Wikipedia* for general overviews. In the case of *Wikipedia*, I have usually chosen well-referenced entries. (In the case of some very arcane material, I have not always been able to follow this rule.)

Please note that I have elected to follow the citation example of George R. Stewart and most contemporary scholarly works aimed at a general audience in these ways. I do not use the older "op. cit.," "loc. cit.," but do use "ibid." for convenience; and the notes for all chapters are gathered at the end of the main work. These decisions are done to make the reading of the main text easier and more coherent for readers.

Preface

1. Carlos Ruiz Zafron, *The Shadow of the Wind*, trans., Lucia Graves (New York: Penguin Press, 2001), 8.

PART I. WANDERING TOWARD WISDOM

Chapter 1

1. Thoreau, Henry David, *Walking*, 1862.
2. http://philosopedia.org/index.php/Henry_David_Thoreau.
3. John Muir, *Wild Wool*, 1875.
4. Horace Albright, letter to the National Park Service staff, 1933. The letter is online at http://www.thebackpacker.com/trailtalk/thread/28396,-1.php. It can also be found in Horace Albright, et al., *National Park Service: The Story Behind the Scenery* (Wickenburg, AZ: KC, 1987).
5. The story of *Storm*'s success comes from a conversation with Theodosia Stewart. See also OH, p. 38. Jill Stewart Evenson still has the telegram in her personal collection.
6. "H+E+X=L." AB, 2 —1–2.

Chapter 2

1. For more on the Oyster Club, see John McPhee, *Basin and Range*, pp. 99–100; or DM. Also see Jenny Uglow's fine book, *The Lunar Men*, about an English club of the era.
2. AH, p. 120.

3. JU, p. 82.

4. For more on Bishop Berkeley: http://www.ci.berkeley.ca.us/clerk/charter/history.htm and http://www.utm.edu/research/iep/b/berkeley.htm and http://en.wikipedia.org/wiki/George_Berkeley. His poem is online at: http://math.berkeley.edu/aboutus_viewpoints_berkeley.html.

5. Witherspoon: JB, p. 74. For more on Dr. Witherspoon, see http://etcweb.princeton.edu/CampusWWW/Companion/witherspoon_john.html.

6. RLS, p. 211. Stevenson's book is online, at the University of California's Digital Library: http://sunsite.berkeley.edu/Literature/Stevenson/SilveradoSquatters/1silver4.html.

7. Most of the following Wilson family history comes from Andrew Wilson's unpublished autobiography, which is in the GRS Papers.

8. JS, email to the author.

9. The journal is in the Bancroft. GRS Papers.

10. The letters from GRS Sr. to Ella Wilson Stewart are in GRS. October (date unclear) 1889, December 4, 1889, January 20, 1890.

Chapter 3

1. Willa Cather's "A Gold Slipper" is online at: A Gold Slipper by Willa Cather. See *Sewickley Valley Historical Society: Events and Programs* for a mention of Mary Roberts Rinehart; read one of her books, set partly in Sewickley, at *The Case of Jennie Brice by Mary Roberts Rinehart— Full Text Free Book (Part 3/3)*.

2. Young Jeffers and his family were the Stewarts' friends and neighbors in Sewickley. The Jeffers family moved before young George Jr. was born, so Robinson Jeffers and George R. Stewart Jr. didn't meet in Sewickley. But their literary paths would cross decades later. The Jeffers-Stewart connections were close ones. George R. Stewart's paternal uncle, Robert Wilson, was student, friend, and colleague of the Rev. Dr. William Hamilton Jeffers, Robinson Jeffers's father, at the Western Seminary in Pittsburgh. (Robinson Jeffers was born in the seminary.) Stewart mentions the Jeffers family in the introduction to his grandfather Andrew Wilson's memoirs, in GRS. In a letter to Stewart, dated October 24, 1938, now in the GRS Papers, Jeffers discusses their connections. Their families' homes in Sewickley were only a half-block apart. Robinson Jeffers's connections with Sewickley are described at Robinson Jeffers — Wikipedia, the free encyclopedia. Ironically, both Robinson Jeffers's

brother, Hamilton, and George R. Stewart would wind up working for the University of California — Hamilton Jeffers became an astronomer at the University's Lick Observatory.

3. AB, page 1. (Much of the following is from Stewart's "Autobiography" or his maternal grandfather Andrew Wilson's autobiography, both unpublished.)

4. GP.

5. AB. See especially Chapters 1 and 4.

6. AB, 1— 8-10.

7. AB, 4 — 5-7.

8. AB, 3 —1-10.

9. He was probably not schizophrenic. From what we now know, if Stewart had any disorder it was a mild case of Asperger's Syndrome. People with Asperger's have been described as "brilliant, eccentric, absent-minded, socially inept, and a little awkward physically," all of which could describe George R. Stewart. They often have "a 'different' way of using language," which could explain Stewart's lifelong interest in new ways of using language in his books. "[They] … desire interaction with others but have trouble knowing how to make it work," which could explain why he was a loner who sought the approval of readers and colleagues. So perhaps George R. Stewart had Asperger's Syndrome … or perhaps not. It is just as likely that George R. Stewart was the kind of person who becomes a loner because few people can keep up with the intricate genius of his mind. My thanks to Dr. Carol Edwards, professor at the British Columbia Institute of Technology, who first suggested that GRS may have been a victim of Asperger's. The quotes, from Dr. Freisleben-Cook, are found at: http://www.udel.edu/bkirby/asperger/aswhatisit.html#LOIS.

10. Jones, p. 187.

11. Robert Louis Stevenson, in HARV, p. 39.

12. AB, 3 — 5-6.

13. AB, 6 —1.

Chapter 4

1. AB, 6 — 5.

2. For more about Buddy DeSylva, see the following websites: http://en.wikipedia.org/wiki/Buddy_DeSylva and http://us.imdb.com/name/nm0221865/bio. You can hear snippets of several of DeSylva's songs at http://www.allmusic.com/cg/amg.dll?p=amg&sql=11:odd4vwdva9l4~T3.

3. The "Bridge to Nowhere" is described in articles at: http://www.ci.azusa.ca.us/general/bridgetono.asp, http://en.wikipedia.org/

wiki/Bridge_to_Nowhere_(San_Gabriel_Moun
tains). Visit http://kcet.org/explore-ca/huells/
and click on the "Bridge to Nowhere" on the
adjacent map to see a short documentary about
the bridge.

Chapter 5

1. AB, 7 — 22.
2. Much of the information about the Arts
and Crafts Movement and other information
about Pasadena came from the web, especially:
http://www.usc.edu/dept/architecture/greene-
andgreene/aboutgreenes.html and http://en.
wikipedia.org/wiki/Greene_and_Greene. I am
also indebted to Arts and Crafts scholar/
builder John Lucia for his information about
the movement.
3. AB, 8 — 8.
4. Definitions and the ancient meanings:
DICT, 809 & 810. For more about Proto-
Indo-European, see http://colfa.utsa.edu/
drinka/pie/default.htm and http://en.wiki
pedia.org/wiki/Proto-Indo-Europeans#Ori-
gins.
5. AB, 9 —1. GRS did not remember the
inspirational speaker who defined "educate" for
him, but the list of Pasadena High School
speakers in the 1913 Yearbook indicates it was
Henry Van Dyke.
6. AB 9 —10-11. I have slightly rearranged
the order of the quotes without changing the
meaning.
7. DICT, p. 732.
8. AB, 8 —10.

Chapter 6

1. AB, 11—1.
2. F. Scott Fitzgerald, "Princeton," *College
Humor*, December 1927, pp. 28–29, 130–
31.
3. AB, 11— 8.
4. GRS in the Orphic Order and Whig-
Clio membership PC. For more on the Whigs
and Whig-Clio Society see http://en.wiki
pedia.org/wiki/Covenanter#Engagers_and_Wh
iggamores http://en.wikipedia.org/wiki/Whig
and http://en.wikipedia.org/wiki/American_
Whig-Cliosophic_Society.

Chapter 7

1. GRS, letter from Stewart's mother, dated
February 1, 1917.
2. Letter to Gladys Knowlton.
3. PICK. Also see GRS, letter dated November 8, 1962.
4. OH, 18.
5. GRS, letter from Justin A. Wood, April
22, 1952.

Chapter 8

1. WEIN, http://www.fhwa.dot.gov/in-
frastructure/trails.htm#2.
2. Quote and information about the
Southern California Auto Club signage expedition is from WEIN, http://www.fhwa.dot.
gov/infrastructure/trailsf.htm#6.
3. GRSD.
4. The same month that Stewart headed
west on the early National Old Trails Road,
the "Motor Convoy" left Washington, D.C.,
heading for San Francisco on the Lincoln
Highway. Ike Eisenhower was a member of the
convoy; the deplorable conditions of the roads
convinced him in later years to build the Interstate Highway System. See Davies, *American Road*. Also see WEIN, http://www.fhwa.
dot.gov/infrastructure/convoy.htm, an online
site containing Ike's notes from the convoy.
5. GRS.
6. OH, 255.
7. Photos of the hitchhiking trip to Berkeley are in PC.

Chapter 9. *Fiat Lux*

1. See the following website, http://www.
uri.edu/library/inscriptions/enlighten.html
and note the following quote: "These words
are from Thomas Jefferson's letter to Count Pierre Samuel du Pont de Nemours, dated April
24, 1816 (paragraph 3, sentence 4). (Correspondence between Thomas Jefferson and Pierre
Samuel du Pont de Nemours, 1798–1817. Dumas
Malone, editor. [Boston, 1930, page 186].)"
2. http://www.thebaileyhotel.com/Din-
ing/letter.html.
3. Letter from Margaret Bayard Smith.
Friis, "Visit," p. 30; as cited online by Baron.
4. Helferich, p. 322.
5. The *American Review*, as quoted in,
Helferich, p. 324.
6. NAMES, pp. 347–48.
7. http://www.yosemite.ca.us/john_muir
_writings/the_life_and_letters_of_john_muir/
chapter_6.html.
8. http://www.wilderness.net/index.cfm?
fuse=NWPS&sec=wildView&wname=John%
20Muir.
9. Quote from Le Conte's Journal. Much
of the information about University Summer
Mountaineering Party is also from the Journal.
The Journal is online at the Sierra Club Site:
http://www.sierraclub.org/history/key_figures/
leconte/ramblings.asp.
10. Most of the information about Hubert
Howe Bancroft is from an online exhibit about
Bancroft and the Bancroft Library: http://ban-
croft.berkeley.edu/Exhibits/bancroft/.

Chapter 10

1. DEPT, p. 16.
2. Hart, p. xlviii.
3. From *Treasure Island*. Chapters 13, 14, 22, available online at: http://www.4literature. net/Robert_Louis_Stevenson/Treasure_Island/ or here: http://www.gutenberg.org/etext/120.

Chapter 11

1. BIKE, 5/14/21. Most of the information that follows comes from his journal of the trip, and cards and letters which he sent to his parents every day. In the GRS Papers.
2. BIKE, 6/12/21.
3. BIKE, 6/14/21.
4. GRS, postcard dated 6/17/21. (Note that on the original cards Stewart uses the European style for the dates, putting the day before the month: 17/6/21. For consistency's sake I use the American format.)
5. At the end of the novel, in Chapter 30. See http://www.gutenberg.org/files/421/421-h/421-h.htm.
6. GRS, postcard to mother dated 9/3/21.
7. Ibid., 8/13/21.
8. Ibid., 8/13/21.
9. Ibid., 8/18/21.
10. Ibid., 8/20/21.
11. Ibid., 9/21/21.

Chapter 12

1. OH, p. 23.
2. OH, p 169. Theodosia was always known as "Ted" to family and friends.
3. GRS, letter from Charles Evans Hughes to Nina Burton, dated June 22, 1922.
4. This and the other photos mentioned are in the Anna Evenson PC.
5. GRS: Letter and humorous sketches to Eleanor Clark, dated May 18, 1924.
6. OH, pp. 171–72.
7. Author's conversation with Theodosia Burton Stewart.
8. WILA, as are the following quotes from Ted about the trip.
9. The Lincoln Highway Association's 1916 *Official Road Guide*, quoted in WEIN2. The suggestions for motorists are also from this source.

PART II. A GIFT OF ORDEALS

Chapter 13. "The California Enlightenment"

1. Emmanuel Swedenborg's ideas influenced many people, including Ralph Waldo Emerson, Carl Jung, and Stephen King. Johnny Appleseed was a Swedenborgian. The Stewarts' friend Robert Frost was married in a Swedenborgian ceremony.
2. Bernard Maybeck, *Hillside Building* (Berkeley: Berkeley Hillside Club, 1906); *Homebuilding on Hillsides* (Berkeley: Berkeley Hillside Club, 1907). These booklets (and other Maybeck works) are online at: http://www.oregoncoast.net/maybeckhill.html.
3. The information about the National Park Service is from SHAN and ALBR. See also TWEE. The Steven Tyng Mather papers, in the Bancroft, include more information. I am also very indebted to conversations with Stephen Mather McPherson II, about connections between the University of California and the National Park Service, during my National Park Service years. See Also Carl Russell's "One Hundred Years in Yosemite" for a good overview of the University of California–National Park Service connections, online at: http://www.yosemite.ca.us/library/one_hundred_years_in_yosemite/interpreters.html.
4. SHAN, p. 7.
5. ALBR, p. 16.
6. SHAN, p. 10

Chapter 14

1. DEPT, 24, 29–31.
2. OH, pp. 23–24.
3. GRS, letter from Frances C. Trimble to Stewart, dated August 6, 1948.
4. GRS, MS, "George Rippey Stewart, Teacher," attached to a letter from Robert Fogerty dated November 28, 1977. The comment about the influence of GRS on Creedence Clearwater Revival is included in the letter.
5. WS, letter from Joel Hedgpeth, dated February 27, 1982.
6. JE.
7. GRS, letter from Marion L. Lehnert, dated January 27, 1942.
8. Ibid., letter from Mary Maxwell Hidalgo, dated June 28, 1965.

Chapter 15

1. GRS, letter from Marion LeRoy Burton, dated September 7, 1924.
2. Ibid., letter from Robert Frost to Nina Burton, dated November 12, 1924.
3. Fisher-Smith interview with Wendell Berry. Available online at: http://arts.envirolink.org/interviews_and_conversations/WendellBerry.html.
4. Stewart, "Color in Science and Poetry," *Scientific Monthly*, January, 1930, p. 72.

5. The Instructions are available from many sources. This is from the Monticello website at: http://www.monticello.org/site/jefferson/jeffersons-instructions-to-meriwether-lewis.

Chapter 16

1. JE: interview.
2. DEPT, p. 32.
3. Ibid., p. 33.
4. OH, p. 25.

Chapter 17

1. OH, p. 26.
2. OH, p. 254.
3. Ray Boynton: JE. Boynton was a distinguished artist, with works in the fine arts museums of San Francisco. He did a mural for the Faculty Club at Berkeley. Boynton also did a pencil portrait of Jill Evenson when he was doing field research for *Ordeal by Hunger* with her father. It still hangs on her wall. See IM, Ray Boynton.
4. JE, oral interview.
5. Later research indicated the logs Stewart found were probably not from the Donner camp. Still, his interest in the trail never faded. Son Jack Stewart remembers that, years later, studying the hard granite of Donner Pass, he and his father found the faint rust tracks of wagon wheels.
6. GRSO, p. 269.
7. OH, p. 26.
8. *Ordeal by Hunger*, Foreword, p. 3. (Stewart used a different foreword in a subsequent edition; then returned to this one when the space age began.)
9. The Ed Lu/"GeoS" images are available online at: http://eol.jsc.nasa.gov/ Mission ISS007, roll E, Frame 16687. Although astronaut Ed Lu kindly volunteered to take several images of the Lewis and Clark campsites for educational purposes and although the foreword from *Ordeal by Hunger* was sent up to the ISS with a request to photograph the "GeoS" image, I cannot verify that this image results from the request. On the other hand, if he did take the images to photographically interpret the foreword, thanks to him and NASA.

Chapter 18

1. Letter quoted by Susan Riess, OH, p. 30.
2. JS, oral interview.
3. OH, p. 39.
4. JS, letter in his personal collection. The letter was written to the Hatfields, who appear in *Earth Abides* as Ish's neighbors. Most of the rest of this discussion about family difficulties

comes from the author's oral interviews with Jack and Jill Stewart.
5. THEO, conversation with the author.
6. JE, oral interview.
7. Ibid.
8. JS, oral interview.
9. JE, oral interview.
10. Putting the children's needs second is common in families of the famous, according to Social Psychologist Dr. A.H. Harrison of UC Davis.
11. GRS, letter from Dan Rogers dated July 18, 1934.
12. JS, oral interview.
13. JE, oral interview.

Chapter 19

1. "Writer" defined, DICT, pp. 800–01; "Author" defined, DICT, p. 48.
2. The unpublished novels include "Detective Story," "If," and "The Dry Country." "The Shakespeare Crisis" was written decades later.
3. EAST, p. 123.
4. The information about the film version of *East of the Giants* is from Robert C. Lyon.
5. From an interview with Bill Cassady, son of Ed and current resident of the Dutch Flat cabin. Bill Cassady was kind enough to show me around the place, to point out where Stewart's "Scholar's Tent" had been, and to tell me the history of the family's relationships with GRS.

PART III. "THE MAN WHO NAMED THE STORMS"

Chapter 20

1. OH, p. 135.
2. Ibid.
3. STORM, "Introduction" to the second edition, pp. xiii.
4. WILA: interview with Theodosia Stewart, 1986, pp. 223–26.
5. There's an interesting story about the writing of *Storm*. According to an article in *American Bungalow*, Stewart did some of the writing while staying in a cottage owned by Dr. Paul Taylor and Dorothea Lange. But when I asked Jack and Jill Stewart about this, they tended to discount it. It may have a kernel of truth to it, in the sense that GRS may have spent a weekend or two house-sitting there while working on the novel. He did know Taylor quite well, and the cottage is an arts and crafts gem, a good place to write. See Ribo-

vich, *American Bungalow*, No. 56, p. 39. Jill
Stewart Evenson's and Jack Stewart's comments
are from conversations with this author.
    6. STORM, p. 12.
    7. OH, n. p. See also OH, pp. 139–52.
    8. STORM, p. 16.
    9. Always one to give credit where it's due,
Stewart acknowledged in *Storm*'s introduction
that he borrowed the idea from pioneering meteorologist Sir Napier Shaw.
    10. Information about Lawrence, Seaborg,
the discovery of plutonium, and the nuclear
age can be found at the following: http://issw
prod.lbl.gov/Seaborg/start.asp http://www.lbl.
gov/Science-Articles/Research-Review/Maga-
zine/1981/. "Lawrence and his Laboratory,"
originally printed in *LBL Magazine*, fall 1981.
Stephen I. Schwartz, *Atomic Audit: The Costs
and Consequences of U.S. Nuclear Weapons Since
1940* (Washington, D.C.: Brookings Institu-
tion Press, 1998). Abstracted online at: http://
www.brook.edu/fp/projects/nucwcost/sites.htm.
    11. The Bohemian Club, the University,
and the Bomb. See Sides, p. 91.
    12. Ernest Callenbach, foreword to the
California Legacy edition of George R. Stewart's *Storm*, p. viii.

Chapter 21

    1. THEO. That the Steinbecks were the
ones waving the paper: from a conversation
with one of the extended Stewart family, Barney Phair. The Stewarts knew the Steinbecks,
and John Steinbeck sometimes lived in the
New York area, so the story may well be true.
    2. JS.
    3. OH, pp. 159–61, 252.
    4. The information about Vic Moitoret
comes from Robert Lyon. Lyon was kind
enough to send letters and other materials de-
tailing the information, including some items
published by Moitoret on his small press when
he lived in Silver City, New Mexico. See letter
from Vic Moitoret to Robert Lyon, dated
March 4, 1989, in Lyon's collection.
    5. WS, letter from GRS to WS, dated
April 22, 1945.

Chapter 22

    1. OH.
    2. GRSN, p. 7.
    3. California place naming history: Chap-
ter XXXIX, "Flavor of California." NAMES,
pp. 346–52.
    4. The letters are in GRS. See bibliogra-
phy for details.
    5. Annie Laurie Williams' comment, for-
warded to the author by JS Evenson.

    6. OH, p. 232.
    7. GRS, letter dated April 18, 1945.

Chapter 23

    1. WS, letter from Theodosia (Ted) Stew-
art to Mary Stegner. Undated; based on internal references, it was probably written in the
spring of 1945.
    2. GRS, letter dated May 7, 1945.
    3. Stewart told me this, but did not spec-
ify the date. I have been unable to discover
which writers' conference it might have been,
or the exact date; but from known dates of
their friendship, this seems to be about the
right time for their meeting. It may have been
connected with Princeton's Lewis Center for
the Arts.
    4. JS.
    5. PC, photo of Jack and Jill Stewart in
Greensboro, Vermont, with Wallace and Mary
Stegner in the background.
    6. JS.
    7. Email correspondence from Page Steg-
ner to the author.
    8. JS.
    9. Page Stegner email correspondence.
    10. Letter from Wallace Stegner to GRS.
    11. Most of the following is from Stegner's
Wolf Willow. Stegner's autobiographical novel,
The Big Rock Candy Mountain, also discusses
(and dramatizes) his frontier childhood.
    12. Dick Banford, whose house neighbors
Stegner's boyhood home, remembers older residents telling him the Stegner place had so
many books that it became the unofficial lend-
ing library for the town.

Chapter 24

    1. The poem is from a letter to this author.
    2. JS.
    3. MAN, p. 297.
    4. Neal Gabler, *Walt Disney: the Triumph
of the American Imagination* (New York: Vintage, 2007), pp. 481–89.
    6. Letter from Walt Disney to GRS.
    7. For more about Anthony Boucher, see
Wikipedia: http://en.wikipedia.org/wiki/An-
thony_Boucher.
    8. "The Ghost Town Mortuary" script:
GRS. Apparently, no recording of the episode
exists.
    9. Beaty, *Lookout Wife*, p. 67. In his own
OH, Stewart says nothing about being lost. A
good hillman, he always knew exactly where
he was.
    10. OH, pp. 162–63.
    11. Ibid., p. 161.
    12. Ibid.

13. FIRE, pp. 62–63.
14. Ibid., p. 336.
15. GRS, Josephine Miles's note to George Stewart, 1948.

Chapter 25

1. During his time as chair, Stewart recommended that the Bancroft Library establish a "Regional Oral History Office" to collect oral interviews like those done decades earlier by Hubert Howe Bancroft. The Bancroft eventually did so; one of its projects would be George R. Stewart's oral history, *A Little of Myself.*
2. Conversation with Jill Stewart Evenson. She also offered one of the best evaluations of EA: "It's a very moving book."
3. EA, p. 41.
4. Ibid., p. 373.
5. Philip Aaberg: from conversations with this author. The influence of *Earth Abides* on Jimi Hendrix is from Egan, *Jimi Hendrix and the Making of* "Are You Experienced?" (Chicago: Chicago Review Press, 2002), p. 95.
6. Competition from video chains forced Ligda to close his video store in 1995. He sold his video collection to pay the back rent on the building. Ligda died in 2008.
7. S. M. Stirling, *The Sunrise Lands* (New York: New American Library, a division of Penguin Group, 2008), p. 234.
8. Kim Stanley Robinson, email to the author.
9. Stephen King, *Danse Macabre* (New York: Gallery, a division of Simon and Schuster, 2010), pp. 424–25.
10. Keith Ferrell, email to the author.
11. Author's transcription of a telephone conversation with Richard Brenneman.
12. James Sallis's column from the *Boston Globe* about *Earth Abides.*

PART IV. "OF FREEDOM AND FRIENDSHIP"

Chapter 26. *Fiat Nox?*

1. OATH, p. 144.
2. Ibid., p. 146.
3. OH, p. 187.
4. Carl Sandburg to GRS. "Go to it....," Dr. Chauncey Leake to GRS. "We, the resident professors...," signed by the academics — including Einstein and von Neumann — of the Princeton Institute for Advanced Studies, to GRS. See bibliography for details.
5. GRS.
6. Ibid.

7. Ibid. Letter from Raymond T. Birge dated June 22, 1968. Birge, Chairman of the Physics Department from 1932 until 1955, he hired Ernest O. Lawrence and J. Robert Oppenheimer; Harold Urey was his student.
8. OATH, p. 94.
9. GRS.

Chapter 27

1. GLOBE, p. 400.
2. OH, p. 176.
3. DICT, p. 141. "College" and "colleague" derive from the Latin *Collega.*
4. WILA.
5. Edward Abbey, *Desert Solitaire* (New York: Random House, 1968), pp. 245–46.
6. GRS. See also IM, Josephine Miles; and OH, pp. 17, 122.
7. JS.
8. Ibid.
9. Wilson, p. 31.
10. JS.
11. THEO, conversation with the author. Also see OH, p. 170.
12. SR, p. 283
13. The discussion of the trip to Nevada comes from OH, pp. 274–81.
14. Interview with Dr. Jeffrey Gritzner.
15. Parker Trask, IM, p. 87.
16. JS.
17. SR, p. 285.
18. Ibid., p. 33.
19. OH, p. 198.
20. Inspired by the novel, Stegner and his wife, Mary, went camping at "Sheep Rock." (Lage, Stegner OH, ROHO Bancroft Library.)
21. OH, p. 190.
22. SR, various pages. The poem was printed by Tim Gorelangton, then of the University of Nevada, Reno, in a limited edition of 50 copies.
23. OH, p. 190.
24. SR, p. 264.
25. Ibid., p. 257.
26. Ibid., pp. 283–84.
27. WILA, interview with Ken Carpenter.
28. GRS, essay by Josephine Miles, dated May 21, 1962.
29. SR, p. 279.
30. Ibid., p. 256.
31. Ibid., p. 284.

Chapter 28

1. OH, p. 194.
2. WS, letter dated February 12, 1947.
3. Ibid., letter dated Jan. 31, 1949.
4. Ibid., letter dated May 12, 1951.
5. *U.S. 40*, p. 28.

6. William Least Heat-Moon, *Blue Highways: A Journey Into America* (Boston: Atlantic Monthly Press/Little, Brown, 1982). Influence of GRS on Least Heat Moon: Conversation and correspondence with the author.

7. Thomas Vale and Geraldine Vale, *U.S. 40 Today: Thirty Years of Landscape Change in America* (Madison: University of Wisconsin Press, 1983).

8. Brusca's communication with the author.

9. Hartmut Bitomsky, communication with the author.

10. *Cars.* Directed by John Lasseter, Joe Ranft (Burbank, CA: Walt Disney Productions, 2006). McMurtry, *Roads*, 2000. *Amiland*, Schewe and Pokorny, 2008.

11. William Least Heat-Moon, *Roads to Quoz: An American Mosey* (Boston: Little, Brown, 2008), p. 9.

12. Ibid., pp. 352–74.

13. Ibid., p. 329.

Chapter 29

1. GRS.

2. This is part of my story, too: The offending question had been red-lined out of the practice version of the test given us by our high school English teacher. See also: http://sfgate.com/cgi-bin/article.cgi?f=/c/a/2002/06/09/MNCF2.DTL.

3. GRS.

4. PICK, p. xii.

5. OH, p. 203.

6. Ibid., p. 214.

PART V. "EMERITUS"

Chapter 30

1. GRS, letter dated June 17, 1962.

2. TRAIL, p. 260.

3. Ibid., p. 182.

4. Ibid., p. 188. Trubody lived into the 20th century, long enough to tell stories of the westering to Charlie Camp.

5. COMM, p. 318.

6. RICH, pp. 216–17. See Chapter "Waste Without Weight" in RICH.

Chapter 31

1. JE. Obituary for Theodosia Burton Stewart.

2. Baiba Strads, email to the author.

3. OH, p. 222.

4. GRS. My copy comes courtesy of LYON.

5. OH, p. 66.

6. Ibid., p. 175.

7. Wheat, Carl I., article in the *Pacific Historical Review* XVIII (1949): pp. 67–69. Excerpts are online at: http://www.phoenixmasonry.org/masonicmuseum/fraternalism/e_clampus_vitus.htm and http://en.wikipedia.org/wiki/E_Clampus_Vitus.

8. OH, p. 218.

9. From a manuscript collection in the Bancroft Library; The Club records, BANC MSS 76/75 c. The quotation is also online at: http://content.cdlib.org/view?docId=tf6199n87c&chunk.id=bioghist-1.3.4&query=The%20Club&brand=oac. See also OH, pp. 217–22.

10. Stewart, "The Four Letter Words." GRS.

11. Sloss, "Foreword," *Only On Monday*, p. xi.

12. See Sides, "In Darkest Bohemia." In Sides, *Americana*. I am also indebted to independent scholar Kerry Richardson, who studies the Bohemian Club. A phone conversation with Richardson was one source for this chapter.

13. JS.

14. DEPT, "Foreword."

15. Ibid., p. 37.

16. Ibid., p. 47.

17. Ibid., p. 54.

18. OH, p. 300.

Chapter 32

1. The information about Rene Weaver comes from our conversations, and the web: http://www.bbhgallery.com/Weaver_Rene_Tuolumne_River.htm (*Bodega Bay Heritage Gallery*) and http://www.askart.com/AskART/artists/search/Search_Repeat.aspx?searchtype=IMAGES&artist=7475 (*Ask Art: The Artist's Bluebook*).

2. Wilder Bentley's son, Wilder Bentley the younger, provided much of this information, sent in manuscript. See also Turnage, "Introduction" to the 2006 edition of *Adam's Sierra Nevada: The John Muir Trail*, pp. xiii–xvi. And http://www.berkeleyheritage.com/berkeley_landmarks/bentley_house.html. The Wilder Bentley Papers are in the William Clark Andrews Memorial Library at the University of California at Los Angeles. Finding Aid is located at http://findaid.oac.cdlib.org/findaid/ark:/13030/tf9b69p2cw.

3. For more about Chiura Obata, see the following: Ross and Smith-Griswold, Nature Art with Chiura Obata. Also see IM, Chiura Obata. And http://obata.wilderness.net/. The Ken Burns series on the national parks also showcases Obata.

4. Letter to this author from H. Wilder Bentley the Younger.

5. Bancroft Phonotape 1655 C.

6. Wallace Stegner, "George R. Stewart and the American Land," in *Where the Bluebird Sings to the Lemonade Springs* (New York: Penguin, 1992).

Chapter 33

1. Most of the following discussion comes from online articles at: http://bancroft.berkeley.edu/FSM/, http://www.sfgate.com/campus/, http://www.fsm-a.org/, http://www.writing.upenn.edu/~afilreis/50s/berkeley.html. An excerpt from David Burner's *Making Peace with the Sixties* can be accessed at: http://berkeleypubliclibrary.org/system/Chapter9.html. Berkeley Public Library's online history of the Free Speech Movement. http://content.cdlib.org/xtf/view?docId=kt687004sg&doc.view=frames&chunk.id=d0e804&toc.depth=1&toc.id=d0e353. This is the University of California Libraries' history of the Free Speech Movement.

2. Part of Mario Savio's speech, recorded in many places. See http://www.fsm-a.org/stacks/mario/mario_speech.html for a more complete version. His speech has become so iconic that it has been used in at least one work of literature: The episode of the new *Battlestar Galactica* entitled "Lay Down Your Burdens, Part 2."

3. Jon Carroll's obituary for Mario Savio, from the November 8, 1996, *San Francisco Chronicle* (date is uncertain). Available online at: http://web.archive.org/web/20000815065929/http://www.physics.sfsu.edu/savio-obit.html#JON.

4. Mario Savio, at: http://www.fsm-a.org/stacks/mario/savio_studrebel.htm (quoted with the permission of his widow, Lynne Hollander).

5. OH, p. 54.

6. GRS, letter dated April 23, 1970.

7. Ibid., letter from Dr. James Hart, dated February 8, 1969.

8. *New York Times*, February 21, 1967. There are several stories, beginning on the front page, and continuing on pp. 32–33.

9. The Bolton Memo is online at http://www.cia-on-campus.org/witanek.html.

10. Rosenfeld, "Trouble on Campus." Online at: http://www.sfgate.com/campus/. For more information, see McCartney, pp. 61–70.

11. OH, p. 248.

12. CRISIS, p. 142.

13. Ibid., p. 145.

14. Ibid., p. 216.

15. Ibid., pp. 275–76.

Chapter 34

1. PLACE, p. xi. The definitions are from the dictionary.

2. GIVEN, p. 42.

3. GLOBE, p. 86.

4. Ibid., p. 391.

5. Ibid., pp. 393–94

6. Ibid., p. 400.

PART VI. "OPUS PERFECI"

Chapter 35

1. GRS, 70/88c (carton 1:38 Personal papers 1974).

2. OH, p. 215; JS.

3. JS.

Chapter 36

1. The letter from Stegner is in Jack Stewart's personal collection; a copy is in GRS.

2. EA, p. 373

3. McMurtry, *Roads*, pp. 81–82.

4. Stegner, "George R. Stewart and the American Land," p. 155.

5. Conversation with the author.

6. Williams, "The Year of the Pilgrim." Unpublished manuscript emailed to the author.

7. Dr. James D. Burke, "Effect of 'Storm' on a Teenager." Paper delivered in *The Heritage of George R. Stewart* Symposium at CONTACT 2005. NASA–Ames Research Center, California. (This and the following talks were videotaped and are in the author's possession.)

8. Dr. John H. Stewart, "George R. Stewart and Science: The Perspective of a Scientist, His Son," George R. Stewart Symposium, CONTACT 2005.

9. Aaberg, Philip, "A Soundtrack for Earth Abides," Paper and performance, George R. Stewart Symposium, CONTACT 2005.

Chapter 37

1. Correspondence with Tim Tokaryk.

2. *Eclectic*, DICT, p. 225.

3. "Finding the Place," and "Letter, Much Too Late," in *Where the Bluebird Sings to the Lemonade Spring*, pp. 30–32.

4. Stegner, "The Sense of Place," in *Where the Bluebird Sings to the Lemonade Springs*, p. 205.

5. See the quote at the following website:

http://eol.jsc.nasa.gov/, the "Gateway to Astronaut Photography of Earth."

6. James R. Hansen, *First Man: The Life of Neil Armstrong* (New York: Simon & Schuster, 2005), p. 564.

7. John Young's quote is published in Albert H. Harrison, *Spacefaring: The Human Dimension* (Berkeley: University of Berkeley Press, 2002), p. 114.

8. SR, pp. 263–64.

Epilogue

1. Wendell Berry, *Jayber Crow* (Washington, D.C.: Counterpoint, 2000), p. 133.

2. The definitions are from DICT, pp. 808, 813.

3. Nicolas Lux Fawzi, conversation with the author.

4. The end quote by Dr. Jill Tarter is published on the Mike and Denise Log http://web.me.com/michaelokuda/michael_okuda/Blog/Entries/2010/6/5_SYMPHONY_OF_SCIENCE.html. The quote is from Dr. Tarter's talk at TED accepting the TED prize for 2009. The Okudas modified it somewhat for their log.

Bibliography

Manuscripts, Papers, and Collections of Papers

Aaberg, Phillip. "Writing a Soundtrack for *Earth Abides*." Unpublished paper presented at the George R. Stewart Symposium of CONTACT 2005.

Burke, James D. "The Influence of 'Storm' on a Teenager." Unpublished paper presented at the George R. Stewart Symposium of CONTACT 2005.

The Club records, BANC MSS 76/75 © The Bancroft Library, University of California, Berkeley.

Stegner, Page. Collection of materials relating to the life and work of Wallace Earle Stegner and Page Stegner. Personal collection.

Stegner, Wallace Earle. *The Wallace Earle Stegner Papers*. MS 676, Manuscripts Division, Special Collections. University of Utah Marriott Library, Salt Lake City, UT, 84112.

Stewart, George Rippey. *George Rippey Stewart Papers*. BANC MSS C-H 13. The Bancroft Library, University of California, Berkeley. The main collection (17+ linear feet of material). This collection, which covers the years 1914–1984, contains his manuscripts and research notes and correspondence. In the Bancroft Library, University of California, Berkeley. A finding aid is online at http://oac.cdlib.org/findaid/ark:/13030/kt9n39r1hp.

Stewart, George Rippey. *George Rippey Stewart Papers*: *Additions*. BANC MSS 70788c. The Bancroft Library, University of California, Berkeley. This covers the years 1750–1984. A finding aid to the *Additions* is online at: http://oac.cdlib.org/findaid/ark:/13030/kt7s 2027gr. (Note that most of the GRS materials are stored off-campus and must be requested in advance of use through the Bancroft Library's website.)

Stewart, George Rippey. "George R. Stewart Trail Dedication." Bancroft Phonotape 1655 C. The Bancroft Library, University of California, Berkeley.

Stewart, G. R., et al. "Parker Davies Trask, Engineering: Berkeley." *In Memoriam*, 1963. Berkeley, the University of California Senate, 1963.

Stewart, John H. "George R. Stewart and Science: The Perspective of a Scientist, His Son." Unpublished paper presented in the George R. Stewart Symposium at CONTACT 2005.

Williams, Stephen, Phonotape 1957 C [Interviews concerning George R. Stewart] [phonotape].

Oral Histories

Stegner, Wallace. *The Artist as Environmental Advocate*. Typescript of an interview conducted by Ann Lage. With an "Introduction" by Ansel Adams. Regional Oral History Office, the Bancroft Library, University of California, Berkeley, 1982. Copyright 1983 by the Regents of the University of California and the Sierra Club.

Stewart, George R. (1895–) Author, *A Little of Myself,* 1972, vii, 319 p. BANC MSS 73/155. Typescript of an oral history. Interviewed 1971, 1972 by Suzanne B. Riess. Introduction by James D. Hart, Professor of English, University of California, Berkeley. Regional Oral History Office, the Bancroft Library, University of California, Berkeley, 1972. (Available online at: http://www.archive.org/details/alittleofmyself00stewrich.)

Individual Manuscript Items

Boucher, Anthony, and Dennis Green. *The Ghost Town Mortuary.* Undated. BANC MSS 70/88c. The Bancroft Library, University of California, Berkeley.

Stewart, George Rippey. Handwritten note about illness. 70/88c carton 1:38 Personal papers 1974.

_____. "The Four-Letter Words." Undated. BANC MSS C-H 13. The Bancroft Library, University of California, Berkeley.

_____. "In a democratic society." BANC MSS C-H 13. The Bancroft Library, University of California, Berkeley.

_____. "On University Government." BANC MSS C-H 13. The Bancroft Library, University of California, Berkeley.

_____. "Sex and the Sexagenarian." The collection of Robert Lyon, Stewart scholar.

_____. "The Shakespeare Crisis," unpublished ms. BANC MSS C-H 13. Undated. The Bancroft Library, University of California, Berkeley.

_____. Untitled autobiography. BANC MSS C-H 13. The Bancroft Library, University of California, Berkeley.

_____. Untitled journal of 1919 hitchhiking trip. In the collection of John H. Stewart.

_____. Untitled journal of 1921 European bicycle trip. In the collection of John H. Stewart.

Stewart, John H. *Pages from Civil War Journal.* BANC MSS 70/88c. The Bancroft Library, University of California, Berkeley.

Wilson, Andrew. *Memoirs* (undated). BANC MSS 70/88c. The Bancroft Library, University of California, Berkeley.

Letters

Birge, Raymond T. Letter dated June 22, 1968. BANC MSS C-H 13. The Bancroft Library, University of California, Berkeley.

Burrill, Meredith F. Letter dated September 6, 1945. BANC MSS C-H 13. The Bancroft Library, University of California, Berkeley.

Burton, Marion Leroy. Letter to George R. Stewart, dated September 7, 1924. BANC MSS C-H 13. The Bancroft Library, University of California, Berkeley.

Einstein, Albert, Robert Oppenheimer, John von Neumann, et al. Letter regarding *The Year of the Oath,* 1950. Princeton Institute for Advanced Studies, Princeton University.

Fogerty, Robert. Letter with attached manuscript, April 29, 1978. BANC MSS 70/88c. The Bancroft Library, University of California, Berkeley.

Frost, Robert. Letter to Nina Burton, dated November 12, 1924. BANC MSS 70/88c. The Bancroft Library, University of California, Berkeley.

Hart, James. Letter dated February 8, 1969. BANC MSS C-H 13. The Bancroft Library, University of California, Berkeley.

Hedgpeth, Joel. Letter dated June 17, 1962. BANC MSS C-H 13. The Bancroft Library, University of California, Berkeley.

_____. Letter dated February 27, 1982. Stegner, Wallace Earle, Papers. Dates: 1935–2004 (inclusive). Collection Number: UU_Ms0676. J. Willard Marriott Library, University of Utah, Special Collections. Salt Lake City, Utah.

Hidalgo, Mary Maxwell. Letter dated June 28, 1965. BANC 70/88c. The Bancroft Library, University of California, Berkeley.

Holstrom, J.D., Chief of Police, Berkeley. Letter dated July 13, 1955. BANC MSS 70/88c. The Bancroft Library, University of California, Berkeley.

Hughes, Charles Evans. Letter to Nina Burton, June 22, 1922. BANC MSS 70/88c. The Bancroft Library, University of California, Berkeley.

Jeffers, Robinson. Letter dated October 24, 1938. BANC MSS 70/88c. The Bancroft Library, University of California, Berkeley.

Leake, Chauncey. Several letters, dated from 1950–1968. BANC MSS 70/88c. The Bancroft Library, University of California, Berkeley.

Lehnert, Marion L. Letter dated January 27, 1942. BANC MSS C-H 13. The Bancroft Library, University of California, Berkeley.

Marcus, H. Stanley. Letter dated July 30, 1945. BANC MSS C-H 13. The Bancroft Library, University of California, Berkeley.

Mencken, Henry Louis. Several letters, dated from 1941–1948. BANC MSS 70/88c. The Bancroft Library, University of California, Berkeley.

Miles, Josephine. Note to George Stewart, 1948. BANC MSS C-H 13. The Bancroft Library, University of California, Berkeley.

_____. Essay dated May 21, 1962. BANC MSS 70/88c. The Bancroft Library, University of California, Berkeley.

_____, and George Rippey Stewart. Poems: "'Seventy' is hard to rhyme…. 'Someone has blundered.'" Undated, although it must be 1965, Stewart's 70th birthday year. BANC MSS 70/88c. The Bancroft Library, University of California, Berkeley.

Neylan, John Francis. Letter dated 1950. BANC MSS C-H 13. The Bancroft Library, University of California, Berkeley.

Rogers, Dan. Letter dated July 18, 1934. BANC 70/88c. The Bancroft Library, University of California, Berkeley.

Sandburg, Carl. Letter dated January 8, 1951. BANC MSS 70/88c. The Bancroft Library, University of California, Berkeley.

Shapley, Harlow. Letter dated October 12, 1950. BANC MSS C-H 13. The Bancroft Library, University of California, Berkeley.

Stegner, Wallace. Several letters to George R. Stewart, dated April 18, 1945–January 31, 1949. BANC MSS 70/88c. The Bancroft Library, University of California, Berkeley.

Stegner, Wallace. Undated letter in the John H. Stewart Collection.

Stewart, Ella Wilson. Letter to George R. Stewart, Jr., dated February 1, 1917. BANC MSS 70/88c. The Bancroft Library, University of California, Berkeley.

Stewart, George Rippey, Jr. Letter to Gladys Knowlton, dated November 6, 1917. BANC MSS C-H 13. The Bancroft Library, University of California, Berkeley.

_____. Several postcards and one letter to his parents, written during his 1921 bicycle trip, June 17, 1921–September 21, 1921. BANC MSS C-H 13. The Bancroft Library, University of California, Berkeley.

_____. Letter dated April 22, 1945. Stegner, Wallace Earle, Papers. Dates: 1935–2004 (inclusive). Collection Number: UU_Ms0676. J. Willard Marriott Library, University of Utah, Special Collections. Salt Lake City, Utah.

_____. Letter to Mr. Stern, dated November 8, 1962. BANC MSS C-H 13. The Bancroft Library, University of California, Berkeley.

Stewart, George Rippey, Sr. Letters to Ella Wilson Stewart, dated October (exact date unclear) 1889, December 4, 1889, January 20, 1890. BANC MSS 70/88c. The Bancroft Library, University of California, Berkeley.

Stewart, Theodosia Burton. Letter to Mary Stegner, undated; based on internal references, it was likely written in the spring of 1945. Stegner, Wallace Earle, Papers. Dates: 1935–2004 (inclusive). Collection Number: UU_Ms0676. J. Willard Marriott Library, University of Utah, Special Collections. Salt Lake City, Utah.

Trimble, Frances C. Letter dated August 6, 1948. BANC MSS C-H 13. The Bancroft Library, University of California, Berkeley.

Wilson, Allen. Letter and humorous sketches to Eleanor Clark, dated May 18, 1924. BANC MSS 70/88c. The Bancroft Library, University of California, Berkeley.

Winchester, John. Letter dated April, 22, 1953. BANC 70/88c. The Bancroft Library, University of California, Berkeley.

Wood, Justin A. Letter dated April 22, 1952. BANC 70/88c. The Bancroft Library, University of California, Berkeley.

Books by George R. Stewart

Fiction

Stewart, George R. *Doctor's Oral*. New York: Random House, 1939.

_____. *Earth Abides*. New York: Random House, 1949.

_____. *East of the Giants*. New York: Henry Holt, 1938.

_____. *Fire*. New York: Random House, 1948.

_____. *Man: An Autobiography*. New York: Random House, 1946.

_____. *Sheep Rock*. New York: Random House, 1951.

_____. *Storm*. Berkeley: Heyday, 2003.

_____. *The Years of the City*. Boston: Houghton Mifflin, 1955.

Non-Fiction

_____. *American Given Names*. New York: Oxford University Press, 1979.

_____. *American Place-names: A Concise and Selective Dictionary*. New York: Oxford University Press, 1970.

_____. *American Ways of Life*. Garden City, N.Y.: Doubleday, 1954.

_____. *Bret Harte, Argonaut and Exile*. Boston: Houghton Mifflin, 1931.

_____. *The California Trail, an Epic With Many Heroes*. New York: McGraw Hill, 1962.

_____. *Committee of Vigilance; Revolution in San Francisco, 1851*. Boston: Houghton Mifflin, 1964.

_____. *The Department of English of the University of California on the Berkeley Campus*. Berkeley: The University of California, 1968. Designed and Printed by Lawton and Alfred Kennedy. The Bancroft Library, University of California, Berkeley. BANC MSS C-H 13, Oversize Drawer A, Folder 1.

_____. *Donner Pass and Those Who Crossed It*. San Francisco: California Historical Society, 1960.

_____. *English Composition: A Laboratory Course*. New York, Henry Holt, 1936.

_____. *Good Lives*. Boston: Houghton Mifflin, 1967.

_____. *John Phoenix, Esq., the Veritable Squibob: A Life of George H. Derby, U.S.A.* New York: Henry Holt, 1937.

_____. *Man: An Autobiography*. York: Random House, 1946.

_____. *N.A. 1: The North-South Continental Highway*. Boston: Houghton Mifflin, 1947.

_____. *Names on the Globe*. New York: Oxford University Press, 1975.

_____. *Names on the Land*. New York: Random House, 1945.

_____. *Names on the Land* (3d. edition, revised and enlarged). Boston: Houghton Mifflin, 1967.

_____. *Not So Rich as You Think*. New York: Houghton-Mifflin, 1968.

_____. *Ordeal by Hunger: The Story of the Donner Party*. New York: Henry Holt, 1936.

_____. *Pickett's Charge: A Microhistory of the Final Attack at Gettysburg, July 3, 1863*. Boston: Houghton Mifflin, 1959.

_____. "The Shakespeare Crisis." Unpublished MS. In the George Rippey Stewart Papers, at the Bancroft Library. BANC MSS C-H 13.

_____. "Stevenson in California. A Critical Study." Master's thesis, University of California, Berkeley, 1921.

_____. *Take Your Bible in One Hand: The Life of William Henry Thomes.* San Francisco: Colt Press, 1939.

_____. *To California by Covered Wagon.* New York: Random House, 1954.

_____. *U.S. 40.* Boston: Houghton Mifflin, 1953.

_____. *The Year of the Oath: The Fight for Academic Freedom at the University of California,* by George R. Stewart, in collaboration with Other Professors at the University of California. Garden City, NY: Doubleday, 1950.

Articles and Essays by George R. Stewart

_____. "Color in Science and Poetry," *The Scientific Monthly,* January 1930.

_____. "George R. Stewart: *Author.*" In *There Was Light: Autobiography of a University: Berkeley, 1868–1968,* edited by Irving Stone. Garden City, NY: Doubleday, 1970.

_____. "The United States Army Ambulance Service," *The Princeton Pictorial Review.* December, 1918.

Books by Other Authors

Abbey, Edward. *Desert Solitaire: A Season in the Wilderness.* New York: Simon & Schuster, 1968.

Albright, Horace. *The Birth of the National Park Service: The Founding Years, 1913–33.* Salt Lake City: Howe Brothers, 1985.

Alvarez, Walter, Ann D. Kilmer, Richard A. Muller, and Martin Trow. *The Idea of a Community of Scholars: Essays Honoring the Centennial of the Faculty Club of the University of California at Berkeley.* Edited by John E. Coons. Berkeley: The Faculty Club, 2002.

Badè, William Frederic (1871–1936). The life and letters of John Muir. Boston and New York: Houghton Mifflin Company, 1924. Online at: http://www.sierraclub.org/john_muir_exhibit/frameindex.html?http://www.sierraclub.org/john_muir_exhibit/life/life_and_letters/chapter_10.html.

Beahm, George. *Stephen King from A to Z: An Encyclopedia of his Life and Work.* Kansas City, MO: Andrews McMeel, 1998.

Beaty, Jeanne Kellar. *Lookout Wife.* New York: Random House, 1953.

Benson, Jackson J. *Wallace Stegner: His Life and Work.* New York: Viking, 1996.

Berry, Wendell. *Jayber Crow.* Berkeley: Counterpoint, 2000.

Brookes, Tim. *"A Hell of a Place to Lose a Cow"—An American Hitchhiking Odyssey.* Washington, D.C.: Adventure Press of the National Geographic Society, 2000.

Brooks, Phyllis. *Art at the Club.* Berkeley: The Faculty Club, 2003.

Bruce, Duncan A. *The Mark of the Scots.* Secaucus, N.J.: Birch Lane, 1996.

Buchan, James. *Crowded with Genius: The Scottish Enlightenment.* New York: HarperCollins, 2003.

Caldwell, John. *George R. Stewart.* Number 46 in the *Western Writers Series.* Boise: Boise State University, 1981.

_____. "George R. Stewart, Jr.: A Checklist." *Bulletin of Bibliography.* Vol. 36, No. 2, April–June, 1979.

Callenbach, Ernest. "Foreword," to the *California Legacy* edition of George R. Stewart's *Storm.* Berkeley: Heyday, 2003.

Doig, Ivan. *English Creek.* New York, Athenaeum, 1989.

Egan, Sean. *Jimi Hendrix and the Making of Are You Experienced.* Chicago: Chicago Review Press, 2002.

Fishgall, Gary. *Pieces of Time: The Life of James Stewart*. New York: Scribner, 1997.

Freudenheim, Leslie M. *Building with Nature: Inspiration for the Arts and Crafts Home*. Layton, UT: Gibbs Smith, 2005.

Gabler, Neal. *Walt Disney: The Triumph of the American Imagination*. New York: Vintage, 2007.

Garfield, Simon. *Mauve*. London: Faber and Faber, 2000.

Goines, David Lance. *The Free Speech Movement: Coming of Age in the 1960s*. Berkeley: Ten Speed Press, 1993. Also available online at: http://content.cdlib.org/xtf/view?docId=kt 687004sg&brand=calisphere&doc.view=entire_text. Revised by the author for electronic publishing, 1993.

Hansen, James R. *First Man: The Life of Neil Armstrong*. New York: Simon & Schuster, 2005.

Harrison, Albert H. *Spacefaring: The Human Dimension*. Berkeley: University of California Press, 2002.

Harvey, Miles. *The Island of Lost Maps*. New York: Random House, 2000.

Helferich, Gerard. *Humboldt's Cosmos*. New York: Gotham, 2004.

Herman, Arthur. *How the Scots Invented the Modern World*. New York: Three Rivers Press, 2001.

King, Stephen. *Danse Macabre*. New York: Gallery Books, 2010.

Least Heat Moon, William. *Blue Highways: A Journey into America*. Boston: Little, Brown, 1982.

_____. *Roads To Quoz: An American Mosey*. Boston: Little Brown and Company, 2008. (See especially "On Motoring," p. 329, "Ten M to B," p. 352, "Building a Time Machine," p. 358, and "Finding the Kaiser Billy Road," p. 366 — sections about U.S. 40, George R. Stewart, and Stewart scholar Frank Brusca.)

LeConte, Joseph. *A Journal of Ramblings Through the High Sierras of California by the "University Excursion Party."* Yosemite: Yosemite Association, 1994. Also online at: http://www.sierraclub.org/history/key_figures/leconte/ramblings.asp.

McMurtry, Larry. *Roads: Driving America's Great Highways*. New York: Touchstone/Simon & Schuster, 2000.

McPhee, John. *Basin and Range*. New York: Farrar, Straus, and Giroux, 1981.

Moheit, Ulrike, ed. *Alexander von Humboldt: Briefe aus Amerika. 1799–1804*. Berlin: Akademie Verlag, 1993. (As cited and quoted online in Baron.)

Partridge, James Gilbert. *A History of the Faculty Club at Berkeley*. Berkeley: The Faculty Club, 1990.

Perlman, James S. *The Atom and the Universe*. Belmont, CA: Wadsworth, 1970.

Putnam, Robert D. *Bowling Alone: The Collapse and Revival of American Community*. New York: Simon & Schuster, 2001.

Robinson, Kim Stanley. *The Wild Shore*. New York: Tom Doherty, 1984.

Ross, Michael Elsohn, and Wendy Smith-Griswold. *Nature Art with Chiura Obata*. Minneapolis: Carolrhoda, 2000.

Shankland, Robert. *Steve Mather of the National Parks*. New York: Knopf, 1970.

Sloss, Frank H. *Only on Monday: Papers delivered before the Chit-Chat Club*. San Francisco, Frank Sloss, 1978.

Smith, Margaret Bayard [Mrs. Samuel Harrison Smith]. *The First Forty Years of Washington Society*, edited by Gaillard Hunt. New York: Scribner's, 1906.

Stegner, Page. "Introduction." In *Wolf Willow: A History, a Story, and a Memory of the Last Plains Frontier*, by Wallace Stegner. New York, Penguin, 2000.

_____, ed. *The Selected Letters of Wallace Stegner*. Berkeley: Shoemaker Hoard, 2007.

Stegner, Wallace. *All the Little Live Things*. New York: Viking Press, 1967.

_____. "Introduction." In *Storm*, by George R. Stewart. Lincoln: University of Nebraska Press, 1983.

_____. *Where The Bluebird Sings To The Lemonade Springs: Living and Writing in the West*. New York: Penguin, 1992.

_____. *Wolf Willow*. New York: Penguin, 2000.

Stevenson, Robert Louis. *From Scotland to Silverado*. Edited by James D. Hart. Cambridge, MA: The John Harvard Library, 1966.

Stewart, Dr. John H. *The Geology of Nevada: A Discussion to Accompany the Geological Map of Nevada*. Reno: Nevada Bureau of Mines and Geology, 1980.

Stone, Irving, ed., *There Was Light: Autobiography of a University*; Berkeley: 1868 —1968. Garden City, NY: Doubleday, 1970.

Turnage, William, "Introduction." In Adams, Ansel, *Sierra Nevada: The John Muir Trail*, by Ansel Adams New York: Little, Brown, 2006.

Tweed, William C. "Parkitecture: A history of rustic building design in the National Park System: 1916–1942." Unpublished, 1978.

Uglow, Jenny. *The Lunar Men*. New York: Farrar, Straus, and Giroux, 2002.

Vale, Thomas, and Geraldine Vale. *U.S. 40 Today: Thirty Years of Landscape Change in America*. Madison: University of Wisconsin Press, 1983.

Waage, Fred. *The Crucial Role of the Environment in the Writings of George Stewart (1895–1980): A Life of America's Chief Literary Ecologist*. Lewiston, NY: Edward Mellen Press, 2006.

Wilson, Garff. *The Unidentified Man on the Right: The Story of Fabulous People and Events on the Berkeley Campus of the University of California During the Past Four Decades*. Berkeley, CA: Privately published by GB Wilson, 1987.

Periodicals and Articles

Anonymous. "A Walker's Guide to the Geology of San Francisco." Special Supplement to *Mineral Information Service*. San Francisco: California Division of Mines and Geology, November 1966. (This is now out-of-print but can be obtained at the new Division of Mines store, located in the U.S. Geological Survey store, Menlo Park, CA.)

Anonymous. "Friends Honor...." *The Independent and Gazette*.... In the George Rippey Stewart Papers, The Bancroft Library.

Brusca, Frank. "Old Trails Tale." *American Road* (Spring 2005): 42.

_____. "Old Trails Tale, Two," *American Road*. (Summer 2005): 50.

Caldwell, John. "George R. Stewart, Jr.: A Checklist." *Bulletin of Bibliography* 36 (April–June 1979).

Clifton, H. Edward, and Ralph E. Hunter. "Depositional and Other Features of the Merced Formation in Sea Cliff Exposures South of San Francisco, California." In *Geologic Excursions in Northern California: San Francisco to the Sierra Nevada*, edited by Sloan and Wagner. San Francisco: California Dept. of Conservation, Division of Mines and Geology, 1991.

Denby, David. "Critic at Large: The Scottish Enlightenment." *New Yorker*, October 11, 2004.

Fitzgerald, F. Scott. "Princeton," *College Humor*, December 1927.

Hall, N. Timothy. "Late Cenozoic Stratigraphy Between Mussel Rock and Fleishhacker Zoo, San Francisco Peninsula." In "A Walker's Guide to the Geology of San Francisco." Special Supplement to *Mineral Information Service*. San Francisco: California Division of Mines and Geology, November 1966.

McIntyre, Donald B. "James Hutton's Edinburgh: The Historical, Political, and Social Background." *Earth Sciences History*, Vol.16, No.2 (1997): 100–157. (Available online at: http://www.dbmcintyre.pwp.blueyonder.co.uk/ (in the "geology" section.) A pdf version is at: http://sp.lyellcollection.org/content/150/1/1.full.pdf.

Perrin, Noel. "Unlisted." *American Scholar* 72 (Spring 2003): 109–16.

Ribovich, John. "Artist's Retreat: Maybeck and Magic in the Berkeley Hills." *American Bungalow* 56 (November 2006–February 2008): 33–43.

Sell, David J. "Roll On Columbia!" *American Road* III, No. 3 (Fall 2005): 14.

Online Articles, Websites

Anderson, Dan. *Yosemite Online.* Links to history, exhibits, publications, etc., related to Yosemite National Park. © 1997–2007. http://www.yosemite.ca.us/.

Anonymous. http://en.wikipedia.org/wiki/Bishops' Wars.

Anonymous. "E Clampus Vitus." *Wikipedia.* Describes George Ezra Dane's role in the reestablishment of ECV; also discusses an event which included GRS and Charles Camp. http://en.wikipedia.org/wiki/E_Clampus_Vitus.

Anonymous. *The Columbia River Highway: A Poem in Stone.* Oregon State Archives 50th Anniversary Exhibit. http://arcweb.sos.state.or.us/50th/columbia/columbiaintro.html.

Anonymous. "History of the National Park Service." *National Park Service History.* http://www.nps.gov/history/history/hisnps/NPShistory.htm.

Anonymous. "Joseph LeConte: Scientist and Savant (1823–1901)." *Key Figures in Sierra Club History.* http://www.sierraclub.org/history/key_figures/leconte/.

Anonymous. "List of Greek words with English derivatives." *Wikipedia.* http://en.wikipedia.org/wiki/List_of_Greek_words_with_English_derivatives.

Anonymous. Realeyz essay on the film *Amiland.* http://www.realeyz.tv/en/florian-schewe-vojtech-pokorny-amiland_cont4142.html.

Anonymous. *Tolman Hall: Past, Present, and Future.* http://www-gse.berkeley.edu/admin/publications/tolmanhistory.html.

Anonymous. "University of California, Berkeley." *Wikipedia.* http://en.wikipedia.org/wiki/University_of_California_at_Berkeley.

Arjanik, David L., Gary Bertchume, et al. *Greene and Greene Virtual Archives.* http://www.usc.edu/dept/architecture/greeneandgreene/aboutgreenes.html.

Ask Art: The Artist's Bluebook. http://www.askart.com/AskART/artists/search/Search_Repeat.aspx?searchtype=IMAGES&artist=7475.

Baron, Dr. Frank. "Humboldt in Washington: Encounters, Exchanges, and the Lewis and Clark Connection (1804)." http://www2.ku.edu/~maxkade/humboldt/main.htm.

Bodega Bay Heritage Gallery. http://www.bbhgallery.com/Weaver_Rene_Tuolumne_River.htm.

Borah, Woodrow W., John Leighly, James J. Parsons, and Lesley B. Simpson. "Carl Ortwin Sauer, Geography: Berkeley." http://sunsite.berkeley.edu/uchistory/archives_exhibits/in_memoriam/.

Brusca, Frank, *U. S. Route 40: America's Golden Highway.* 1996. http://www.route40.net/index.shtml.

Clark, David G. *On the Trail of the Named Highways from Chicago to the Southwest.* http://windycityroadwarrior.com/Stories/Pontiac_Trail.html.

Dale, Peter, Scott Jonas Barish, C. T. Christ, I. C. Hungerland, and B. F. Ritchie. "Josephine Miles, English, Berkeley." http://sunsite.berkeley.edu/uchistory/archives_exhibits/in_memoriam/.

Droz, Robert V. "U. S. Highways: From U.S. 1 to (U.S. 280)." http://www.us-highways.com/1998–2007.

Ecker, Pam S. *The Historic Context of the Dixie Highway.* In Zimmerman, Thomas, "The Dixie Highway." http://www.us-highways.com/tzimm/ecker.htm.

Elliston, Jon. "CIA's Man on Campus." *The Independent Weekly*, November 29, 2000. Available online at: http://www.indyweek.com/gyrobase/Content?oid=oid%3A15208.

Fisher-Smith, Jordan. "Field Observations: An Interview with Wendell Berry." *Orion Magazine*, Autumn 1993. http://arts.envirolink.org/interviews_and_conversations/Wendell-Berry.html.

Friis, Herman R. "Baron Alexander von Humboldt's Visit to Washington," Records of the Columbia Historical Society 44 (1963): 1–35. As cited in Baron.

Hardwick, Bonnie, Merrilee Proffitt, et al. *Building Bancroft: The Evolution of a Library.* Bancroft Library, University of California, Berkeley, 2002. http://bancroft.berkeley.edu/Exhibits/bancroft/.

Harper, Douglas. *Online Etymology Dictionary*. http://www.etymonline.com/ (accessed January 10, 2008).

Hart, James D., Travis M. Bogard, William B. Fretter, and John H. Raleigh. "George Rippey Stewart, English: Berkeley." http://sunsite.berkeley.edu/uchistory/archives_exhibits/in_memoriam/.

Johnson, J. W., J. A. Putnam, and G. R. Stewart. "Parker Davies Trask, Engineering: Berkeley." http://sunsite.berkeley.edu/uchistory/archives_exhibits/in_memoriam/.

Kantorowiscz, Ernest H. *The Fundamental Issue. Documents and Marginal Notes on the University of California Loyalty Oath*. Berkeley: the Regents of the University of California. © 1999–2005. http://sunsite.berkeley.edu/uchistory/archives_exhibits/loyaltyoath/symposium/kantorowicz.html.

Lauher, Joe. *The Road Ahead. A Collector's Look at North American Road Maps*. http://www.chem.sunysb.edu/lauher/roadmaps/.

Lin, James. *About Via*. http://www.ugcs.caltech.edu/~jlin/links/ 1998–2002.

Moore, Matt. *The Great Nature of Chiura Obata*. http://obata.wilderness.net/.

Regents, University of California, Berkeley. *Student Protest, UC Berkeley: Free Speech Movement*. http://bancroft.berkeley.edu/FSM/ © 2005.

Rosenfeld, Seth. "The Campus Files." *San Francisco Examiner*, 2007. Online at: http://www.sfgate.com/campus/.

Rossman, Michael, et al., *FSM-A*. http://www.fsm-a.org/ Archives of the Free Speech Movement, © 1999–2004.

Ruhaak, Marty. *New Left Beginnings: The Free Speech Movement at Berkeley in 1964*. http://www.eiu.edu/~historia/2003/berkeley.htm.

Sallis, James. "Earth Abides: Stewart's Dark Eulogy for Humankind." *Boston Globe*, February 16, 2003. Also available online at: http://www.grasslimb.com/sallis/GlobeColumns/globe.06.earth.html.

Savio, Mario. *The Berkeley Student Rebellion of 1964*. http://www.fsm-a.org/stacks/mario/savio_studrebel.htm.

Schul, David, *North American Auto Trails*. http://www.marion.ohio-state.edu/fac/schul/trails/trails.html.

Thompson, Daniella. "Rev. Dr. Robert Irving Bentley House." *Berkeley Architectural Heritage Association, Berkeley Landmarks*. http://www.berkeleyheritage.com/berkeley_landmarks/bentley_house.html.

Varner, S. *American Roads*. http://www.americanroads.us/ ©2002.

Vaux, H. J., R. F. Dasmann, D. R. McCullough, W. W. Middlekauff, W. C. Russell, and D. E. Teeguarden. "Aldo Starker Leopold, Zoology; Forestry and Conservation: Berkeley." *In Memoriam*. Berkeley: University of California Press, 1985.

Weingroff, Richard. *The Lincoln Highway*. U.S. Department of Transportation, Federal Highways Administration. http://www.fhwa.dot.gov/infrastructure/lincoln.htm.

_____. *The National Old Trails Road*. U.S. Department of Transportation, Federal Highways Administration. http://www.fhwa.dot.gov/infrastructure/trails.htm.

Wollenberg, Charles. "Chapter 9: Heritage of the Sixties." *Berkeley, A City in History*. © 2002. http://berkeleypubliclibrary.org/system/Chapter9.html.

Maps

Everhart, Mark R. "Lost Highways: Auto Trails and Markers circa 1924." Poster showing all the transcontinental highways the year the Stewarts took their honeymoon trip. May be viewed online at http://www.users.qwest.net/~everhart/highways.htm.

Media

Aaberg, Phillip, *Earth Abides*. Performance of his own musical composition. On the CD "Christmas." Sweetgrass Music, Chester, Montana.

Anonymous. "Mars Dead or Alive." *NOVA*. PBS. WGBH, January 4, 2004. http://www.pbs. org/wgbh/nova/programs/ht/tm/3101.html?site=1&pl=qt&rate=hi&ch=6.

Bitomsky, Hartmut. *Highway 40 West*. German documentary based on Stewart's *U.S. 40*.

Hauser, Dwight. *A Fire Called Jeremiah*. Directed by James Algar. Burbank, CA: Walt Disney, 1961.

Lasseter, John. *Cars*. Burbank, CA: Pixar/Walt Disney, 2006.

Nelson, Kenneth, Director. *A Storm Named Maria*. Burbank, CA: Walt Disney, 1959.

Pokorny, Vojtech, and Florian Schewe, Directors. *Amiland*, 2008.

Interviews and Correspondence

Bitomsky, Hartmut. Interviewed by the author, by email, about his film *U.S. 40 West*, and the influence of George R. Stewart.

Bliss, Anthony. Personal conversations about Pasadena culture in the 1920s, and the influence of George R. Stewart on his family.

Bentley, Wilder, the Younger. Email and mail correspondence, 2007. Interviewed by mail about Wilder Bentley the Elder, Chiura Obata, and Bentley family history.

Brenneman, Richard. Phone interview and email correspondence with the author about George R. Stewart's influences.

Broughton, Robert. Several conversations and an informal interview in 2006, about films produced by Disney Studios in the late 1940s and early 1950s.

Brusca, Frank. Several email conversations with the author about *U. S. 40* and Stewart's influence on Brusca's and others' work.

Butler, Philip. Personal conversations with the author about the Black Rock Desert and land management agency history and culture.

Cassady, William. Video interview with the author about his life in the Stewart's former Dutch Flat cabin. Dutch Flat, California. Summer 2006.

Callenbach, Ernest. Email communications with the author about George R. Stewart's influences.

Doig, Ivan. Brief conversation and subsequent mail correspondence with the author about George R. Stewart's influences.

Edwards, Dr. Carol. Personal conversation with the author about effects of Asperger Syndrome. Spring 2005.

Evenson, Anna. Video interview by the author about family, and memories and influences of George R. and Theodosia Stewart.

Evenson, Jill Stewart. Video interview by the author; also subsequent phone and mail communications with the author. Interviewed about family memories and Jill Stewart Evenson's career.

Ferrell, Keith. Brief conversations with the author about George R. Stewart's influences. Interviewed by email, by the author, on the same topic.

Gritzner, Dr. Jeffrey. Conversations and email correspondence with author, about Dr. Carl Sauer and Sauer's way of thinking.

Least Heat Moon, William (William Trogdon). Brief conversation and subsequent mail correspondence with the author about George R. Stewart's influences.

Lucia, John. Personal conversations with the author discussing the Arts and Crafts Movement and Thornton State Beach.

Lyon, Robert C. Extensive email and mail correspondence and many personal conversations about George R. Stewart's influences, and George R. Stewart's life and work.

McIntyre, D. B. Email communications with the author, about the Scottish Enlightenment.

Robinson, Kim Stanley. Correspondence. Several brief conversations. Email interview for book by author about the influence of George R. Stewart.

Rossman, Michael. Email correspondence about the Free Speech Movement.

Savio, Lynne Hollander. Email correspondence about the Free Speech Movement.

Stegner, Page. Email interviews about his memories of the friendship between the Stegner and Stewart families.

Stewart, George R. Several personal conversations between 1974 and 1980, which included brief, informal interviews.

Stewart, Dr. John H. Video interview by the author. Also extensive phone, email, and mail communications with the author about family memories, and Dr. John H. Stewart's career.

Stewart, Theodosia. Extensive personal conversations between 1974 and 1989 about life with George R. Stewart, as well as the man's works.

Strads, Baiba. Personal conversations with the author. Email interview, by the author, for the book, about her memories of the Stewart family.

Williams, Stephen. Many personal conversations with the author about George R. Stewart's influences.

Index

Numbers in *bold italics* indicate pages with photographs.

227